THE GODS OF GENERATION

THE
PANURGE PRESS
New York

SOME RECENT PRIVATELY PRINTED
AND LIMITED EDITIONS

¶BLACK LUST *by* JEAN DE VILLIOT

The love and hate of a white woman for a black Mohammedan chief forms the overtone of this historic novel whose background paints the native tribes in the Valley of the Nile before the turn of this century. This diabolic novel is an encyclopedia of venery, a kaleidoscope of perversions, a jungle of horrors.

Limited to 2000 press-numbered copies.

¶ CHASTITY BELTS *by* ESAR LEVINE

The only full-length account ever written of one of the strangest methods devised to bridle the privates of women. This volume is a factual encyclopedia of the subject for the author has included anecdotes, secret memoirs, court trials, short stories, newspaper accounts and numerous full-page illustrations of these belts.

Limited to 2000 press-numbered copies.

¶EUNUCHS, ODALISQUES AND LOVE
by NICOLAS FROMAGET

A fascinating novel of oriental passion dealing with a Frenchman's amatory adventures in Turkey. The protagonist is an insatiable lover who slakes his lust at every opportunity and whose venereal hazards reveal the extravagance of harem sexuality and the parts played by eunuchs and odalisques.

Limited to 2000 press-numbered copies.

¶ MADAME SEX *by* Dr. Isaac Goldberg

Modern sex psychology has opened the door to a new gallery of women, passion-driven erotomaniacs of different types. This is the first collection of short stories ever written about them. Gruesome perversions rub shoulders with normal love, while the comic profundity of these stories recalls Pantagruel and Panurge.

Limited to 2000 privately printed copies.

¶ PRAEPUTII INCISIO

A complete history of MALE and FEMALE CIRCUMCISION with additional chapters on Hermaphrodism, Flagellation, Eunuchism, Infibulation, Priapism, etc. The anonymous doctor-traveller-author uncovers the phallic habits of unknown races and intrigues the reader by his incredible revelations of savage ethnology.

Limited to 1500 press-numbered copies.

¶ EROTIC FAIRY TALES *by* the Abbe de Voisenon

These superlative fairy tales are for adults only. They discuss the eternal battle of the sexes and are liberally sprinkled with high lights on marital indelicacies, the higher mysteries of esoteric passion, complicated cuckoldry, sophisticated tomfooleries, indiscreet virgins, and hilarious erotic adventures of all sorts.

Limited to 1000 press-numbered copies.

¶ THE HINDU ART OF LOVE *by* Edward Windsor

The only attempt ever made to record and classify all the refinements of passion as practised among the immemorial Hindus. This volume covers dozens of the most esoteric works of Hindu sages and eroticists which surpass the wisdom of the French and Greeks even more than the latter surpass that of the Americans.

Limited to 1500 press-numbered copies.

¶ THE MERRY NIGHTS of Straparola

This collection of panurgic stories is a veritable handbook on amorous intrigue but it is vastly more facetious than the Heptameron or the Decameron. Its contents include: Trust Not a Friend, The Way of All Wives, A Mistake in the Dark, The Revenge Indelicate, Cuckolds Will Be Cuckolds, etc.

Limited to 1000 press-numbered copies.

ALL PANURGE PRESS PUBLICATIONS
ARE $5.00 EACH

*Of this American edition,
the first in English, only
2000 copies have been issued
for private collectors of
erotica*
✳

JACQUES-ANTOINE DULAURE

* * * * * * * * * * *

THE
GODS OF
GENERATION

A HISTORY OF PHALLIC CULTS
AMONG ANCIENTS & MODERNS

TRANSLATED FROM THE FRENCH BY A. F. N.

* *
*

1933
Privately Printed
THE PANURGE PRESS : NEW YORK

* * * * * * * * * * *

Philip Golding

*Copyright, 1933, by
The Panurge Press, Inc.
New York*

*

PRINTED IN U.S.A

CONTENTS

*

*

TRANSLATOR'S FOREWORD

TRANSLATOR'S FOREWORD

IN *the biographical article on Dulaure herein translated, Alcide Bonneau concludes with the statement: "Dulaure does not occupy the rank among mythologists which is legitimately due him." To this I both subscribe and disagree. Among mythologists themselves and students of phallicism and the history of religion, Dulaure, I believe, is properly estimated and valued. However, beyond the confines of this very restricted circle, he is almost unknown, particularly as a mythologist and antiquarian; his chief bid to fame being as a historian, through his* Histoire de Paris. *Even the amateur in phallicism and the history of manners is likely grossly to underestimate, or perhaps remain in complete ignorance of our author and his works; although he will not have been able to read much along those lines without having encountered some of Dulaure's material, usually it is quietly included by some writer without acknowledgment. I recall the sense of breaking dawn I experienced when first I read the work in hand; in every chapter I met with facts or conclusions which in various other works on the same subject had impressed me with that author's erudition. Being unacquainted at that time, as many at present still are, with Dulaure at first hand, I was unable to recognize the imposture. Had I the time, and would it serve any purpose, I might draw up a list of these different plagiarisms of various degrees; I promise it would be no short one. For example, at this moment I can recall that Campbell in his* Phallic Worship *translates paragraph after paragraph, word for word, from this book and includes them under his own name, merely mentioning in his introduction that he has drawn on Dulaure as he saw fit: his entire treatment of the*

xi

Bacchanalia and Phallophoria derives from this source. Wherever the Feast of Fools is mentioned, Dulaure's material is brought in, but seldom his name. His discussion of the phallic Saints of France is almost classic, and like the classics has come to be regarded as common property. I have frequently been amused when some "polite scholar" has thought to astound a wide-eyed public by impressively declaring in a "believe it or not" manner that there are twelve foreskins of Jesus Christ extant! But he does not stop there; his learning goes even farther: he rattles off the resting places of six of these holy prepuces, and then, intimating that surely these will suffice, concludes with an off-hand etc. These six places are always those that Dulaure gives, and in the same order; even the etc. is his.

But to get on. The prime reason for Dulaure's personal oblivion, as I see it, has been his inaccessibility. Even in France, in the Parisian book-stalls, either part of his Histoire abrégée is by no means easy to locate. As for translations, it is a constant source of wonder to me how the Divinités Génératrices has escaped being Englished for all these years; it is so often referred to in works pertaining to phallicism that one would think there would be sufficient curiosity aroused to cause something to be done about it. However, that translation finally being at hand, let us hope that the above mentioned curiosity has merely been held in abeyance and is now all ready to break out in glad welcome of the following efforts.

Need we estimate Dulaure? He is sometimes dismissed as being inexact and fantastic. This, while partly true, is hardly fair. His fantastic qualities, I believe, will prove on examination to be largely the result of his enthusiasm, while most of his inexactness can easily be traced to his covering ground almost entirely untouched. It is on the foundations put down by such pioneers that later writers, much later, erect their "exact" systems and hypotheses. That Dulaure has some oddities, I readily grant: his stand on the non-phallic origin of the cross, for example, will forever remain an enigma to me. But what can we in some sense consider as contributions from him? First, regardless of our personal leanings in the matter, we have a definite, logical, and pleasingly clear presentation of the astronomic origin of phallicism. Secondly, though this really concerns his Des cults qui ont précédé etc. more than the present volume, he gives us the introduction of human figures into worship as a distinct step and development in religion, which to me makes many things clearer. Thirdly, he advances what I feel to be a point of extreme importance in phallicism, and one which seems to have gone unnoticed by other writers: that the worshipped phallus is derived from the virile organs of the sacred bulls and goats and not from those of man. Over and above all this, he presents so much interesting esoteric and recondite material that his work can almost be considered a source-book, for which it is frequently used.

As for Dulaure's life and works, I scarcely need go into that since I have translated and included Alcide Bonneau's biographical notice on him. If Bonneau has left anything unsaid, I certainly am not able to supply it.

Is it part of a translator's duty to run down editions of the work he is translating and give a complete bibliography of it? I sincerely hope not, for if so it is a duty I fully intend shirking. I have not the means at hand for this task, nor do I believe the necessary efforts would be justified.

xiii

Translator's Foreword

Suffice it to say that Dulaure first brought this book out in 1805. A second edition, somewhat revised and edited, came out in 1825. Isidore Liseux reissued this 1825 edition in 1885. It was to this 1885 edition that Bonneau's Notice was affixed, and it was this edition which served for my translation. Also, an edition newly edited by A. van Gennep was brought out in Paris in 1905. Beyond this I say nothing. In all probability there have been other editions, but I can with safety assert that they have not been numerous.

If for a moment I may cast my habitual modesty aside (it comes off readily, like an old glove, though it hardly fits me as gracefully) and bring myself to speak of my translation, I wish to say that while it is in no sense elegant, it will be found to be both literal and faithful, which perhaps come to the same thing. I have kept my editing and amplifying of the text down as well as I could, not wishing to thrust myself in under Dulaure's name and fame. Such notes as I have felt to be necessary will be found duly signed. And then a word as to the italics. Dulaure, like most Frenchmen, employs italics on impulse, as a means of artistic expression, I sometimes feel; but at any rate, excessively and inconsistently. I have straightened these out according to orthodox usage as well as I could; but as Dulaure seems to use Phallus *in two senses: one, universal, in the sense of a god or religious abstraction or principle; and the other particular, as the mere image of the virile member, I have reserved the italicized form for the abstract sense.*

In conclusion, I wish to acknowledge the aid of my friend Robert D. in the checking over of my manuscript. My thanks are due him.

A. F. N.

St. Louis, Mo.
August, 1932.

A BIOGRAPHICAL NOTE

JACQUES-ANTOINE DULAURE

A BIOGRAPHICAL NOTE

JACQUES-ANTOINE DULAURE was one of those modest and industrious scholars of an open and searching mind, of a remarkable variety of aptitudes, of a facility for work, of an astonishing fecundity, such as made up the majority of the school of philosophy for the XVIII century, the Encyclopedists, and who for the most part were lost in the whirlpool of the Revolution. "What did you do during the Reign of Terror?" some one asked Sieyès.—"I lived," he answered. That was indeed a great deal, that of managing only to live; but Sieyès succeeded in this while remaining until the end in the midst of parties who were killing each other. Dulaure escaped the guillotine only by exiling himself.

Born at Clermont-Ferrand in 1755, he had thought at first to make an architect of himself, and he came to Paris to place himself under the direction of Rondelet, the continuator of Soufflot. These studies, which he did not carry to their complete achievement, were useful to him, however, in that they developed in him a taste for archeological researches. Notices on three theatres of recent construction: the *Odéon* (1782), the *Théâtre-Italien* and the *Cirque du Palais-Royal* (1787), that famous circus later transformed into a naumachia and which has become, by a last metamorphosis, a water-garden, attracted attention to him, and the bookseller Lejay intrusted him with the compilation of a *Description des curiosités de Paris* (1786-9, 3 vol.), soon followed by *Singularités historiques ou Tableau critique des moeurs, des usages et des évènements de differents siècles, contenant ce que l'histoire de la capitale et des autres lieux de l'Ile de France offre de plus piquant et de plus singulier* (1788), interesting collections with which he preluded his most extensive work, the one which has remained popular, the *Histoire physique, civile et morale de Paris*. He undertook at the same time to extend his researches to the whole of the kingdom and published the *Description des principaux lieux de la France, provinces, villes, bourgs, monastères et châteaux* (1788-89).

Meanwhile the Revolution was approaching; it was going to interrupt for a long time the peaceable labors of the scholar. Dulaure was named assistant to the National Assembly by the province of Marche, and utilized his leisure in composing violent pamphlets against the old regime: the *Evangélistes du jour* (1790), a publication which had sixteen numbers and which answered the *Actes des Apôtres*, by Peltier and other Royalists; the *Histoire critique de la noblesse, où l'on expose ses préjugés, ses crimes, ses brigandages* (1790); the *Liste des noms des ci-devant nobles* (1790-91, 3 parts), where he showed that the majority of the noble titles had been acquired only through fraud; he founded and drew up all alone the *Thermomètre du jour*, a periodical sheet which lived from August 11, 1791 to May 25, 1793. His constituents sent him to sit at the Convention; but already the horizon was beginning to darken. "It was not with joy," he writes in his *Mémoires*, which have remained unpublished, "that I received the news of my election as representative of the people. On reading the record which declared it, I was struck with astonishment and fright. I was not frightened by the progress of our enemies, whose troops were advancing to within twenty leagues of Paris, but it was by the birth of a bloody faction, which seemed to threaten entire France with its disastrous exploits and which had just signalized itself in an atrocious manner by the massacres of the first days of September. That is what I feared, and my fears were realized."

Dulaure was of those wise, balanced spirits who would have wished peaceably to found a new regime of liberty, equality, and justice, and to lead the Revolution into a regular path. He combated the dictatorship of the Jacobins and the *Comités* with as much ardor and severity as he had previously used in demolishing the privileges and in decrying the clergy and nobility. This was not what his electors had expected, or at least the most turbulent, the most fiery portion of them. The revolutionary Society of Clermont-Ferrand signified to him that, "weary of seeing that his journal, instead of breathing forth the purest patriotism, contained only anti-civic principles, tending to foment trouble and division," it refused from that time on to receive the *Thermomètre*. This was a first warning for Dulaure; he suspended his journal, but he did not break his pen for this, and he published two brochures: *Physionomie de la Convention National* (1793) and *Du fédéralisme en France* (1793), which answered preoccupations of the moment. Without belonging to the Girondin party, he was connected with the principal persons among them, especially with Roland and his wife, with whom he sometimes went to dine. During their trial, he received this anonymous note right at the Convention, which he ever afterwards believed to be from Mme. Roland: "Thunder, brave Dulaure; your colleagues are going to be victims of the most atrocious injustice. Remember that the tribunal which judges them is not named by the people."—"But then," he adds, "I no longer had a journal, I no longer had any thunder at hand; already the storm was rumbling over my own head; I was going to be struck by it." He was decreed for accusation October 15, 1793, five months after the Girondins, and escaped the fate of his friends only with great trouble, by hiding himself from the searching of the police. He lived for some time hidden at Paris, then at Saint-Denis, and undertook to win to the frontier, on foot, under a disguise. Having arrived in Switzerland, by way of the Jura mountains, he presented himself at a printed calico mill where, hired at first as a workman, he subsequently found himself able to utilize his talents as a designer. "Why," he said, "am I banished from the soil of liberty, I who for many years have acted, thought, and written only for it? Before and after the Revolution, I have constantly fought the triple tyranny of the priests, nobles, and kings!" He lived there completely unknown, allowing no one to suspect either his name or identity, until the fall of Robespierre. After the ninth of *Thermidor*, he went back to France and peaceably took possession again of his seat in the Convention. Three departments, Puy-de-Dôme, which held him in the highest esteem, Corrèze and Dordogne where, having been sent on a mission by the Convention, he had been able to win all approbation by his honesty, moderation, and patriotism, elected him deputy to the *Cinq-Cents*; he held his seat there until the eighteenth of *Brumaire*, which put an end to his political life.

During this period he published only a *Discours prononcé à Brives à l'occasion de la fête funèbre en l'honneur du représentant du peuple Féraud* (year III) and, in the same year, the *Supplément aux crimes des anciens comités de gouvernement*, a collection full of interesting facts on the revolutionary excesses. Back to private life, provided with a modest employment which assured him food and lodging, he returned to his favorite studies and brought out the remarkable work entitled: *Des cultes qui ont précédé et amené l'idolâtrie ou l'adoration des figures humaines* (Paris, 1805) followed the same year by the volume which completes it: *Des Divinités génératrices, ou du culte du Phallus chez les Anciens et les Modernes, des cultes du dieu de Lampsaque, de Pan, de Venus*, etc. This was the Voltairian who was protesting against the Catholic reaction which the reopening of the churches had given the signal, and against the infatuation which the *Génie du Christianisme* was carrying to the skies. To the poetic fictions of Chateaubriand, Dulaure opposed real and precise facts going back to the origin of religions, and he showed that they had all issued from a coarse or monstrous fetishism. The old Republican, the Convention member awakened at the Restoration; he published a *Défense des propriétaires des biens nationaux* (1814), and a virulent pamphlet which at the same time is an historical document: *Causes secrètes des excès de la Rèvolution* (1815), where he held the *émigrés* and priests as the instigators of the death of Louis XVI, and even held them responsible for the Reign of Terror. This pamphlet appeared in the *Censeur*, the seizure of which it motivated, and raised hatred against its author which found occasion for satisfying itself when, ten years later, Dulaure reprinted, under the general title of *Histoire abrégée des differents cultes*, his two volumes of mythology. The one which treats of the *Gods of Generation* had been, at its appearance in 1805, the object only of criticisms and contradictions more or less vigorous: in 1825 it was judged

outrageous to public and religious morality, the edition
was seized, condemned, and in part destroyed[1].

At this period Dulaure was in process of publishing his
great work: *Histoire physique, civile et morale de Paris*
(1821-22, 7 vol.), which in succeeding editions he carried
to ten volumes, and which was, along with the *Esquisse historique des principaux événements de la Révolution* (1825,
4 vol.), the work of the entire last part of his life. The *Histoire de Paris* has justly remained esteemed, and, it can be
said, popular. Less prolix than Sauval in all that concerns
Parisian topography, the successive enlargements of the
city, its civil buildings, its churches, its pious foundations,
less copious than D. Fèlibien and Lobineau in charts, ordinances, regulations, etc., Dulaure is greatly superior to his
predecessors by the manner in which he draws these eru-
dite materials together. Paris naturally having been the theatre of the principal events of our history, it is a history of
France viewed as a whole which he presents to us in retrac-
ing that of the capital. Dulaure has not the flame of a Mich-
elet, but he is exact and veracious, advancing scarcely a
fact, an assertion, which he does not support with a document. He is especially curious as to peculiarities, anecdotes:
he is a man who has with the greatest care collected from
chronicles, memoirs, the registers of the *Parlement* and the
Chambre des Comptes, and the sermons of preachers, all
that which was able to demolish religious superstition and
discredit the morals and institutions of the monarchy.

Besides these vast enterprises, Dulaure had had a great
number of notices and articles inserted in the bulletins of
the *Académie Celtique* and in those of the *Société des Antiquaires de France*. At his death, in 1835, he left a consid-

erable mass of manuscripts, including among other things his *Mémoires*, which has not been printed, and the materials for a *Histoire de l'Auvergne* for which he had made immense researches. His manuscripts, bought from his widow by the municipality of Clermont-Ferrand, are deposited in the library of that city.

Such was the troubled and at the same time industrious life of the political man and the historian; it remains for us to say a word of the mythologist. Dulaure has brought to this variety of research, in which he excelled, the clearness of opinions, the conscientiousness, and the exactitude which were peculiar to him. He assembles around the questions which he proposes to elucidate such a quantity of texts, of citations borrowed from ancient and modern authors, that one marvels at the variety and extent of his reading. His work is all the more worthy of praise as he travelled along a way scarcely marked out and found but feeble support either in the *Origine des cultes* of Dupuis, from whose system he deviates considerably, or in the monographs of the Abbé Mignot, Count de Gébelin, and the president De Brosse, who had treated only very special points. A comparison of Dulaure's system with those of his predecessors and of the more recent mythologists, Creuzer, Guigniaut, and Alfred Maury, would carry us too far afield; let us say merely that he has the advantage over them of being very simple and of offering, consequently, the greatest chance of probability, for man of ancient ages ought not to have been the subtle metaphysician that the *Symbolique* of Creuzer supposes. Contrary to Dupuis, who sees in Sabeanism, that is to say in the adoration of the stars, the origin

Jacques-Antoine Dulaure:

of all the cults, Dulaure shows as far as his evidence goes that there were cults a good bit prior to the astronomical knowledge of which Sabeanism shows man in full possession; that the first objects of his superstitious adoration were natural objects: the mountains which limited his horizon, the impenetrable forests which served as barriers to the tribes, the rivers, the beneficent springs where he drank, the sea impassable for him and which struck him with a-mazement, the stones taken from sacred mountains, the boundaries solemnly posed as frontiers between nations, as limits between patrimonies.

As for the cult of the *Phallus*, by a derogation of his system Dulaure gives it a planetary origin; it is, in fact, associated with the zodiacal sign of Taurus in the most ancient documents to be had. This point of view is perhaps contestable; but this justice at least will be rendered Dulaure, that he has neglected nothing to give us the most ample and luminous account of this singular cult. He has followed its developments and ramifications in all times and in all countries, up to our day where it is secretly perpetuated under various names. He alone is complete; let one read after him the few scattered pages on this subject in the *Symbolique*, the few lines that Alfred Maury devotes to it in his *Histoire des religions de la Grèce antique*! Besides, he knows how to interest by variety, abundance of information and citations, and clarity of recital. Dulaure does not occupy the rank among mythologists which is legitimately due him.

Alcide Bonneau

Paris, 1885.

THE GODS OF GENERATION

Aut igitur tunicam parti prætende tegendæ,
Aut quibus hanc oculis adspicis, ista legæ.

Priapeia.

DES DIVINITÉS

GÉNÉRATRICES,

ou

DU CULTE DU PHALLUS

CHEZ LES ANCIENS ET LES MODERNES;

Des cultes du *dieu de Lampsaque*, de *Pan*, de *Vénus*, etc.;
origine, motifs, conformités, variétés, progrès, altéra-
tions et abus de ces cultes chez différens peuples de la
terre; de leur continuation chez les Indiens et les Chrétiens
d'Europe; des mœurs des nations et des tems où ces cultes
ont existé.

Ce sont les besoins des hommes qui ont créé les vertus des dieux.

PAR J. A. D******.

～～～～～

PARIS.

1805.

AUTHOR'S PREFACE

AUTHOR'S PREFACE

THIS is the first work of its kind in our literature. The mythologists, the investigators of antiquity will here find some hints, some new facts, some explanation on the origin, up till now unknown, of several deities, some discoveries, and above all the combination of a great number of points scattered through an immensity of uncommon books, of unpublished ideas, drawn from manuscripts or furnished by amateurs, the whole of which will offer an aspect of history which has not yet been perceived.

I do not limit myself to the history of the cult of the *gods of generation*, to disentangle the chaos of its origin, to a pursuit of its ramifications, its differences, its connections in each country. I join to this a description of the opinions, manners and institutions which directed the different nations where this cult had flourished. One will see that a perfect harmony existed between them and it. I also treat all the deities created by the same motive, adored for the same purpose. I establish their common source, their connection, and their various alterations.

When the history of manners, institutions, cults, and customs is separated from political events, it presents humankind in a new light, opens a vast field for reflection, enlarges the course for conjectures, and prepares the way for discoveries in the ocean of the past. It no longer relates to a single people, to a single country; it does not limit itself to particular points. It spreads itself over all the nations of the earth; it embraces all the relations which unite them, which divide them; it classes the different primitive families which, in separating, have formed the different races; it indicates the sources from which each of them has proceeded, as well as the alterations in character due to climate, sun, events, and laws.

The comparison of customs, cults, dialects, even dress; that of the means of transmitting language or of writing it; that of the superstitious ceremonies observed at the time of births, marriages, and deaths; the practices calculated to

31

turn away troublesome accidents, calamities, maladies, to bring on abundance and prosperity, to implore the god to render himself favorable; these comparisons, I say, can procure more certain knowledge on the origin of different races than can for the most part be drawn from our historical traditions.

But an obstacle can arrest the pen of the historian of manners and cults; and this obstacle results from the great difference established by time and place between the opinions, decencies, and languages of past centuries and foreign countries, and those of the present century and the country for which one writes. Is it permitted to say today, and among us, without fear of straining the conventions, what it was formerly permitted to say and do, and which still goes on now among certain peoples far away from us? Must one brusquely pass over this obstacle by braving the decencies, or must one indeed renounce in the history of manners the lessons and wisdom which result from it?

It is important for me to clarify these doubtful questions.

These two positions are extreme, but there is a middle ground where I must stop. It is necessary to tell everything, because in order to know a matter fully, one must hide nothing; but one must tell everything suitably to our manners; and, in telling, not to go against traditional forms. For the extreme delicacy of our language, our hypocrisy, or, if you will, our decencies, imperiously demand that these forms be respected. I shall therefore submit my expressions to them; they shall be as a light veil which, satisfying decency, covers shocking nudities without stealing away the outlines.

It is at this middle boundary that I halt. I shall describe institutions, practices, and deities which are indecent to our morals; but I shall describe them decently.

History would not exist, or would present only a dried corpse, only a sad skeleton, if one banished from it the facts which shock reason or justice, which wound decency, or which revolt human nature. No lesson would come out of history if the corruption, errors, and crimes which have so long stained the human species were passed over in silence. How judge the merit of similar religious or civil institutions, if one allows the baneful or fortunate influence that they have exercised on the conduct of man to be ignored? How appreciate the value of causes if their effects remain unknown?

To retrace crimes, the historian is not criminal; to retrace indecencies, the historian is not indecent. To the historian, imbued with his duty, indecency signifies only coarseness of expression and falsehood.

It must be admitted that in certain respects our reason has made little progress, and that our manners still feel the effects of our original barbarism. The words *executioners*, *assassins*, etc., represent nothing of indecency for us. Our delicacy is not wounded when we name a *dagger*, a *sword*, a *stiletto*, *poison*, etc. We pronounce without shame the names of the instruments which give death, and we blush to designate, to pronounce the names of those which give life[1].

This inconsistency in our manners ought not to prevent the writer's submission to them. He ought, in depicting errors and vices, to disapprove of them and make his reader share the horror they inspire in him. He ought, in order that the expression may not be judged as criminal as the action expressed, present it in words and phrases which do not wound the feeble eyes of the reader. If reason condemns our extreme delicacy, reason requests also that this delicacy, since it exists, be respected.

Such are the principles which have guided me in the composition of this work; and in order to reconcile the truth of the facts with the delicacy of our language, it has been necessary for me never to lose sight of them.

There are persons whose shame is comparable to an inflamed sore which is irritated at the least touch; persons who, in the time of Molière, would have been named *collets montés*, *précieuses ridicules*, who, without having re-

33

gard for the decency maintained by my expressions, engaging themselves solely with the material of this work, would apply to it that maxim of Isocrates: *That which is improper to do is improper to say*.

This maxim is not applicable here; moreover, it is false in the greatest number of cases. It is not applicable because the institutions, the ceremonies, the idols of which I speak in my work, were and still are very decorous matters, since they were and are sacred and religious matters, objects of the veneration of various peoples for a long succession of centuries. It is false because in following it one would produce more evil than he would prevent. It would be necessary to burn all the histories and all the works on morality which present pictures of the depravation of manners, all the books on criminal jurisprudence, and an infinitude of others, because these books often contain accounts of highly improper actions. If the Athenian rhetorician had said: *One ought never, without disapproving them, report improper actions*, his less decisive maxim would have been more reasonable.

What I am going to expose will make the plan of my work known, and will justify the motive which made me undertake it.

Everything which can enlarge the field of human knowledge, everything which tends to increase our information, is incontestably useful; and the efforts of those who, through long meditations and laborious researches, devote themselves to such enterprises, can only be praiseworthy. Their results, were they only errors, ought still to merit public gratitude, because it is only by advancing toward the center of the whirlpool of errors which hide it that one discovers truths; and errors, well recognized, are further steps toward its sanctuary.

The numerous difficulties of mythology are of a nature to pique the curiosity, to exercise the mind, to fire the courage of amateurs of antiquity, and of all those who view with inquietude the veil which still covers our origin. I attempt to raise a corner of this veil, to explain some difficulties, and to bring to light some unknown truths.

People knew of the existence of the *Phallus* and of *Priapus*, but they were ignorant of their origin. They knew that among the ancients they were the emblems of fecundity, because their figures very clearly indicated this motive; but they did not know why these emblems were established. They had no other ideas but those furnished by their fables, that is to say, they were reduced to proving the certain by the uncertain and truth by falsehood.

They knew that the cult of the *Phallus* existed among different peoples of the earth; but they had not observed the alterations that it had undergone nor its constant union with the sun-gods of each country, a union which assists in linking together the different parts of the system which establishes the origin of the deity.

They were ignorant of the fact that, in principle, the *Phallus* had been completely isolated. They were ignorant of the cause of its disproportion to the human body, to which they later united it. They were ignorant of the fact that its attachment with different bodies, such as tree trunks, boundary markers, human figures, had given births to various deities: *Hermes, Phallus, Priapus, Pan, Fauns,* and *Satyrs.* They surmised the affinity of these various deities, but they had not yet perceived the bond which united them, nor their common origin. No more did they know, or they knew it but vaguely, that the cult of the *Phallus* had been preserved in Europe up until our times.

They had never compared this cult with that of the other gods of generation, nor shown the identity of their principles. They had not compared it with institutions and manners, which bear an important relation to it, a comparison which demonstrates a uniformity of purposes among the ancients, and which explains practices otherwise isolated and obscure. My work has for its object the elucidation of these points of ignorance, the dissipation of these doubts, and the clarity of these incertitudes.

35

I prove, in an incontestable manner, the origin of the *Phallus*. I follow its cult through its ramifications, its alterations, and its abuse, for many centuries and among the different peoples of the earth where it has been established. I find it almost wherever the sun was adored, where astronomic religion flourished.

This cult has long existed among the modern peoples of Europe; they have preserved the form of the *Phallus*, and have believed, like the ancients, in its fecundating virtues; but they have disguised its name and have applied other names appropriate to the times and to the dominant religion. I have carefully gathered together the different material that history and monuments have furnished me on the continuation of this cult. This part of my work, which is not the least interesting, shows the strength of religious customs, since they can maintain themselves for a very long time in spite of the efforts of contrary religions.

In order to render the existence of this indecent cult among the Christians more probable and to prove that it was not as foreign to their manners as one thinks, it is necessary to depict the manners contemporaneous with this cult and to join to it that of several practices whose indecency coincides with that of the *Phallus*. One will easily conclude from this that a people habituated to such manners and such institutions, far from rejecting them, would readily welcome the obscene cult and figure of the god of the gardens.

According to this statement, one might believe that it is necessary for me to enter into details which, by their nature, will alarm timid and skittish spirits. However, let them be reassured: they will find in this work no description capable of stimulating the senses; moreover, its scientific tone will repel readers who, by their age, might otherwise obtain some premature instruction from it. I shall be decent, I repeat, and I shall be more so than the majority of respectable authorities from whom I draw support. I shall be more decent than are certain books of the Bible, more than certain of the Church Fathers, whom I have cited only by employing circumlocutions. I shall be more decent than was Arnobius, one of the first defenders of Christianity, than were Saint Clement of Alexandria, and many other ecclesiastical writers; more decent than many prelate compilers of penitential Canons, whose expressions are of an amazing naïveté and liberty, and which, out of respect for our manners, I have carefully guarded against translating.

My expressions will be in conformance with genuine propriety; but ought I to sacrifice to the faint-heartedness of certain readers such colors as the verity of the picture demands? Anything that shame can find to rebuke in my work does not belong to me, but most often belongs to ecclesiastical writers, commendable for their piety and doctrine. And if, in this connection, my work has some blame to incur, it is not upon me, it is upon them that it ought to fall[2]. For the rest, my purpose, which I have expounded, is my excuse. I feel that, on this point, I have already said too much for reasonable readers, and that it would be in vain that I should say more about it for those who are not such.

TABLE OF CHAPTERS

*

TABLE OF CHAPTERS

*

THE TEXT

Chapter 1

ORIGIN OF THE PHALLUS. THE CULT OF THE BULL.
THE ZODIACAL GOAT[1]

IN order to represent, by a physical object, the regenerative power of the sun in the spring and the action of this
power on all the beings of nature, the ancients adopted the
image of masculinity, which the Greeks named *Phallus*.
Although this image appears indecent to the majority of
moderns, it was not so in antiquity; its sight awakened no
obscene ideas. On the contrary, people venerated it as one
of the most sacred objects of the cult. It must be admitted,
in spite of our prejudices, that it would be difficult to imagine a sign more simple, more energetic, and which better
expressed the thing signified. This perfect fitness assured its
success and obtained an almost general acceptance of it.

The cult of the image of masculinity spread over a large
part of the globe. It flourished for a long time in Egypt,
Syria, Persia, Asia Minor, Greece, Italy, etc. It was and still
is vigorous in India and some parts of Africa. It has even
propagated as far as America. When the Spaniards made the
discovery of that part of the world, they found this cult established among the Mexicans. What is more surprising, it
has been preserved almost up to our own times among the
Christians of Europe. It existed in France in the sixteenth
century; one finds traces of it even today in some parts of
Italy.

A cult which appears so strange to us, a cult so universal
in spite of the actual indecency of its object, well merits that
one occupy himself with it, that he search out its origin, its
condition among different peoples, the variations it has experienced, its influence on manners and its abuses. The history of man is in great part made up of his errors, his follies,
his crimes; and it is likewise the true picture of them which
produces the most efficacious lessons. If ancient and modern writers have unblushingly depicted the fury of the passions which divide, desolate, and annihilate societies, why

43

should reason oppose itself to an institution which, having a contrary purpose, produces less fatal results, the knowledge of which can throw new lights on the history of the human mind, and whose faithful exposition ought also to give rise to a moral lesson? One can, then, without blushing, seek out the origin, draw up the history, and blame the abuses of a cult whose primitive object tended, not to break, but to strengthen the bond of societies, to preserve them and augment them.

Some ancient and modern writers have spoken of the *Phallus* without saying anything of the origin of its cult. Some of these last, moralists more zealous than capable in the art of examining antiquity, sparing themselves a great deal of research and meditation, have quite simply attributed this origin to the corruption and libertinage of certain peoples. Even if I had not collected proofs contrary to that opinion, reason would make me reject it. Never have religious institutions in their beginning motivated a depravation of morals. One must therefore seek this origin elsewhere.

I believe it is found in the cult of the stars, or astronomic religion. In that case, one can say that the *Phallus* is of celestial origin. In order to establish this origin, I must go back to the times when astronomic religion began to make great progress. It is about four thousand five hundred years ago that the sun, through the effect of a third movement of the earth from which the precession of the equinoxes resulted, came, at the spring equinox, within the sign of the zodiac called *Taurus*. The sign of the celestial constellation which carried this name, represented on artificial zodiacs, was considered as the symbol of the vernal sun, of the regenerating sun of nature.

The birth of spring is the most attractive of all the times of the year; no other procures livelier or sweeter emotions. Triumphant over frost and the long nights, the sun, higher on the horizon, prolongs the days, spreads its fecundating warmth over the earth, imbues plants and animals with it, resuscitates nature, and everywhere sows life, verdure, hope, flowers and love. This precious time, and the numerous benefits of the vernal sun, were keenly sensed by all the peoples adoring this star. Also they celebrated it by joyous fêtes. The priests of this cult vested it with the imposing prestige of religion; and, in spite of the differences of climates and peoples, in spite of the numerous alterations the ancient cult of the stars experienced, in spite of the ravages of the centuries, the vernal fêtes have endured up to our times.

Popular gratitude, and the homage rendered to the gods of the day, to the sun for bringing the spring back, moved naturally toward an object more within the reach of the senses, toward the sign of the zodiac which was its symbol, toward the sign of *Taurus*, which, participating in some manner in the action of the regenerating sun, was in this respect identified with that star. They attributed its virtues to *Taurus*, its power, its benefits; they bestowed its honors on it. This sign counterbalanced the object signified, became a god, and representations of the celestial bull were adored.

Religious enthusiasm for this sign of the spring equinox went much further. People adored not only representations of the zodiacal bull, but later a living bull obtained the divine honors. Such is the march of the human mind. Once engaged on a career of error and superstition, it advances along it and never turns back; an admitted error then calls other errors to its aid.

It is thus that the bull, the sign drawn, painted, or sculptured on artificial zodiacs, was identified with the spring sun, became bull-sun, and then, represented by a living bull, was adored as a god. I shall describe under what names; I shall speak of the sort of worship rendered him, and I shall report the testimony of writers of antiquity who state that from the zodiacal sign of the bull are derived the bulls, cows, or oxen adored by partisans of the cult of the stars, and notably by the Egyptians[2].

45

The Gods of Generation:

In the same division of the zodiac where the bull is found, and close by it, is found another constellation called the *Celestial Charioteer* or the *Goatherd*. It is today represented by a man with goat's hoofs, carrying a she-goat and kids. At its origin, this sign was only the figure of a goat.

The same causes which elevated the sign of *Taurus* to the rank of the gods, procured a similar honor for the sign of the Goat[3]. These two signs equally indicated the return of spring: they had the same charm, carried the same name, but were adored in different cities. Thus, the vernal sun had two living animals for its emblem. The sacred goat was adored under the name of *Pan* at Mendes, a city which, as well as the Mendesian Nomos, owes its name to that animal deity; for *mendes* signifies *goat*. "The goat or god Pan," says Herodotus, "is called *Mendes* in Egyptian[4]." It is the same for the city of *Thmuis* or *Chemmis*[5], where the cult of the goat flourished. Saint Jerome tells us that this word signifies goat[6]. Arcadia, and even Italy, placed this goat in the rank of the great gods, and named it *Pan*. The sacred bull and goat often carried the same name: this novel conformity is attested to by Plutarch, who expressly says that the Egyptians gave the name of *Apis* to the goat of Mendes[7].

It is certain that these two living animals, the goat-god and the bull-god, had the same extraction and came from the same zodiacal division, where their signs were joined.

Iamblichus says that it was the system of the ancients to represent the sun under the forms of the animals that occupy the signs of the zodiac[8]. Lucian, in his Treatise on Astrology, explains with more precision: he says, speaking of the bull *Apis*, the object of the Egyptians' veneration, that if they worship that animal, it is to honor the celestial bull or the bull of the zodiac; and he adds that the cult of Ammon, the god with the ram's head, owes its origin to the celestial ram and to the knowledge of that sign of the zodiac[9]. Thus the animals worshipped in Egypt were the living symbols of the animals figured in the zodiac.

It is from these two worshipped animals, these two deities of the same making: the sacred bull called *Apis* and the sacred goat likewise called *Apis*, that the cult of the *Phallus* is derived, which is also called *Priapus*. It is the image of their genital parts, and not of those of man, as is generally believed, that became an object of worship.

First, I find a decided connection between the name *Apis*, given to those two sacred animals, and the name *Priapus* or *Priapis*, which was borne by the Phallus, isolated or attached to a herma. *Apis*, according to the most capable etymologists, signifies *high, elevated, powerful*; or this word is the same as *ab, abis*, from which was made *ap, apis*, which in oriental tongues expresses *father, chief, master*. In both cases, *Apis* would be an honorable name given the sun. As for the syllable *pri* or *pré*, it signifies, in the same languages, *principle, production, first source*; thus the word *Priapus, Priapis*, could be translated as *principle of production* or *fecundation of Apis*.

This etymology, furnished me by the savant Court de Gébelin, though it is highly probable and conforms with the genius of oriental languages, would be a feeble proof if it were not strengthened by several others more decisive. A great number of antique monuments demonstrate that it was an accepted custom to render worship to the separate parts of a sacred animal, to make images of them, to worship them in isolation, or to attach them to the trunks of trees, columns, or boundary-markers, called *Hermæ* by the Greeks, or, when human figures were introduced into religion, to unite different parts of these sacred animals to them.

It is thus that *Jupiter Ammon* had the horns of a ram, that *Pan* had the legs and hoofs of a goat, and sometimes its ears and horns. It is thus that *Bacchus*, the sun-god, was often represented with the head of the celestial bull, or only with its horns, and sometimes with its hoofs. That is why this god was often named *Bacchus Tauricorne* or *Tauriforme* by the Greeks and Romans. These figures were

47

monstrous: but this monstrosity had a mysterious motive, and without it the idol would have signified only a man.

The ancients were persuaded that these parts, joined on a tree-trunk, a boundary-stone, a herma, or a human figure, not only gave a divine character to such objects, but moreover communicated to them a sublime virtue, an influence comparable to that which was atributed to the sacred animal from which they were copied, and the constellation or star of which they were the symbol.

The horns were accepted as the symbol of the active power of the sun; thus the sun-gods, such as *Bacchus, Harpocrates*, and *Achelous*, his son[10], were represented with their foreheads adorned with bull's horns; a bull's horn was placed in the hand of *Achelous*, indicating his extraction from the celestial bull. Conforming to the idea of fecundity and strength attached to this attribute of the regenerating sun, the poets and sculptors evolved the *horn of plenty* or *cornucopia* out of these horns. In consequence of this principle, and in order to represent strength and dominance, they placed horns on the foreheads of many deities, on river-gods, demi-gods, and even some heroes of antiquity.

From these examples, it ought not to seem strange to see the sexual parts of the sacred bull and goat gain the same honors as their hoofs, head, or horns, since these parts expressed to mind and eye, in a peculiar and striking manner, the regenerative force, the source of fecundity attributed to the spring sun, and to those animals which were its symbols.

Another fact adds a new point of probability to my opinion: it is the importance which the Egyptian priests attached to the genital parts of the bull *Apis*[11]. When this animal-god had died, the priests chose with very great care a worthy successor for him. Among the marks which should, in the eyes of the people, signalize its divinity, the size of sexual parts of the new elect was highly commended. Porphyry says that the bull chosen to fill the rôle of god at Heliopolis had generative parts of an extraordinary size, in order better to designate the generative force that the sun exercises on nature through its heat. Also, Ammianus Marcellinus says that the bull worshipped at Memphis had evident signs of its generative faculty[12].

The Phallus was isolated in its origin and did not adhere to a human body. This adherence first took place a long time afterward, when the worship of human figures had made some progress. It even appears that at the period when the Greeks received the Phallus from the Egyptians, it was not joined to any body, and that the Greeks, even in the time of Herodotus, had not yet adopted this union. That historian, describing the ceremonies of this cult in Egypt, was astonished that a small human figure had been joined to the Phallus. "They have invented," says he, "human figures of an arm's-length in height to which genital parts, almost as large as the rest of the body, are adjoined[13]."

From this fact I draw a new proof of my opinion. If the Phallus had belonged to the human body, it would have been united to it from the very origin of this institution. But we notice that there was a time in Egypt when it was completely isolated, and that the Greeks, who took this cult from the Egyptians, had maintained its isolation.

The tale of Herodotus proves that the Phallus, joined to a human figure, was of a size disproportionate to that figure. He knew the mysterious cause for this disproportion but, through religious scruple, did not publish it. After having said that this human figure, an arm's-length high, was furnished with a Phallus almost as large as the rest of the body, and that in the towns and villages women carried several of these figures in procession, making the Phallus move by means of a cord, he adds: "But why do these figures have the genital member of a size so little proportionate, and why do these women move only that part? A holy reason it given for it; but I must not report it[14]." This reserve of Herodotus implies that he was initiated into the mysteries of the *Phallus*; that he knew its origin but could not divulge it. It appears that the human figure to which the *Phallus* was adjoined was a quite indifferent accessory which the priests had devised in order to put one on the wrong scent and hide the true origin of this cult from the eyes of the vulgar.

The disproportionate size of the Phallus proclaims plainly enough that it did not belong to the human figure to which it adhered. Besides, this disproportion was a mystery, and if the Phallus had belonged to the human figure, the matter would have been simple. Herodotus would not have been able to find anything mysterious in it. This disproportion as well as the proper size of this Phallus with the sexual parts of the bull, are new rays of light which, joined to the rays already brought forth, light up the tenebrous origin of the Phallus, and concur in proving that this object of worship was the image of the genital parts of the bull or goat *Apis*.

But the most positive proofs remove the least doubts which might arise against this fact. I have spoken of the affinity which is found between the bull and goat deities. I have said that both have the same origin, carried the same name, and owe their extraction to the same zodiacal division which marks the spring equinox; that both are the worshipped symbols of the regenerating and fecundating sun of nature. From this common identity of the cult I should be able to conclude that the origin of the *goat-Phallus*, fully established, ought sufficiently to establish that of the *bull-Phallus*. The origin of the first is attested to by a serious historian and one profoundly versed in mythology, who declares, in a precise manner, that the image of the genital parts of the goat was worshipped as the symbol of the nature which gives birth to all beings. Here is the passage: "The goat," he says, "because of its genital member merited, among the Egyptians, being placed in the rank of the gods for the same reason that the Greeks rendered divine honors to *Priapus*. That animal being strongly inclined to the acts of Venus, people judged *that the member of his body, which is the instrument of generation, merited wor-*

ship because through it alone Nature gives birth to all beings[15]." The same author immediately adds: "Finally, it is not only the Egyptians, but a large number of other peoples, who render worship to the sign of the masculine sex and employ it as a sacred object in the ceremonies of the mysteries, because it is from it that the generation of animals arises."

This worshipped member, this instrument of generation of the goat, this sign of the masculine sex which figured in the ceremonies of the mysteries of large numbers of peoples, could not be the living part of the sacred goat but its image or representation; and these images or representations were of the Phallus. Therefore it was Phalli which were representations of the genital parts of the sacred goat worshipped at Mendes and Chemmis. It was not men but two worshipped animals which furnished the model for the Phallus and the figure for its cult. This truth, until now unknown, acquires additional proofs in the following portion of this work.

People attributed to this isolated image the same virtue that they attributed to the vernal sun. They believed, and this opinion is expressed by the philosopher Iamblichus, that wherever Phalli were located they brought on abundance and fecundity and warded off accidents which are contrary to them. This sacred symbol received different names, according to the language of the peoples among whom it was worshipped, according to the use for which they destined it, and according to the object to which it was applied and joined. Called *Phallus, Priapus,* or *Priapis* among the Egyptians, Phoenicians, and Greeks, it also carried the name of *Tutunus, Mutinus,* and *Fascinum*[16] among the Romans; it is named *Lingam* among the Indians. But, whatever its name and its variations among different nations, the motives of this cult were always related to the fecundating action of the spring sun. Most often it was found joined with, and sometimes even confused with, the cult of the stars.

The Gods of Generation:

Suidas testifies that among the Egyptians *Priapus* was named *Horus*, sun-god of the spring; that he was represented in human form, holding a sceptre in his right hand, and in his left his Phallus in an energized state: "Because it is he who develops, who germinates the seed hidden in the earth. The wings he wears proclaims the celerity of his movement; the disk he holds represents the roundness of the universe. It is believed that he is the same as the sun[17]." In the monuments of Thebes, described by the Egyptian commission, an Osiris of gigantic stature is seen holding his Phallus in his right hand, the ejaculation of which produces men and animals. The Gnostics represented their sun-god *Jao* in the same attitude and with the same attributes. They added to it a serpent biting its tail, a symbol of eternity[18].

I shall give, in detail, positive proofs of the constant union of the cult of the *Phallus* with that of the sun. The sun, in the spring, kindles ardor and spreads light which, in autumn and winter, always passes away. The languor that nature experiences through the impotence of the sun has been as keenly felt and expressed by the mythologists of antiquity, but not so much venerated, as the regeneration which takes place in the spring. They therefore represented the Phallus, the symbol of the autumn and winter sun, in a state suitable to the sterility of those seasons; and the sad event which brought back the shortening days and the cold, has been allegorized in different mythologies by various fatal accidents which happened to the organs of generation of the sun-deities: accidents which caused the sterility of these deities.

Osiris, the sun-god of Egypt, was shut up in a chest and then cut up into many pieces by his brother Typhon, who threw his generative part into the Nile. *Attis*, sun-god of Phrygia, mutilated himself, or was mutilated by others. *Adonis*, sun-god of Phoenicia, was wounded by a boar in the generative parts. *Bacchus* or *Dionysus* wanted to descend into Hell in order there to seek his mother. A young man offered to lead him there, but this young man died; a sterile Phallus plays, in the fable, a highly indecent rôle. Saturn, an ancient sun-god, cut the generative organs off his father *Uranus*, god of the Heavens. *Jupiter*, another sun-god, subjected his father Saturn to the same operation. *Ixora*[19], *Brahma*, and *Vishnu*, the principal deities of India, underwent the same humiliation and were temporarily reduced to the same sterility. *Odin*, sun-god of the Scandinavians, being asleep in the woods, was, according to some, deprived of his generative organs by the teeth of a boar, or, according to others, he deprived himself of them with his own hands. He recovered them through the attentions of his wife. Olaus Rudbeck explains this allegory very well: "It signifies," he says, "that the sun, after having travelled the high regions of the Heavens, is forced to descend into the lower hemisphere, where it seems to rest during the winter[20]."

I shall not multiply examples of these allegories, which are almost alike, and which signify the vicissitudes of the sun during the course of the year; simple allegories drawn from nature, born in the imaginations of different peoples far from each other without intercommunication.

Thus the organs of virility, in a state of energy or impotence, have served in almost all religions of astronomic origin to signify the regenerative force of the sun in the warming season and the weakness of this star during the season of frost. Religion offered images of these organs of virility to public veneration; but I believe these symbolic images were prior to the mythological fables. Here is, according to reason, the geneology of these various institutions:

Knowledge of the course of the stars and agricultural needs brought about the divisions of the zodiac. The signs of the bull and the goat, placed in the division of the spring equinox, led to the worship of these animals and their sexual parts as principles of the regeneration of nature. Popular belief went farther and attributed a fecundating virtue to the mere images of the sexual parts of these celestial animals.

Later these figures of the zodiac, the images of their sexual parts, and the annual course of the sun developed into mythologic allegories. Upon this foundation each nation embroidered the legend of its deities.

I shall seek out and expose the fables and the forms of this cult in the various countries where it has flourished. It will always be found joined with and confused with the cult of the sun. The *Phallus* has played an important *rôle* in the religious \history of antiquity, has given birth to various deities, and has served to characterize many others. The numerous uses of this object of worship have greatly embarrassed writers on mythology who, clinging always to mythological fables and seeking truth in falsehood, have presented in this respect no satisfying explanation and have not dissipated the cloud obscuring its origin.

Chapter 2

THE CULT OF THE SACRED BULLS AND GOATS, ITS CONNECTION
WITH THE CULT OF THE PHALLUS OR PRIAPUS

BEFORE engaging upon the history of the cult of the
Phallus among the different peoples of the earth, it
would be wise to explain a few matters on the cult rendered
the two animals from which it arose, and the nature of the
religious homage addressed to the divine bull and goat,
archetypes of the *Phallus*.

The bulls, worshipped in Egypt under different names,
were, as has been said, the living images of the celestial
bull, figured in the zodiacal division in which the spring
equinox is located; and, through that circumstance, this
sign of the zodiac was the symbol of the sun which at that
period of the year, fecundates nature. People attributed
not only the fecundating faculty to the bull but also the
power of communicating this same faculty to humankind.

As soon as one of the *Apis* bulls was dead, the priests of
Egypt hastened to find a successor which, according to
popular opinion, was to be born of a cow fertilized by a ray
of the sun. Certain spots on its hide determined its election.
Its discovery changed the mourning into which the death
of its predecessor had plunged the Egyptian people, into rejoicing. At the very place where the new god had been
found a magnificent stable was constructed for him, facing
the direction of the rising sun. There, for four months, the
bull was fed on milk; then a troupe of priests conducted it
in procession to the banks of the Nile, embarked it on a
richly decorated ship, and brought it to Nicopolis. Here
women had the right, for forty days, to visit the new god.
According to Diodorus Siculus, they would take off their
clothing and offer the divine bull that which shame orders
to be hidden[1]. The aim of these women in this ridiculous
ceremony was evidently to obtain fecundity from the
bull-god.

This tale suggests another connection between the sacred

bull and the *Phallus* or Priapus, and confirms the origin of
the *Phallus* as the image of the genital parts of the deified
bull. If this animal was fed with milk, milk was also offered
to Priapus, and the libations that were made in his honor
were ordinarily of that substance. If Egyptian women, in
order to become fecund, showed themselves naked before
the bull, women observed this custom before the idol of
Priapus, and sometimes did still worse, as shall be seen in
the following part of this work.

The bull *Apis* left Nicopolis in a ship in which a golden
chamber was prepared for it. It was disembarked at Memphis where a temple, magnificently built by King Psammitichus, served it as stable. Its nativity was celebrated with
pomp, and it was led through the city accompanied by an
escort of magistrates and preceded by children who sang
hymns in its honor. This last ceremony was doubtless a-
dopted by many peoples. The custom of parading a fatted
calf decorated wth flowers and ribbons and accompanied
by music, which was and still is practised in many cities
of France, appears to be an imitation of it.

Let us pass to the cult of the goat, the living image of the
celestial goat or goatherd which is located in the zodiacal
division of the bull, and which, like it, was the symbol of
the vernal sun and of the fecundating and regenerative
powers of that star. The cults of these two sacred animals
have all the bonds of union arising from their common origin.

"The Mendesians," says Herodotus, "have a great deal
of veneration for goats and she-goats, and still more for the
former than the latter; and it is because of these animals
that they honor those who take care of them. They hold
one goat in especial veneration and when it dies, the whole
Mendesian Nomos is in mourning[2]." He adds that in the
Egyptian language *mendes* signifies *goat* and *Pan*, and
proves, consequently, the identity of that animal with god.
The mourning that the death of the goat caused recalls that
which the Egyptians manifested at the death of their bull

56

Apis. Milk was offered to that bull; likewise milk and honey were offered to the goat or to Pan, who was its idol, as well as to Priapus, who was of the same family. Pan, says the fable, accompanied the sun-gods *Osiris* and *Bacchus* on their expedition to India. Priapus also followed Bacchus on his trip to India[3], and had a dispute along the road with the ass of Silenus which that god rode[4].

The sacred goat had other conformities with Priapus. The Greeks, under the names of *Pan, Faunus, Silvanus, Satyr*, etc., worshipped rural deities whose figures represented various parts of the goat and the most characteristic attribute of Priapus. They had the horns, sometimes the ears, and always the thighs, legs, and hoofs of that animal, and also its Phallus in a state of ardor. "Temples have been erected to them", says Diodorus Siculus, speaking of these deities with horns and hoofs of a goat, "They are represented in a state of ardor and lubricity in order that they might appear to imitate the natural lasciviousness of the goat[5]." That is why Priapus often has the form of a goat; that is why he is often confused with the gods *Pan, Silvanus* and *Satyr*[6], all of whom have the same origin as he.

The women uncovered themselves quite indecently before the bull Apis. They did the same thing before the goat of Mendes or *Chemmis*, and even carried their strange devotion a great deal further. In the intention, doubtless, of destroying the supposed charm which held them in a state of sterility, they offered themselves up to its brutal passion.

"Nothing is so certain," says the translator of Herodotus, "as the infamous custom of shutting up women with the goat of Mendes. The same thing was practiced at Chemmis (a city of the Delta). A thousand authors have spoken of it[7]." Some verses of the poet Pindar, cited by Strabo, a passage from Clement of Alexandria, and several other writers of antiquity, attest to the existence of this religious and revolting practice[8].

"Whilst I was in Egypt," says Herodotus, "an astonishing thing happened in the Mendesian Nomes: a goat publicly had commerce with a woman; and this adventure was known to everyone[9]." This monstrous union did not take place every time it was solicitated; and here the gross instinct of an animal showed itself superior to the human mind, degraded by religion. "It must not be astonishing," Plutarch informs an interlocutor, "if the goat of *Mendes* in Egypt, shut up with many beautiful women, shows no desire for them, and is inflamed only for she-goats[10]."

There still exists at Chemmis some traces of this disgusting prostitution. "One sees there," says Vivant Denon, "an edifice almost completely covered over. Doubtless it is the temple dedicated to the god *Pan,* formerly consecrated to prostitution. One encounters there today, as at Metabis, a number of *halmès* and public women who, if not protected, are at least recognized and tolerated by the government. I have been assured that every week they gather together on a fixed day in a mosque, near the tomb of the Sheik *Haridi,* and that, mixing the sacred and profane, they there commit all manners of lewdness[11]."

The Jews, whose legislator had applied himself to forming institutions entirely contrary to those of the Egyptians, quite far from worshipping goats, presented two of them each year before the tabernacle. One was sacrificed to the Lord; and the other, charged with the imprecations of the High Priest and the iniquities of the people, was sent into the desert.

It was not thus with the Samaritan sectarians. The first verse of their Pentateuch proves that they worshipped the goat as the creator of the universe: "In the beginning," it reads, "the goat *Azima* created Heaven and Earth."

This cult passed into India. In the monuments of the grottoes of *Iloura,* which go back to the greatest antiquity, the cult of the goat is found, to which the Indians gave the name *Mendes,* which it bore in Egypt. The goat was worshipped in Greece and Etruria. The Romans modified its worship and greatly diminished its brutal aspects. Here is what Ovid tells in this respect:

58

A History of Phallic Cults

The Romans, vexed at seeing the Sabine women they had stolen remain sterile, went to invoke Juno in the sacred forest of the Esquiline Hill. Scarcely had they finished their prayers, when they saw the tops of the trees shake and heard this oracle: *Let the women of Italy be fecundated by a goat.* That was to prescribe the revolting practices of the cult of *Mendes* to the Romans. They did not seem disposed to obey the oracle. Then a soothsayer of Etruria interpreted it and lessened its severity: *Arrangements are to be had with Heaven.* He proposed to the sterile women to have themselves beaten on back and belly with thongs made of goat's skin. Accordingly, this took place in the fête of the Lupercalia.

On February 23, the day set aside for this solemnity, young men, almost or completely naked, went through the city armed with the knife by which they had sacrificed the goats, and a whip made from thongs taken from the hides of these animals, and struck those they encountered with it. The women, far from fleeing, hastened to the front and offered their naked bellies to the blows of these young floggers, in the hope of becoming fecund and producing fine children. It should be noticed that the ceremony among the Romans differed from that of *Mendes*. Here the goat did not play the principle rôle, merely a part, but the motive was the same.

If one could lend belief to those tales, mingled with so many ridiculous stories, related by our credulous ancestors about the nocturnal assemblies called *sabbat*, one would be tempted to believe that the cult of the goat continued for a long time among modern nations. In these assemblies it is always a goat that presides; it is a goat that is worshipped there; it is a goat that is joined with women assistants. If one could separate the truth from the chaos of falsehood, strip it of the exaggerations with which the accounts of these mysterious assemblies are charged, one would perhaps find therein the practices of the cult of *Mendes*; one might form judicious opinions about the existence of these sabbath as-

59

sembles, attested to by many authorities, by many judicial proceedings, and so strongly contested by many illustrious writers. A good history of the mystic societies of all nations would dissipate many uncertainties and clear up the obscure origin and filiation of human institutions.

Chapter 3

THE CULT OF THE PHALLUS AMONG THE EGYPTIANS

IS it India, Phœnicia, Ethiopia, Chaldea, or Egypt that saw this cult born; or rather was the model for it furnished the inhabitants of those countries by a nation still more ancient? The various opinions advanced on this matter are subordinated to the question of astronomic religion, of which this cult is an appendage. Many savants have thoroughly examined it without much success but their opinions are contradictory.

Abbé Mignot, who with a pertinacious constancy has carried on research in the religious antiquities of the Assyrians and Phœnicians, thinks that the *Phallus* was original with Assyria, and with Chaldea, which was part of it, and that from that country the custom of consecrating this symbol of generation passed into Egypt. He believes, according to the savant Le Clerc, that the name of this symbol is Phœnician; that it derives from *Phalou*, which in that language signifies a *secret* and *hidden thing*, and from the verb *phala*, which means *to be admirable* and *to be held secret*. He concludes from this that the origin of the *Phallus* is not Egyptian[1].

Whatever it may be, it is in Egypt that the most numerous monuments of this ancient cult are located; it is from this country that it spread through Asia Minor, Greece, and Italy; and Egyptian history offers us more ideas on the *Phallus* than that of other peoples of the Orient. All this decides me to draw the first strokes of the picture I am going to present from the Egyptians.

Among that nation the *Phallus* received divine honors; it was placed in the temples. It was taken about in procession in the country; and it figured with distinction at the fêtes celebrated in honor of the sun-god Osiris or Bacchus. Herodotus, who attended this ceremony, describes it for us in this manner: "The Egyptians celebrated the fête of Bacchus in almost the same manner as the Greeks; but, in place

61

of a Phallus, they invented figures of about an arm's length in height, which were made to move by means of a cord. In the towns and villages the women carry these figures, the virile member of which is scarcely smaller than the rest of the body, and which they move about. A flute-player walks at the head. They follow him singing the praises of Bacchus, etc[2]."

It is remarkable that this custom of carrying a large Phallus in procession, and of making it move whilst thus carrying it, exists even today in a region remote from Egypt. In 1787, M. de Grandpré was witness of a fête celebrated in the Congo States. He there saw masked men executing a pantomime and primly carrying an enormous Priapus which they shook with a spring[3].

This similarity of custom among peoples whose existence is separated by more than two thousand years, whose countries leave vast deserts between them and a distance of more than a thousand French leagues in a straight line, evokes many conjectures as to the authentic origin of the cult of the *Phallus*. Could it have reached the East Coast of Africa from Egypt through Ethiopia? Or rather could Ethiopia which, as many writers of antiquity witness, furnished its gods to Egypt, have been the common source from which the Egyptians and the inhabitants of the Congo drew this cult? I shall not undertake to resolve a question so difficult; but the comparison I have just made can suggest a new direction to the ideas of the students of antiquity.

The first of the epagomenal days[4], or five days before the first day of the Egyptian year, the birth of the sun-god Osiris was celebrated; and in honor of the same god on the 25th of the month *plaménoth*, which corresponds to the spring equinox, were observed. The *pamyles*, a word which, according to the savant Jablonski, signifies the *announcement of good tidings*. Then, says Plutarch, a figure of Osiris whose Phallus was triple was carried in procession: "For this god," he adds, "is the principle of generation; and each principle, through its producive faculty, multiplies everything that goes out from it." According to this author, the number three expresses indefinite plurality[5].

In Egypt there were some affected mysteries of the private cult of the *Phallus*. Diodorus Siculus informs us that those who wished to attain the priesthood began by having themselves initiated into them.

The ancient monuments of the Egyptians which bear witness to the existence of this cult are very numerous, and their manner of representing the *Phallus* is quite varied. Many of them are seen isolated, or sculptured on a landmark in a horizontal direction. Vivant Denon, in his *Voyage d'Egypt*, saw these isolated Phalli sculptured in the temples, and frequently repeated[6].

The most remarkable of isolated Phalli is doubtless the one that the same traveller discovered at Thebes in Upper Egypt, in the tomb of a woman. This Phallus, which had been alive, was embalmed and wrapped in little bands. It was found resting on the corresponding part of the female mummy. The engraving he gives of this mummy and Phallus proves that the latter was larger than natural size and did not belong to the human species. I should imagine that this mummy was that of a woman of high dignity, and that the embalmed Phallus belonged to one of the sacred bulls, which had been removed after the death of the animal and placed in the tomb as a preservative, as a proper means of warding off evil spirits, which the ancients believed were solely occupied with tormenting the souls of the dead[7]. The Greeks and Romans also sometimes placed figures of the Phallus in sepulchures for the same reason: many Greek and Etruscan vases, found in tombs, offer Phalli in painting, and even licentious scenes, called *Priapées*[8]. Isolated Phalli of very small size are found in great numbers in Egypt. Ordinarily they are of porcelain of different colors, and were worn as amulets.

I cannot leave these details on isolated Phalli without speaking of a very strange opinon, relative to a figure that

is assured to be their representation, nor without combat-
ing this opinion advanced by distinguished savants. They
pretend that the figures of the cross that one so frequently
sees on Egyptian and Indian monuments, are figures of the
Phallus. Thus, those crosses, placed on the top of the covers
of many Egyptian vases consecrated to religious ceremonies; those crosses, with which the vestments of the
priests and deities of Egypt are often strewn; those crosses
or crosslets, enclosed in a circle, which are seen on a great
number of ancient monuments; and finally, those crosses
encircled or surmounted by a ring, which the figures of
priests, Osiris, and especially Isis, almost always hold in
their hands, etc., therefore should be so many Phalli. This
opinion, which would give an impure origin to the cross of
the Christians, has been supported by the savants Jablonski,
in his *Panthéon Egyptien*[9]; Delacroze, in his Histoire du
Christianisme des Indes[10]; Carli, in his *Lettres sur l'Amérique*[11]; and finally Larcher, in his notes to the translation
of Herodotus[12]. This last even gives the figure of these supposed Phalli; and this figure is exactly the same as that of
the crosses which hang on the bosoms of our devout and
genteel women and on bishops. He also gives the figure of
the triple Phallus or *triphallus*; and this figure recalls that
of the triple crosses which are carried in procession before
the Pope or before eminent prelates.

Crosses are extremely ancient and appear to have originated in Egypt. The sacred sign of the *Tau*, the image of
the worshipped cruciform pillars, which the Egyptians
called *Thoth* and of which they made a deity, was a cross.
This sign also formed an alphabetic character, of which
our T represents, if not the exact figure, at least the accen-
tual value. When, toward the end of the fourth century,
the Christians demolished the famous temple of *Serapis* at
Alexandria, they found there many crosses engraven on the
stones. It is this circumstance, says the historian Sozomen,
that determined many pagans to embrace Christianity[13].
As for the cross surmounted by a ring, it was and still is

the sign of the planet; and the Tau, which is adjoined to it, distinguishes it[14].

Those who are perfectly acquainted with the form of the Phallus will not be able to persuade themselves that a cross is its image. Moreover, in the same Egyptian monuments one sees quite simple crosses and Phalli according to nature. The Egyptians would not have represented the same object at the same time by figures so dissimilar. But let us come back to the history of the *Phallus* among the Egyptians.

Phalli were added to the figures of animals, men, or deities. A singular example of those additions has been published by Knight; it is a figure representing the solitary head of the bull *Apis*, ornamented with the disc of the sun, which characterized that divine animal. From the two sides of its mouth appear the forms of two Phalli of equal size which extend horizontally in the same line[15]. It is the symbol of strength joined together with that of a double power of fecundity.

Egypt still offers Phalli adhering to the deity Terminus. Vivant Denon has described a bas-relief where a man is seen with the head of a wolf making offerings to a Terminus. At the same time this wolf-headed man is placing a hand on the Phallus of that deity[16].

Phalli joined to human figures are very frequent in Egyptian monuments. One finds representations of figures of seated children to whose bodies an enormous Phallus adheres, which rises above their head, or the extremity of which they support on their shoulders. Caylus has had one of these figures engraved: "It represents," he says, "the most terrible Phallus that has been seen, in proportion, on any other work[17]." Although those who passed on this antiquity to him affirm that it was Egyptian, Caylus has judged it to be Roman. This savant, elsewhere very circumspect in his decisions, has evidently spoken with too much precipitation. Vivant Denon has published two figures entirely similar to that of Caylus which he found in Egypt[18].

The following portion of this work will prove that similar figures existed in the temple of Hierapolis in Syria. Thus, the model for these little figures with large Phalli came from Egypt or Syria.

The intimate relations which exist between the vernal sun and the symbol of generation led the Egyptians, when they had adopted the custom of giving human figures to their deities, to represent the sun-god, Osiris or Bacchus, with a Phallus in a state proper for fecundation. The majority of the ancient monuments offers us this sun-god holding his Phallus quite freely in his hand and seeming, by this attitude, to prove to his worshippers his resurrection in the spring and his renewed vigor. Caylus had four antique figures of Osiris engraven which are all in this mystic attitude[19]. In the collection of antiquities at Paris, several of this variety are to be seen. There a naked Osiris can be seen, with a mitre on his head, raising a veil wth his right hand and holding his Phallus with his left. A sulphur impression, made from an engraven amethyst, represents the same god in the same position[20].

The figure of Osiris, with a mitre on his head, holding in his hand the scourge or whip which characterizes him, and furnished with a quite salient Phallus, figured in religious ceremonies. Twelve priests would carry on their shoulders a rich litter covered with a carpet strewn with blossomed lotus flowers, upon which the idol of this sun-god was raised. Bas-reliefs seen in the temple of Hermonthis, in that of Karnak at Thebes, and in several other places of Upper Egypt, represent this processional ceremony and the god with the Phallus thus carried in triumph[21].

Sometimes the same figure of this god is found before an altar laden with offerings of fruit or fowl. A very striking bas-relief which ornaments a bronze vase brought from Egypt, the engraving of which has been published by Caylus, represents a nude Osiris in that manner: his Phallus is found in contact with the offerings laden upon the altar[22].

A quite similar scene was reproduced in the Egyptian monuments published by Vivant Denon[23]. A very rare peculiarity of this cult is noticed in a bas-relief at Tentyra. It represents an Osiris, his mitre on his head, completely nude and lying horizontally, whilst his Phallus is raised in a vertical direction[24].

It would be too long, it would be too tedious to describe all the variety of figures which the Egyptians gave the cult of the *Phallus*. The cabinets and collections of antiquities present many other varieties of this type of worship among this nation. I have limited myself to the principal ones.

Now I ought to relate, and it will be curious to learn, under what allegorical veil Egyptian priests hid from the vulgar this powerful symbol of the regenerative sun, its astronomic origin, and by what fable they justified the cult of the *Phallus*.

Osiris (or the Sun), the principle of good, the spirit of light, had as enemy his brother Typhon, the principle of evil, the spirit of cold and darkness. This latter managed to seize Osiris and shut him up in a chest, which he threw into the waters of the Nile. This disappearance of Osiris is a crude allegory of the rigorous season, in which the nights, longer than the days, the absence of vegetation, and the torpor of nature, proclaim the triumph of the spirit of darkness and death over the spirit of light and life.

Isis (the Moon), wife of Osiris, made extensive travels in order to recover the body of her husband. It was at Byblus, in Phœnicia, at the time of spring, that she discovered it. She at once carried off the chest which contained this precious burden; but, wishing to visit her son *Horus* (god of the day), she deposited it in a secret spot, far from the gaze of mortals. Typhon, hunting during the night, noticed the chest, recognized the body of Osiris, took possession of it, cut it up into fourteen or twenty-six parts, and scattered them hither and thither[25]. Isis, sorely afflicted, very carefully searched for the scattered parts of the body of her dear Osiris. Wherever she recovered each part she raised a monument in its honor. She managed to recover them all except the sexual part, which Typhon had thrown into the Nile, and which had become the prey of the fishes. In order to replace this lost part the goddess had a representation of it made, and rendered it the same funereal honors that the other parts of the body of Osiris had received. She even marked her predilection for this image of virility by having it placed in the temples and exposing it to the adoration of the people.

It is affirmed that this part of Osiris's body, the Phallus, was originally made of fig wood because that tree contained to a great degree the principles of moisture and reproduction. Be that as it may, Isis set up this image of wood as a deity. "She consecrated," says Plutarch, "the Phallus, whose fête the Egyptians still celebrate[26]." He adds that "Isis made it herself. She had it carried in the sacrifices in order to inform us that the productive virtue of the sun-god had moist substance for its prime material; and that through it this virtue is communicated to everything that is susceptible to it."

It was by this fable, which was invented at a period when the Phallus was still isolated and unattached to any body, that the Egyptian priests sought to give the people reason for the worship of this symbol. It was under this allegorical veil that they hid the mechanism of their dogma and the changes of the sun, or rather of the earth, during its annual revolution. It will be observed hereafter, that the fables invented by priests of each nation to justify the cult of the *Phallus* were not more ingenious.

Such are the progressive variations which this image underwent in Egypt. First, the simple and isolated Phallus, then the double Phallus, then the triple; the Phallus joined to any body, tree, boundary-marker, landmark, etc.; the Phallus adhering to a human figure, without designation; finally, adhering to that designated under the name of the god Osiris.

Thus was the Phallus shaped in Egypt. The cult could not elevate this symbol to a more eminent degree than by adjoining it to the idol of the sun-god. This adjunction did not alter the simplicity of the primitive cult, and the isolated Phallus continued to be venerated; for, in ancient religions, an admitted novelty never established itself at the expense of ancient practices, and cults from the most remote times, from the most barbarous times, often existed alongside of cults enriched and ornamented by civilization. The crude and simple Phallus lost nothing in public opinion, whilst the Phallus rendered illustrious by its adhesion to the figure of the sun-god Osiris, was pompously honored and venerated.

This cult continued in Egypt up to the end of the fourth century of the Christian era. Cambyses, king of the Persians, conqueror of the Egyptians, killed the ox *Apis* and had its priests flogged. He was a worshipper of a single god. The Greeks, conquerors of Egypt, and who reigned there in the name of Ptolemy, changed nothing of the Egyptians' cult, submitted to it, and embellished and strengthened it. They were imitated by the Roman emperors: the Greeks and Romans worshipped many gods. The Christians imitated neither the Greeks nor the Romans; they followed the footsteps of Cambyses, resolved to annihilate the religion of Egypt, and their perseverance assured their success.

In 389, the bishop Theophilus obtained permission from the emperor Theodosius to destroy Egyptian idolatry. Furnished with his powers, and escorted by a crowd of monks, he set the priests to flight, broke the idols, and demolished the temples or established monasteries in them. The famous temple of Serapis at Alexandria was razed on this occasion. The temple of Osiris or Bacchus, falling into ruins, was converted into a Christian temple. This expedition did not take place without exciting bloody emotions among the people. In the subterranean vaults of the temple of Bacchus were found, says the historian Socrates, many of those infamous figures named *Phallus* by the Greeks[27].

Such were the beginnings, the progress, and the ruin of the cult of the *Phallus* in Egypt. I am now going to examine what became of this cult among other nations.

Chapter 4

THE CULT OF THE PHALLUS IN PALESTINE AMONG
THE HEBREWS

IN geographic order, Syria presents itself first; and the
part of Syria bordering most closely upon Egypt is
Palestine. What was the cult of the *Phallus* in this last
country, which was inhabited by the Hebrews, God's
chosen people, who, always directed in the holy way by
the divine hand, never ceased to swerve from it; whose
laws altho, it is said, composed by their god, were so poorly
suited to their character and national customs that they
were almost continually violated?

The Moabites and Midianites, neighboring peoples of
Palestine, worshipped a god called *Baal-Phegor* or *Beel-
Poor* [*Baal-Peor*][1]. The earliest Christian writers who
have spoken of this deity, such as Saint Jerome, Rufinus,
Isidorus of Seville, and many other learned commentators
on the Bible, agree that this deity was the same as *Priapus*.
Always fond of imitating the superstitious practices of their
neighbors, the Hebrews had themselves initiated into the
cult of *Baal-Peor*: they fornicated with the Moabite girls;
they ate of their sacrifices; they worshipped their gods[2].

The god of the Hebrews or Israelites, greatly irritated
by this conduct, said to Moses: "*Take all the chiefs of the
people, and hang them up before the Lord against the
sun*[3]." Moses did not follow the order of God, who wished
to spare the people and punish the chiefs; he did not hang
them, but he said to the judges of Israel: "*Slay ye every
one his men that were joined unto Baal-Peor. . . .*" There
were then twenty-four thousand men killed[4].

This was not all; the Lord further said to Moses: "*Vex
the Midianites, and smite them: For they vex you with
their wiles, wherewith they have beguiled you in the matter of Peor*[5]." Thus the blood streamed in Israel: relatives
slaughtered relatives; twenty-four thousand Hebrews were
put to death, as well as all the Midianites, for having paid

71

homage of that which gives life[6]. For it need not be doubted that this *Baal-Peor* was a phallic idol, situated on the mountain of *Phegor* or *Phogor* [*Peor*], the name of which was given to this deity. It was the Priapus of the Greeks and Romans, as various writers agree[7].

This terrible method of converting a people did not produce the effect expected of it by the law-giver Moses. By killing men, one does not always kill their opinions; and several centuries later the Hebrews were seen to renew their adoration of the idol of Baal-Peor. Here is how the Lord made the prophet Hosea speak: "I found Israel like grapes in the wilderness; I saw your fathers as the first-ripe in the fig-tree at her first time: but they went to Baal-Peor (or they were initiated into the mysteries of Baal-Peor), and separated themselves unto that shame; and their abominations were according as they loved[8]."

There were women who officiated in the temple of this god: they were named *kedeschoths;* and this name, according to Saint Jerome, had the same significance as that of prostitutes who fulfilled the function of priestesses of Priapus. Saint Jerome represents this idol to us as carrying the characteristic sign of Priapus in its mouth.

The ceremonies observed in the cult rendered to Baal-Peor have exercised the pens of many commentators on the Bible, and other savants. It seems that the principal ceremony consisted of presenting oneself naked before the idol. The worshippers, according to Philo, placed all the body's external openings in evidence before it. The text of the Bible seems to say that they offered themselves to the idol so as to prostitute themselves to it. Beyer, in his additions to Selden, concludes from the text of the Bible that the Moabite girls first prostituted themselves to the idol, then to the Israelites[9]. This infamous ceremony seems to have been closely related to the cult that the Egyptians rendered the bull Apis by uncovering themselves before it.

The rabbi Solomon Jarchi attributes a highly indecent and yet filthier practice to the cult of Baal-Peor. It would be difficult to find a stranger and more disgusting form of worship in the annals of human folly. The worshipper, according to this rabbi, presented his naked posterior before the altar, unburdened his bowels, and made an offering of his stinking excrement to the idol[10].

The books of the Bible say nothing more of Baal-Peor; but they make mention of various other cults which differ in nowise from that of the *Phallus* or of Priapus.

The ancestors of King *Asa* had introduced several species of idolatrous cults into Israel, and that of the *Phallus* or Priapus was among the number. The high priestess of this deity was even the mother of the young king. "Asa took away the sodomites out of the land, and removed all the idols that his fathers had made[11]." He stripped his mother, named Maachah, of the authority with which she was vested, in order that she might no longer preside over the priesthood of Priapus and the sacred grove where the statue of this god was adored. He destroyed the cavern where its mysteries were celebrated, and the image of this crapulous deity, broken into pieces, was burnt near the stream Kidron[12].

This deity, which the Vulgate names *Priapus*, carries, according to the Hebraic text, the name of *Mipheletzeth*. Some commentators have judged it to be of the feminine gender, and believed that it was the goddess *Astarte* or *Venus*. Would the authors of the Vulgate have taken one sex for the other, and Priapus for Venus? This opinion is not firmly supported unless one regards the authority of Rabelais, on such a matter, as very weighty[13].

One finds, in the books of the prophets, another testimonial to the existence of the cult of the *Phallus*. Ezekial indicates, in a precise manner, the fabrication of this indecent image, and the abuse that the women of Israel made of it. "And of thy garments," he told them, "thou didst take, and deckedst thy *high places*[14] with divers colors, and played the harlot thereupon: the like things shall not come, neither shall it be so. Thou hast also taken thy fair jewels of my gold and of my silver, which I had given thee, and madest to thyself images of men, and didst commit whoredom with them[15]. Thus the Israelite women fabricated, doubtless after the example of some neighboring peoples, Phalli of gold and silver, and misused them in a strange manner.

Such is what the books of the Bible and the works of their commentators furnish on the cult of the *Phallus* among the Hebrews. This cult, whose existence was an obvious infraction of this nation's laws, began to manifest itself in the time of Moses and reappeared at different periods until the days of the prophet Ezekiel: about nine hundred years.

Chapter 5

THE CULT OF THE PHALLUS IN SYRIA, PHŒNICIA, PHRYGIA,
ASSYRIA, AND PERSIA

AT the extremity of Syria, and on the banks of the
Euphrates, was *Hierapolis* or the sacred city. Within
its precincts a temple was raised, renowned for its grandeur
and magnificence. Never, in any region of the earth, was
the *Phallus* more honored than at this place; never had
more imposing, more colossal monuments been raised to
it[1].

The author of the *Treatise on the Syrian Goddess*[2], who
has described the temple of this city and its sacred objects,
describes it as follows: "This temple is the vastest of all
those of Syria; there is none more holy; no place is more
consecrated by the devotion of the people. It holds the
most precious works and the most ancient offerings. There
one sees many wonders, statues worthy of the gods whose
image they offer and whose presence they manifest. . . . Its
riches are immense: Arabia, Phœnicia, Babylon, and Cap-
padocia pay it tribute. The Cilicians and Assyrians bring
there the most precious things their countries have. I have
seen the treasury where these riches are deposited: it contains a large number of vestments and a great amount of
other objects which equal gold and silver in value. Moreover, among no nation is celebratedd as many fêtes and solemnities."

This temple, built on an elevation in the middle of the
city, was surrounded by two enclosures. It had an extent
of a hundred fathoms. Riches abounded in its interior. Gold
shone on the doors; the vault was all covered with it. Per-
fumes from Arabia deliciously caressed the nose, and the
eyes were dazzled by golden statues enriched with precious
stones. But the most remarkable things to be seen there
were the throne of the sun and the statue of Apollo, which
the author, from whom I borrow these details, says to have
seen move and raise themselves up to the roof of the temple.

75

In order to maintain and augment the devotion of the people, the priests neglected nothing to tickle the senses, to astonish the mind. But I shall not further follow this enthusiastic and credulous writer in his long and pompous descriptions, which smack of the soil and which offer the ordinary extravagances of oriental imagination.

Before the portico of this magnificent temple rose two colossal Phalli, whose prodigious height causes suspicion of our writer's exaggeration, or error of his copyists. These two images of the masculine sex had, according to him, an elevation of 300 *orgies*: which comes to 1706 feet 3 inches in the measure of France[3]; an extravagant size! These Phalli, then, would have had a height three times the length of the temple, which was only 100 *orgies*, or 568 feet 9 inches. This shocking disproportion between the length of the edifice and the height of the Phalli has caused it to be deemed necessary to cut off a zero and read 30 *orgies* in height instead of 300: which reduces these monuments to the more suitable height of 170 feet $7\frac{1}{2}$ inches, a still very considerable height, since it approaches that of the towers of Notre-Dame at Paris[4].

The inscription engraved on these Phalli read: *Bacchus has raised these Phalli to Juno, his stepmother*[5]. This is one of the examples of the custom, constantly followed by the ancients, of associating the Phallus with the sun-deities. The throne of this star was in this temple; and the most brilliant statue which decorated its interior was that of Apollo, a sun-god. Bacchus, who raised these Phalli, was, as well as Osiris, the sun-god of the Egyptians. For symbols, both have the celestial bull and the Phallus drawn from the figure of this animal.

These two enormous Phalli, which figured before this temple as the two towers before the portals of our gothic churches, seem to have served as the model for this type of construction, so generally adopted in recent centuries. From the time of Vitruvius, round towers whose top represented an egg have been named *phalæ*. The towers which served for the defense of camps and cities also carried the same name in the Middle Ages[6]. The conformity of names, the relations which exist between the forms, and especially the location of these Phalli and that of the towers of our gothic churches, give a great deal of probability to this opinion.

These two Phalli served not only for the decoration of the façade of the temple, but also for the ceremonies of the cult. "Every year," continues our author, "a man mounts to the summit of these monstrous images, and remains there for seven days. He pulls up, by means of a long chain, the provisions he needs, and wood with which he constructs a sort of seat in the form of a nest. A standing priest, placed at the base of the Phallus, receives the offerings of the multitude that comes to the temple, and he repeats very loudly the names of those who have made them. The man perched on the Phallus hears them, and at each name he addresses a prayer to the god for the devotee. During this prayer, he beats on a brazen instrument, which gives out a disagreeable sound."

During the seven days and seven nights that this reciter of prayers remained on the elevated point of one of these Phalli, he had carefully to guard against going to sleep. It is related that if he yielded to the attraction of sleep a scorpion would come to sting him painfully and awaken him[7].

It seems that, at the time the author I cite was travelling in Syria, opinions on the origin of this ceremony were markedly divided. Some believed that this man so highly elevated, being closer to heaven, was able more easily to communicate with the gods. Others thought that his stay on the top of this species of obelisk was an act commemorative of the deluge of Deucalion, when men climbed into trees and on the mountains in order to save themselves from the flood. But our author is of another opinion: he believes that it is in honor of Bacchus that this ceremony is practiced. "All those who raised Priapi to Bacchus," he says, "placed upon them men of wood. For what reason did they

77

place those figures there? That I shall not say; but it seems to me that it is in order to represent that wooden figure that a man mounts the Phallus."

The figure of these wooden men mounted on the top of a Phallus is found in an engraving of the *Antiquitiés* of Caylus. It represents a group composed of an enormous Phallus and two children. One of them is seated and seems to support the Phallus, which he cannot clasp; the other is completely perched on the top. It is evident that the figures described by the author of the *Treatise on the Syrian Goddess,* and those which Caylus retraces for us, were copied from the same model[8].

In describing the various objects contained in the same temple, our author adds that there were to be found there many of these wooden Phalli on which were sculptured little men furnished with "large Priapi," and that these figures were called *Nevropastes,* which is to say, *stiff sinew.* "These Phalli are also seen in the temple, and on the right is found a little man of brass, seated and holding a *Priapus*[9]." This last type of Phallus is entirely similar to that which was in use in Egypt, and which the women paraded in the country. Caylus and Denon have given figures of them[10].

In Phœnicia, the neighboring country to Syria, the *Phallus* was also in honor; and, as elsewhere, it was associated with the cult of the sun. This star was adored there under the name of *Adonis* or *Lord.* This deity is entirely the same as the Osiris of Memphis, and the Bacchus of Thebes in Egypt[11].

It was at Byblus that the same cult was particularly celebrated. There *Astarte,* or the *Byblian Venus,* was worshipped in the same temple. Venus presided over the generation of beings. Like Isis, she represented the symbol of fecundation. In love with handsome Adonis, she offered the symbol of the earth at spring which, avid for the heat of the sun, opens its bosom to its rays and is fecundated by them. After the example of the Egyptians, who celebrated the death and resurrection of Osiris, they celebrated at Byblus the death of Adonis with tears and mourning. Then his resurrection was announced: the mournful fête was succeeded by ceremonies where public joy was manifest. It was during the latter that the Phallus, symbol of the resurrection of Nature at spring, was carried about in triumph[12].

In order to justify the presence of the Phallus in these joyous solemnities, the priests of Byblus contrived the fable of the enraged boar that wounded Adonis in the generative parts: they said that this god, being cured of his wound, consecrated the Phallus, the image of the wounded part. It was this fable that the Greeks, according to their custom, embroidered, amplified, and altered, but the principal features of which they preserved: the death or wounding of Adonis, and his resurrection or cure.

If one turns to Phrygia, he will find the cult of the *Phallus* likewise associated with that of the sun, and founded on a similar fable. The sun-god of this country was named *Attis*; and, in order to explain to the people the reason for the presence of the Phallus in the religious ceremonies that they celebrated in honor of this regenerative deity, the priests composed several fables which agree in saying that the young and handsome Phrygian, named *Attis*, mutilated himself, or was mutilated by others.

According to all these oriental fables, Egyptian, Phœnician, Phrygian, it was always after a fatal and unfortunate event that the Phallus appeared publicly and received divine homage, because it was after the cold and sterility of vegetating nature that the sun appeared and spread vigor and fecundity everywhere.

Diodorus Siculus informs us that the Egyptians were not the only ones who honored the Phallus: several other peoples imitated them in this respect. In Assyria, as in Phœnicia, the Phallus figured in the mysteries and religious ceremonies.

Alexander Polyhistor, speaking of the temple of Belus

at Babylon and the varied and monstrous idols that were to be found there, says that one of these idols had two heads: one of a man and the other of a woman, as well as the generative parts of the two sexes[13]. Similar mixtures of the two sexes in the same figure will be seen elsewhere. The geographer Ptolemæus testifies that the symbol of the reproduction of beings was consecrated, not only among the Assyrians, but also among the Persians. "The members destined for generation," he says, "are sacred among the peoples of Assyria and Persia because they are the symbols of the Sun, Saturn, and Venus: planets which preside over fecundity[14]. Thus it was not only the image of the masculine sex, but also that of the feminine sex, that the Assyrians and Persians consecrated in their religious ceremonies. One will find other examples of this union of the figures of both sexes.

Among the ancient and allegorical bas-reliefs of Mithra, sun-god of the Persians, one finds the symbol of fecundity figured by a man holding his Phallus in his hand, which is in a state proper for fecundation. These allegorical bas-reliefs, which are common enough, represent a man with a Phrygian cap on his head and holding under him a bull whose throat he has just cut. This is the symbol of the sun, conqueror over the celestial bull[15].

In the ruins of Persepolis, according to a modern traveller, several bas-reliefs are to be seen which retrace the same scene, but instead of the bull it is a goat that the man, symbol of the sun, is slaughtering[16]: which proves that the ancient Persians, like the Egyptians, likewise had for symbols of the vernal sun the zodiacal signs contained in the same division: the Bull and the Goat.

Chapter 6

THE CULT OF THE PHALLUS AMONG THE INDIANS

AFTER having gone over all the lands existing between the banks of the Nile and those of the Indus, and having found the cult of the *Phallus* established among the various nations occupying this vast expanse of country, I shall examine what this cult was and still is among the ancient and modern inhabitants of India. This nation differs from those of which we have spoken in that in spite of the efforts of the Mussulman and Christian missionaries, its inhabitants have, for the most part, preserved their ancient religion, its dogmas, and its ceremonies.

Bardesanes saw among them, in a deep grotto, a statue of ten to twelve arm-lengths in height, which represented man and woman in a single body. One-half the face, one arm, one foot, belonged to the masculine sex, and the other half of the body to the feminine sex. On the right breast was to be seen the sun, and on the left the moon in painting; all the rest of the body represented figures of mountains, seas, rivers, plants, and animals. The Brahmins, said that God had given this hermaphroditic statue to his son in order that it might serve him as a model when he created the world. It was the symbol of the active and passive principles of Nature. That is what Porphyry tells us of this symbolic figure of the two sexes, by which the ancient Indians represented the generation of beings[1].

It is quite clear from this description that the two sexes are the symbol of generation; but the sign is lacking there which characterizes the masculine sex, named *Priapus* or *Phallus*, and which the Indians call *Lingam*. The silence of Bardesanes does not prove that this sign was unknown among the Indians at the time when, about fifteen hundred years ago, he travelled among them. Bardesanes obviously did not notice everything there; besides, he may have seen *Lingams* there without mentioning them, because these images may have presented nothing extraordinary to him, nothing that he had not seen many times in his own country; moreover, Porphyry, who cites him, may not have set down everything which Bardesanes had mentioned on the cult of the Indians.

This citation serves to prove that the figure of the two sexes joined together was formerly a sacred object among the Indians. It also proves that these people have scrupulously preserved up to the present day the rites and ceremonies which they observed about fifteen centuries ago, for the figure that Bardesanes remarked in India at that time exists even today in the same form[2]

This vigilance in not altering religious practices enforces my belief that the figure of the Phallus or *Lingam*, which the Indians venerated as a sacred object, was likewise venerated by them in very remote times. This opinion is confirmed by the report of several travellers in India who have seen on the walls of the *pagodas* or temples of that country, the construction of which is of the greatest antiquity, bas-reliefs representing the image of the masculine sex, called *Lingam*, in quite varied shapes. Finally, to say to those who know the Indians' aversion for religious innovations that the cult of the *Lingam* exists, is to prove to them that it has existed for a very long time.

The Phalli, called *Lingams* in India, are found there in many forms: there are some isolated, some combined with the figure of the feminine sex; there are some which, by their smallness, ought to be placed in the rank of amulets; others which are of a size highly disproportionate with the body to which they adhere.

The Indians of the sect of *Chiven* [Siva], one of the three principal deities, hold the *Lingam* in great veneration: it is under this form that the god is worshipped in the pagodas; but when he is carried in procession through the streets, his idol bears the figure of a man[3].

Three symbols joined together ordinarily express, in the places consecrated to the cult, the three principal deities: *Brahma*, *Vishnu*, and *Siva*. This Indian Trinity is characterized by a pedestal on which there is an urn from which a body in the form of a column rises. The pedestal signifies *Brahma*; the urn placed above indicates the figure of the feminine sex and the symbol of *Vishnu*; the column which rises from the heart of this urn designates the masculine sex, symbol of *Siva*.

The interiors and exteriors of the pagodas offer paintings and sculptures well calculated to offend the eyes of all people other than the Indians: scenes are often found there of a revolting indecency. The pagodas, the roads, the places intended to lodge travellers, which the Persians named *caravansaries*, and the Indians *chauderies*, everywhere offer the *Lingam*. The *pagoda* of Villenour, situated two short leagues from Pondicherry, contains within its precincts a tower consecrated to the *Lingam*. This tower is surrounded by colossal and very ancient figures of this image of masculinity[4]. The celebrated and ancient pagoda of *Jaganneth*, and the no less ancient one of *Elephanta* near *Bombay*, the bas-reliefs of which William Alen sketched in 1784, offer the most indecent pictures that a corrupted imagination could conceive[5].

Over the gate of one of the cities of the little kingdom of *Sisupatnum* is to be seen a statue of *Sita*, wife of the god *Vishnu*, incarnated under the name of *Rama*. This statue, of natural proportions, is accompanied by six fakirs or penitent Indians, placed in such a manner that three are on one side and three on the other. These penitents are represented kneeling, entirely naked, their eyes raised to the wife of the god, and each holding his Phallus in both hands, of which they seem to be making an offering to this deity[6].

On the Malabar Coast many pagodas are seen whose façades are laden with bas-reliefs which represent scenes most astonishing to European eyes. Such are those of the celebrated pagoda of *Cuddalore*, situated between Pondicherry and Tranquebar, whose vast edifices form four great series of buildings joined together. Such are those, yet a great deal more remarkable, of the pagoda of *Tri-*

colour, situated between Pondicherry and Madras. The cult of the *Phallus* is there seen expressed with most extraordinary refinements. There the figure of a man is to be noticed armed with a *Lingam* of prodigious size which, twisting about like the serpent of Laocöon, entwines the naked limbs of several women, and comes finally to reach the goal destined for it. The strangest attitudes, which even the lascivious genius of Aretino was not able to imagine, are found in these bas-reliefs consecrated by the cult, as well as in those which decorate the chariots intended for religious ceremonies.

A Frenchman recently arrived from India, who furnishes me these details, assures me of having stealthily penetrated into the most secret sanctuary of the pagoda called *Tréviscarré*[7], which is consecrated to the cult Siva, and of there having seen a species of pedestal, made of granite, composed of a large base and a column supporting a basin from the middle of which rises a colossal *Lingam*, about three feet in height. Below, and on the stone forming the urn, is a large hollow which represents the feminine sex: this symbol characterizes the Trinity of the Indian religion. In this sanctuary, which is lighted only through the roof, and on this sacred stone the priests initiate the young *devadasis* or dancing-girls, which the Europeans call *Bayaderes*, into the mysteries of love; who, consecrated to the cult, also serve the pleasures of the public and are, as were the courtesans of Greece, priestesses and prostitutes.

What is to be said of these indecencies, when one is convinced that it is not libertinism but religion which has prompted them? Regarding these scandalous pictures, a modern traveller makes this sage reflection: "Let us not pass judgment on the customs of peoples with whom we have no resemblance, according to our prejudices and habits: these figures shock Europeans but they inspire the Indians with religious ideas[8]."

The Indians believed to give more expression or power to the symbol of fecundity by joining together the generative parts of the two sexes. This union, which some writers confuse with the *Lingam*, is named *Pulléiar⁰*. It was doubtless a copy of the half male, half female statue that Bardesanes saw earlier in India. "This symbol, as simple as it is forceful," says Sonnerat, "is the most sacred form under which Siva is adored: it is always in the sanctuary of his temples." The votaries of this god have great devotion for the *Pulléiar*: they employ it as an amulet or charm; they wear it hung around their neck, and the monks, called *Pandarams*, never go about without this religious decoration. Others enclose the *Pulléiar* in a silver box, which they attach to their arms. Sonnerat informs us that the votaries of *Vishnu* scorn this practice and regard it as infamous.

The Indians further have a little ornament, of gold or silver, called *Tali*, which the women ordinarily hang around their necks like an amulet. They receive it on the day of their marriage from the hands of their husbands, who themselves obtain it from the Brahmins. These trinkets carry the impression of some hieroglyphs which represent the *Pulléiar* or *Lingam*. It is in connection with them that Sonnerat, from whom I borrow these details, reports the following anecdote:

A Capuchin missionary had a violent quarrel with the Jesuits of Pondicherry, which was taken before the courts. The Jesuits, very tolerant when tolerance favored their ambitious designs, had not opposed the use of this amulet. M. de Tournon, apostolic legate of Saint-Siège, who did not trifle on such matters, and who scarcely loved the Jesuits, rigorously prohibited the *Tali*, and prescribed to the Christian women of India to wear in its place a cross or medal of the Virgin. The Indian women, attached to their ancient practices, refused to make the change. The missionaries, fearing to lose the fruits of their zeal and seeing the number of their neophytes shrink, compounded and took a middle course with the Christian women of India. They engraved a cross on the *Tali*. By this arrangement the symbol of the Christians was joined to the image of the parts of generation of the two sexes[10].

Some *Lingams* of India are, as were certain Phalli of Egypt and Syria, of colossal size and highly disproportionate to the bodies to which they were joined. Such are the *Lingams* of the pagoda of *Villenour*, which are isolated, and those which one sees in the base-reliefs of that of *Elephanta*, which are adjoined to human bodies, etc. A traveller in that part of the world reports a remarkable example of a gigantic *Lingam* affixed to a boundary-marker. In passing opposite the Travancore Coast, near Cape Comorin, this traveller, a naval officer, sent a boat ashore for some information. "On its return," says he, "the boat carried a *Lingam* or*Priapus* that the boatmen had taken from a niche made in a boundary-marker, where it was exposed to public veneration. The design of it was only too well executed, for it was indecent through the studied elegance of its sculpturing. . . . The boatmen had taken it to serve as a tiller for the boat's rudder. They had steered the boat with this *Phallus*, the dimensions of which one can judge from this use[11]."

Every day at the noon hour the priests of Siva decorate the sacred *Lingam* with garlands of flowers and with sandal-wood. And in order to render themselves worthy of this august function, they prepare for it by purifying themselves with a bath. In the ceremony called *Nagapoutché* [*Nagar-panchami?*] or the office of the adder, women replace the priests. They carry a stone *Lingam*, represented between two adders, to the bank of a pool, wash this symbol of generation, after having purified themselves by a bath, burn pieces of wood destined for this sacrifice before it. They throw flowers on it and ask of it riches, a numerous posterity, and long life for their husbands[12]. The Indians firmly believe that if the ceremony is done in the prescribed manner, one obtains all that is asked for.

The monks of Siva are named *Pandarams*. They begrime their face, breasts, and arms with ashes of cow-dung; they go about through the streets asking alms and singing the praises of Siva, carrying a bundle of peacock feathers in their hands and the *Lingam* hung around their necks[13]. The *Cachi-caoris* are a species of *Pandaram* who make the pilgrimage of *Cachi*, from which they bring water of the Ganges in earthern urns. They must carry it to Ramissaram, near Cape Comorin, where there is a very renowned temple of Siva. They pour this sacred water over the *Lingam*, which is adored in this temple under the name of *Ramanada-Suami*[14],which signifies *God adored by Brahma*. The water which has run from the *Lingam* is gathered up and distributed to the Indians, who religiously preserve it and make a custom of pouring a few drops of it on the head and in the mouth of dying persons. They drink it and believe that this water washes them of all impurity and renders them worthy of achieving celestial blessedness after death[15].

The *Andis* or penitents are in India what the Fakirs are among the Moguls. Almost all votaries of Siva, they constantly offer their adoration to the *Lingam*, which is practically the only furnishing with which they are supplied[16]. One further finds in India a peculiar sect of Siva; those who compose it are named *Laris*. They are seen completely nude, covered with ashes, asking alms with the *Lingam* in hand. Among these mendicants, those who constantly hold their two hands on their head while grasping the *Lingam*, are revered as saints. Charitable people give them something to eat and place the food in their mouths[17].

The *Lingam* fresh from the hands of the workman is a furnishing without virtue; it acquires some only after a Brahmin has blessed it and incorporated the deity into it through his prayers and ceremonies[18].

The priests of Siva do not mutilate themselves like those of Vishnu; but they are obliged to approach the *Lingam* entirely nude in the presence of the public. The obscenity of the idol, the voluptuous scenes painted or sculptured on the walls of the majority of this god's temples, do not prevent the most rigorous chasity being enforced upon them.

The Gods of Generation:

When they exercise their office, they must abstain from the desires that these licentious images are able to arouse. If these priests, allowing their thoughts to pause there, experience an emotion which the imagination transmits to the external organs and which their complete nudity would render visible, they are severely punished. "If the people," says Sonnerat, "whilst performing their devotions, should perceive that the priests were experiencing the least stirring of the flesh, they would regard them as infamous and stone them to death[19]."

Sterile women come to place certain parts of their body in contact with the extremity of the *Lingam* consecrated to this purpose. Even cattle are led there and submitted to the same ceremony in order that they may multiply more abundantly. This custom, as we shall notice later, is practiced among the Greeks and Romans through the same motive.

Duquesne saw, in the environs of Pondicherry, newly married girls offer this wooden idol the complete sacrifice of their virginity. In one part of India, called Canara, as well as in the environs of Goa, similar sacrifices are the custom. The young girls, before marrying, offer and give in the temple of Siva the first-fruits of marriage to a similar idol whose *Lingam* is of iron, and this god is made to act the rôle of sacrificer[20].

In some countries of India the priests, more clever, have stolen such a precious function from this god. This sacrifice, quite preferable to the first, doubtless appeared more holy to the sacrificers and sweeter to the victims. The King of Calicut, for example, gives up for one night the maiden he is going to marry to the most highly esteemed among the priests of his kingdom, and pays for this service with a considerable sum[21].

At Jagannath, a young girl, introduced during the night into the pagoda, is supposed there to espouse the deity. A priest, under cover of the shadows, takes possession of her first-fruits which she believes is being offered to a god[22].

Ancient history offers a great number of similar examples, customs, and deceits[23].

Superstition extended the homages rendered the *Lingam* to the priests of that divine object. It was quite natural that the original should share in the honors conferred upon the copy. In the country of Canara, of which I have already spoken, the priests of Siva are naked when they go out from their pagodas, and walk about thus in the streets, making a little bell resound. At this noise the women, even of the highest quality, hasten before these pious personages and devoutly kiss their sexual parts in honor of the god Siva. It is thus that many penitents show themselves as insensible to pain as to the attractions of pleasure, and receive without emotion similar kisses by devout Indian women.

This religious veneration for the virile organ of generation was inculcated in the soul of all oriental peoples. That which appears ridiculous and shameful to us was noble and sacred for them; I shall report some proofs of it later. Egypt furnishes examples similar to those of India; and the Egyptian women still perform the same act of devotion toward those inspired by Heaven as the women of Canara perform with respect to the priests of Siva[24].

In order to justify the adoration of the *Lingam* and the cult of Siva, to whom this part was consecrated, the Indian priests, like those of other nations, thought up several fables, of which the following are the most credited: While Siva was living among men, he stole from the priests or Brahmins several beautiful women attached to their service; for Siva was a god of extremely evil example, as were the majority of Greek and Roman deities. These Brahmins, ill-satisfied, pronounced so many maledictions against the ravisher god that he lost the use of one of his members, highly necessary to this occasion. The god, accursed, could not in consequence satisfy his desires with these women; and the *Lingam* was consecrated as a commemorative monument to this adventure, shameful for Siva and honorable for the Brahmins.

89

In other countries of India the fable is different: One day when this god, lying with his wife, was going to taste the most sprightly pleasures which love has to offer, a devotee came, quite unseasonably, to knock at his door. The god is too busy to open for him. The devotee continues to knock, but knocks without success. Exasperated by this delay, he gives vent to his anger and bursts out in insults against Siva who, having heard them, answers the importunate fellow with violent reproaches. Then the devotee, dismayed, changes his tone, excuses himself profoundly, and asks that those who will worship Siva under the figure of the *Lingam* be more favored than those who adore him only under the human figure: his prayer was granted.

Another fable reports that the sexual part of this god was so large that it reached to his forehead. He was obliged to cut it off and divide it into twelve portions, which gave birth to all human creatures[25]. This last fable seems allegorical; the preceding ones are not. It seems to express the annual revolution of the sun, divided into twelve months. The author who conceived it allowed the truth to be seen through the light veil of allegory. It suggests that the *Lingam* has the same origin and the same connection with the regenerative sun as the *Phallus*, and that Siva is the sun-god of the Indians.

In the neighboring regions which are to the east or north of India, or in Hindustan, the cult of the *Phallus* is no longer found. The references that we have on Pegu, Ava, Siam, or Burma, on Tibet or Bhutan, offer no ideas on this cult. Although the religions of these different nations had numerous connections with those of India, this cult seems never to have been adopted in the vast regions of Tartary. One is tempted to believe that it existed in China, according to an idol witnessed by recent travellers there, and which they qualified vaguely as the idol consecrated to voluptuousness. "Many of these idols," says one of them, "are seen in the temples of *miaos*. They receive a tribute of confidence and respect on the part of Chinese women, very chaste otherwise. Superstition is a veil for these images[26]."

These idols are doubtless those of which Barrow speaks when he says that the sterile women go into the temples in order there to touch their bellies to certain little copper idols, persuaded that in consequence of this contact they will conceive and bear children[27]. That indeed is the cult of an obscene idol, and this cult is rendered by women; but these vague ideas declare neither the sex of the idol nor consequently the Phallus. Thus one must conclude, so long as no new information enlightens us, that the cult of this sacred object extended in Asia from the banks of the Nile to those of the Ganges, and that it did not cross this last boundary.

Chapter 7

THE CULT OF THE PHALLUS IN AMERICA

IT was necessary that circumstances be found in America which existed in Asia in order that they might cause the same cult to be born in these two parts of the world; or rather, it was necessary that Asiatics, presumably Phœnician sailors, thrown by storms on the coasts of the New World, had there taken up their abode and carried over their arts, manners, and religion. This latter opinion, which is very probable, is adopted by many authorities.

That the cult of the *Phallus* had passed from India or Ethiopia into Egypt, from Egypt into Asia Minor and Greece, etc., is no wise astonishing. These peoples were in communication with each other. But that this cult had existed in regions long unknown to the rest of the earth, in many parts of America with which the peoples of the Old World were formerly not in communication, is an astonishing fact, but is none the less true. Here are the proofs of it:

When Mexico was discovered, the particular cult of the *Phallus* was found well established in the city of Panuco. Its image was adored in the temples. Bas-reliefs like those of India were set up in public places, representing different manners of union of the two sexes. At Tlaxcala, another city of Mexico, the act of generation was revered under the united symbols of the characteristic parts of both sexes[1].

Garcilaso de la Vega says, according to Blas Valera, that among the Mexicans the god of luxuriousness was named *Tiazolteuti* [*Tezcatlipoca?*][2]. I must not neglect to observe that the sun was the principal deity of Mexico, and that there, as in Asia, the cult of the *Phallus* was found associated with that of this luminary.

The natives of Tahiti [Haiti?], since named San Domingo, also rendered a cult to the *Phallus*. One can have no doubt of this from the number of these sacred objects discovered in that country in 1790, as is proved by the dissertation made on this subject by Arthault, former physician to the king of France. These Phalli, he says, found in excavations in various quarters, are incontestably the work of the natives of the country. "They had several varieties of them. One of them was found in the great *caverne du Borgne*. It is represented in natural size; the form of it is regular; the glans is perforated; it is flattened at its base in a chisel-form." This chisel-part was pierced; doubtless a cord was drawn through it which served to attach it to or hang it in some holy place. "The material of this Phallus, whose design I have seen," remarks Arthault, "is a species of marble." A second is of harder stone, not as large as the first, finely polished, and equally well formed. The scrotum is expressed here in a natural manner, and forms part of the same piece. A third, smaller, shaped like the preceding one, is pierced at its base; it seems intended to be worn hung on a cord. Arthault possessed seven of these Phalli[3].

These isolated Phalli ought to be ranked in the class of those that the Africans and Asiatics carried in state in religious ceremonies, or rather in that of the *ex-votos* hung up in places intended for the cult, in order to cure the sick part of which the Phallus is the image. Whatever they may be, they certainly belong to the first periods of this cult: their isolation is the proof of it.

The discovery of these Phalli throws a new light on the antiquity and universality of the cult, and enlarges the field for conjectures on the origin of the inhabitants of what we call the *New World*. Let us now pass to Europe and examine the cult of the *Phallus* in that part of the world.

Chapter 8

EGYPTIAN colonies having been established at different periods in certain parts of Greece, brought along their manners and religion which were gradually adopted by the uncivilized inhabitants of that country, in those days known by the name of *Pelasgi*. One of the chiefs of these colonies founded a city in Beotia to which he gave the name of Thebes, a name which another very famous city of Upper Egypt bore, where there existed the worship of the sun under the name of Bacchus, and consequently the Phallus, one of its principal symbols.

Herodotus and Diodorus Siculus agree in saying that the cult of Bacchus was brought to Greece by a man named Melampus, who lived 170 years before the Trojan War. "Melampus, son of Amythaon," says Herodotus, "had great knowledge of the sacred ceremony of the *Phallus*. It is he, in fact, who taught the Greeks the name of Bacchus, the ceremonies of his cult, and who introduced the procession of the Phallus among them. It is true that he did not reveal the basis of these mysteries to them; but the sages who came after him have given an ampler explanation of them. It is Melampus, then," he adds, "who instituted the procession of the Phallus which was held in honor of Bacchus; it is he who instructed the Greeks in the ceremonies which they practice even today[1]."

The same historian informs us that Melampus, instructed by the Egyptians in a great number of ceremonies, including those concerning the cult of Bacchus, introduced them into Greece with slight changes. It is natural for the ceremonies practiced by the Greeks to have a great deal of resemblance to those of the Egyptians. Plutarch likewise says that the *Pamyles* of the Egyptians, fêtes celebrated in honor of the sun-god Osiris and in which the Phallus was carried, did not differ from the *Phallophoria* of the Greeks, celebrated in honor of the sun-god Bacchus, where the Phallus

94

was also carried[2]. The difference which Herodotus finds
between them was that the Greeks did not sacrifice a pig
in their fête as the Egyptians did, and that the Phallus
which they carried in the processions was isolated and did
not adhere to a human figure. Herodotus thinks that the
knowledge acquired by Melampus of the cult of Bacchus
proceeded from his connections with the descendants of
Cadmus of Tyre, and with such Tyrians as came from
Phœnicia in that part of Greece today called Beotia.

The Greeks did not compose their theology solely from
that of Upper and Lower Egypt, but they further combined with it the crude worship of the *Pelasgi*, the ancient
inhabitants of Greece. Herodotus informs us that the
Hermes with the Phallus, or the *Mercury of the rigid
member*, does not come from Egypt, but that the Athenians
retained it from the Pelasgi, who inhabited the same district. "The Pelasgi," he adds, "give a sacred reason for it
which is found explained in the mysteries of Samothrace[3]."

To the cult transmitted by the Egyptians, and to that
which they found established among the Pelasgi, the
Greeks added the cults in flower among the Syrians, Babylonians, Phœnicians, Phrygians, and the other peoples who
founded colonies among them or with whom they had commerce. This confused *mélange* became the material which
the fruitful and unruly imagination of the Greeks employed to give birth to their inextricable maze of mythology: that ocean of ridiculous and marvelous adventures, often contradictory, which are the despair of commentators. Amidst this chaos there nevertheless exist points
of recognition which establish the conformity of the ceremonies and fables of the Greeks with those which were
current among the foreigners. The Phallus, for example,
was among them, as among the Egyptians and other peoples, constantly united with the cult of the sun-god.

In Greece, Bacchus was named Dionysus[4], and his fêtes
Dionysia. There were several fêtes by this name. Those
which were celebrated in the city were called the *Greater*

Dionysia, or the *Urban Dionysia*: they took place at Limnæ in Attica, where Bacchus had a temple, on the twelfth of the month *Elaphebolion*, which corresponds to March 12, and a week before the period when the same fête was celebrated in Egypt under the name of *Pamyles*. The *Greater Dionysia* lasted for three days. Fourteen priestesses, chosen by the archon and presided over by his wife, participated in this solemnity.

Originally these fêtes were celebrated without luxuriousness and without a great deal of magnificence. Here is what Plutarch says of them: "Nothing was simpler, and at the same time merrier, than the manner in which the Dionysia were formerly celebrated in my country. Two men walked at the head of the cortege, one of them carried a jar of wine, the other a vine-stock; a third led a goat; a fourth was laden with a basket of figs; a figure of the *Phallus* closed the procession. Today," he continues, "this happy simplicity is disregarded; it is even made to disappear under a vain magnificence of silver and golden vases, superb vestments, horses yoked to chariots, and bizarre disguises[5]."

The procession was begun by Bacchantes, who carried urns full of water; then came young virgins commendable by the purity of their morals and by their birth, called *Canephori*, because they carried golden baskets filled with the firstlings of all the fruits, in which there were some tame snakes, various flowers, and some mystic objects: as sesame, salt, ferula, ivy, cakes of an umbilical form, placentas, and especially a Phallus crowned with flowers. Following this troupe of virgins appeared the *Phallophori*: these were men who did not wear any mask on their face, but who covered it with a tissue made of the leaves of ivy, wild thyme, and acanthus. A thick crown of ivy and violets encircled their heads. They wore the amice and the augural robes. They held long staffs in their hands, from the top of which hung Phalli. This part of the ceremony was named *Phallophoria*, *Phallogogia*, or *Periphallia*.

Then came a chorus of musicians who sang or with musical instruments accompanied songs which matched the images that the *Phallophori* displayed, crying at intervals: *Evohe Bacche! io Bacche, io Bacche!* This chorus was followed by the *Ithyphalli*. According to Hesychius, they were dressed in women's clothing. Athenaeus represents them with crowned head, their hands covered with gloves on which flowers were painted, wearing a white tunic and a light Tarentine amice, and counterfeiting drunkards by their gestures and countenance. It was the *Ithyphalli* especialy who chanted the phallic songs and who gave vent to these exclamations: *Eithe, me Ithyphalle!* The mystic *van* followed, and other sacred objects.

Groups of Satyrs and Bacchantes often participated in these processions. The Bacchantes, half naked or covered only with a tiger skin worn sling-wise, with dishevelled hair, and holding lighted torches or thyrsi in their hands, abandoned themselves to the most impetuous movements, bellowing *evohe's*, and threatening or even striking the spectators. They sometimes executed dances called *phallic*, the principal characteristic of which consisted of lascivious movements. The Satyrs dragged along goats ornamented with garlands, destined for sacrifice. Behind these, mounted on an ass, followed the figure of Silenus, representing that unsteady and half-drunk foster-father of Bacchus.

One would imagine that such religious scenes degenerated into abuse. Also, everything most disgusting connected with drunkenness and debauchery was audaciously offered to the eyes of the public. A physician of antiquity, Aretaeus, in speaking of the Satyrs who accompanied the ceremonies of Bacchus, says that they presented themselves there in a highly indecent manner, in an apparent state of desire, the amazing continuance of which was regarded as a favor from Heaven, a mark of divine assistance[6]. It is probable that this author has taken fiction for truth and drollery for reality. Various antique monuments which retrace for us scenes with groups of Satyrs, represent men whose heads were covered with a whole mask, or a cap-like one, and whose bodies and legs were wrapped in goat-skin. It can be believed that the travesty was complete and that an artificial Phallus was substituted for the natural one, for without it an erethism so sustained during a long and fatiguing march, would be truly a miracle.

Whether the obscene sports of the groups of Satyrs were real or figurative, they were none the less attempts against public decency. A Father of the Greek church, revolted by these scandalous scenes, expresses himself thusly: "The most debauched man would never dare, in the most secret spot of his home, to give himself up to the infamies that the chorus of Satyrs brazenly commit in a public procession[7]."

This religious procession was followed by games which had a similar character. The youth exercised itself by jumping over goat-skins blown up with air, and by running blindfolded amongst Phalli decorated with flowers and hung from pines or columns. It was regarded as an omen of good fortune when in running the head happened to strike against these images.

The priests of Osiris, Adonis, Attis, Siva, and other sungods, had composed one or several legends for each of these deities, which were recited during their fêtes and also sung in their hymns, and which explained their association with the Phallus. The priests of Bacchus followed this example and composed a fable, of which here is a summary: Bacchus had lost his mother Semele, killed by lightning or dead in a fire; he sought her in many countries, and went as far as Hell in order to find her. During the course of his searches he met a young man, called Polymnus or Prosumus, who promised to lead him to his mother, and to show him the road to Hell if necessary. But having become amorous of Bacchus, Polymnus demanded a shameful complaisance as a price for this service; the god consented without difficulty. It will be seen in what manner he kept his promise. Polymnus died along the road. Bacchus raised a tomb to him, and in memory of the deceased he carved a

Phallus from the branch of a fig tree, and placed it on this monument. The two Church Fathers who supply these details, Arnobius and Clement of Alexandria, add something highly scandalous. Their expressions are so indiscreet that I shall not translate them. I shall limit myself to saying that Bacchus, desirous of fulfilling his obligation, fixed the wooden Phallus on the tomb of the deceased, seated himself naked on its point, and in that position completely acquitted himself of the promise he had made young Polymnus[8].

It was by such obscene tales, which reveal the immorality of the time in which they were invented, that the priests amused the people and deceived them as to the true purpose of the institution of the *Phallus*; as if vulgar falsehoods could be more profitable to religion than simple truths, the knowledge of which was reserved solely to the initiated of the highest classes.

The scholiast of Aristophanes attributes the institution of the *Phallus* in Greece to another cause. He relates that a man named Pegazus having introduced the cult of Bacchus and his symbols into Attica, the inhabitants of that country refused to adopt them. They were punished for it by this god, who struck them in the generative parts with an incurable malady, unresponsive to all remedies, and of which they could rid themselves only by rendering great honors to Bacchus. They then made Phalli as a particular homage paid to this deity, and as a monument to their recognition of and attachment for him.

The Greeks, very kindly disposed to the cult of the *Phallus*, introduced it into the ceremonies consecrated to several other deities. "The custom has been preserved," says Diodorus Siculus, "of rendering various honors of Priapus, not only in the sacred mysteries of Bacchus, but also in those of other gods; and his figure is carried to the sacrifices smilingly and sportively." Venus and Ceres, the first presiding over the fecundity of humankind, the second over that of the fields, naturally assumed a right to the Phallus, the general symbol of fecundity.

The consecration of the *Phallus* by Isis in Egypt, the union at Byblus, in the same temple, of the cults of the Sun, Venus Astarte, and the *Phallus*, and this same union of the images of the two sexes in India, prove that the Greeks did not lack examples for associating the *Phallus* with the cult of Venus. Also, they often united it with the *Mullos*, that is to say, with the image of the female sexual parts, and this union completed the allegory. Also, in the mysteries of the Mother of the Loves at Cyprus, the symbol of virility was represented. Initiates into the mysteries of the Cyprian Venus ordinarily received a handful of salt and a *Phallus*.

A peculiar and little known sect, called the sect of the *Baptae*, celebrated at Athens, Corinth, on the island of Chios, in Thrace, and elsewhere, the nocturnal mysteries of *Cotytto*, a species of popular Venus. The initiated, who gave themselves up to all the excesses of debauchery, employed the Phallus in a peculiar manner; they were of glass, and served as drinking vessels[9].

Those who see in this symbol of reproduction only the character of libertinage, may be astonished that it formed an integral part of the ceremonies consecrated to Ceres, a deity so commended for her purity and surnamed the *Holy Virgin*, and that it figured in the mysteries of this goddess at Eleusis, called the *mysteries par excellence*, into which all the men of antiquity, distinguished for their talents and virtues, were honored to be initiated; from which scoundrels, were they placed on a throne, were rigorously excluded; and the morality of whose dogmas and the wisdom of whose principles are guaranteed by the testimony of Greek and Roman writers known for their veracity and proper action. Tertullian informs us that the Phallus made part of the mysterious objects at Eleusis. "Everything most holy that these mysteries have," he says, "that which is hidden with so much care, that which is permitted to be known only quite recently, and that which the priests of the cult, called *Epoptae*, make so ardently desired, is the image of the virile member[10]." Theodoretus says that in the secret orgies of Eleusis the image of the feminine sex was also venerated[11].

This image also took part in the fête called *Thesmophoria*, in honor of the same goddess. A procession of women was to be seen. Each of them was accompanied by a female attendant carrying a basket, in which was the cake that had to be offered to Ceres and her daughter. Among these pious Athenian women figured, as an incident necessary to the ceremony, the Ithyphallus or Phallus, carried at the end of a pole. All about were heard ithyphallic canticles, that is to say, very obscene songs[12].

In order to justify the presence of these obscene figures in such holy mysteries, in order to explain this association of the cult of Ceres with that of the *Phallus*, here is the extravagant fable that the priests conceived: Ceres was seeking her daughter Proserpina whom Pluto had stolen. In this endeavor, she went about the world holding two torches which she had lighted from the fires of Mount Etna. She arrived tired out at Eleusis, a town of Attica. A woman named Baubo offered her hospitality, made her a gracious welcome, sought through caresses to lessen the grief in which the goddess was sunk, and in order to refresh her presented her with that liquor famous in the mysteries, which the Greeks called *Cyceon*. Ceres, a prey to her grief, disdainfully refused this beverage and repulsed the hand of the one who invited her to quench her thirst with it. Seeing her offers rejected several times, the obliging Baubo, in order to conquer the obstinacy of the goddess, had recourse to other means. She thought that a pleasantry, by cheering her up, would be able to dispose her to take the nourishment she stood in need of. To this end she went away, made her arrangements, then reappeared before the goddess, uncovered herself before her eyes, and had her see all those secret parts which decency forbids naming. At this spectacle, as strange as unexpected, Ceres, burst into laughter, forgot her grief, and consented joyfully to drink the *Cyceon*[13].

In the fêtes of Eleusis a hymn was sung, one strophe of which contained the conclusion of this adventure. Clement of Alexandria and Arnobius have both published this fable; they have, moreover, transmitted this strophe to us, an authentic monument to the coarseness and indecency of the fables which the priests of antiquity spread about.

In the fêtes called *Thargelia*, which were celebrated the sixth of the month of *thargelion* or May, the Phallus also played its part. Its presence in this solemnity ought not to astonish, since it was consecrated to Apollo, a sun-god, and to Diana, a moon-deity, or, according to the scholiast of Aristophanes, to the sun and the seasons. He adds that in this fête young men carried olive branches from which hung bread, vegetables, acorns, figs, and Phalli[14].

It has been remarked that the *Phallus* was constantly bound to the cult of the sun-gods, whatever names they might carry; that it was dependent on them, and that it was present in the mysteries consecrated to that luminary only as a symbol, a secondary object of the ceremony, but not as a particular deity. The inhabitants of Lampsacus[15], a city situated on the banks of the Hellespont, were the first to take it into their heads to draw this symbol from its dependency on the sun-gods, set it up as a deity, and render it a separate cult under the ancient name of *Priapus*. This god was born in that city, says the fable; which, in allegorical language, signifies that this cult took birth there.

Priapus was there represented as a *herma*, the head of which, and sometimes half the body, belonged to the human species. His figure was a copy of those *Hermes* or *Mercurys* furnished with a colossal Phallus which, in Greece, abounded in the fields, on the roads, and in the gardens. They were evidently an imitation of the figures with disproportionate Phallus which the women of Egypt carried in procession during the fêtes of Osiris, and which were kept in the temple at Hierapolis, in Syria.

A History of Phallic Cults

It was such hermae with Phallus which, placed at the intersections of Athens, were mutilated in a nocturnal debauch by Alcibiades and his companions; a profanation which had very grievous results for him. It was also to these hermae with human head and a Phallus that Philip, King of Macedonia, compared the Athenians. They have, said he, like the hermae, only a mouth and parts of generation, in order to express that they are only babblers and libertines[16].

The inhabitants of Lampsacus, being ignorant of the origin of this deity and having no data other than his figure with which to compose a legend or fable for him, and finding striking connections between a certain part of the ass and the feature which characterized Priapus, sacrificed an ass to him and introduced this animal as an actor in the adventures which they excogitated for this god. Here in substance is what that fable was: The birth of Priapus is highly uncertain. According to some, he owed it to Bacchus and the nymph called *Nayade*[17]; others give him the nymph *Chione* for a mother. Hyginus speaks of him as the son of Mercury; and Apollonius, of Adonis and Venus. The view most generally adopted makes him born of Bacchus and Venus. The mythologists who speak of him as the son of Hermes or Mercury, announce by this that the god owed his birth to the stones or the trunks of trees, called *Hermes* by the Greeks, which had served to make up his figure. Those who speak of him as the son of Bacchus or of Adonis, sun-gods, express his origin by an allegory more learned and more in conformity with truth. Jealous Juno, learning that her daughter Venus was pregnant, visited her. Under the pretext of aiding her, she employed, by touching her belly, a secret charm which made her give birth to a deformed child, whose mark of virility was of gigantic proportions. Venus, angry at having given life to a monstrous child, abandoned it and had it brought up far from her at Lampsacus. Having grown up, the god paid court to the ladies of this city, and this deformity did not displease them;

but the husbands, jealous, drove him ignominiously away. They were soon punished for this violence: a cruel malady attacked them in the very place over which the god presides. In this dire extremity, the oracle of Dodona was consulted. Following its advice, Priapus was honorably recalled, and the poor husbands saw themselves constrained to raise altars to him and render him a cult[18].

Such are the fables fabricated on the origin of Priapus. Here are a couple which explain the association of the ass with his cult: One day Priapus encountered Vesta lying on the grass and sunk in profound sleep. He was going to profit by an occasion so favorable to his lascivious tastes, when an ass happened quite opportunely to awaken the sleeping goddess by his braying, and she happily escaped from the pursuits of the libertine god.

Lactantius and Hyginus attribute the custom of sacrificing an ass to this god to another cause; and this cause is still less decent. Priapus, they say, had a dispute with the ass of Silenus, which Bacchus mounted at the time of his trip into India. Priapus pretended to be better endowed by nature in a certain respect than the ass. The question, says Lactantius, was decided in favor of the animal; and Priapus, furious at such a humiliation, killed his competitor. Hyginus, on the contrary, relates that Priapus was the vanquisher, and that the vanquished ass was placed in the ranks of the stars[19].

The people of Lampsacus, says Pausanias, are more devoted to Priapus than to any other deity[20]. He was the tutelary god of this city, the medals of which, preserved to our own day, offer his figure well characterized and further attest to the consideration he enjoyed among its inhabitants. These medals, which are to be seen in cabinets of curiosa, present him most commonly under the form of a herma, to which the monstrous Phallus is fixed. Some of the Roman emperors, not those who have distinquished themselves by their extreme debauchery, wished to eternalize their devotion to the god of Lampsacus, and had medals struck on which their names are associated with the indecent sign of that deity. Among them is found one of Septimus Severus, and another which the city of Lampsacus itself had struck in honor of the emperor Maximinus[21].

The city of *Priapis* or *Priapus*[22], built on the banks of the Propontus, in Troas, owes its name to the cult of this deity. It was at this place, says the fable, that Priapus, driven away by the husbands of Lampsacus, came to seek an asylum. A temple was to be seen there where the sun-god Apollo was adored under the name of *Priapesaeus*. Thus the inhabitants had preserved in their cult the connections existing between the star of the day and the symbol of fecundity. Pliny makes mention of several other places which bore the name of *Priapus*, and where, doubtless, he was venerated as the principal deity. In speaking of the islands of the sea of Ephesus [the Ægean Sea], he mentions one of them called *Priapos*[23]. He also says that in the Ceramic Gulf there is the island of *Priaponese*[24].

Priapus was honored with a particular cult in different cities of Greece: such were *Orneae*, situated near Corinth, which gave this god the surname of *Orneates* and his fêtes that of *Orneania;* and *Colophon,* a city of Ionia, famous for its oracle of Apollo. The fêtes of Priapus were celebrated there with a great deal of pomp; and this god had there for ministers only married women. The Cyllenians also rendered a particular cult to Priapus, or rather they confused this deity with Hermes or Mercury; for, as I have said, the ithyphallic Hermes differed in nowise from the Priapi as to figure: the material, of stone or wood, the places where they were located, and the honors paid them, made the only differences. One of these figures, which Pausanias styles Hermes, received divine honors at Cyllene. It was elevated on a pedestal, and presented a remarkable Phallus[25]. The same author saw another figure of Priapus on Mount Helicon, which, he says, merits the attention of the curious. This god was especially honored, he continues, by those who care for the flocks of goats and sheep, and the bees[26].

All the authors who speak of Priapus are in agreement, along with the numismatic and lapidary monuments, in giving his characteristic sign proportions greater than those of nature. The Greeks had preserved to the human figure to which it adhered, the ancient tradition in respect to that foreign colossal form. They also preserved to the *Phallus*, and to Priapus himself, its original connections with the sun, and their cult was almost never separated from that of this star, under whatever name it was adored. Determined by these principles, they accorded Priapus the title of *Saviour of the World*, which was often given to the sun-gods, and especially to the different signs which have successively marked the spring equinox, such as Gemini, Taurus, Capricornus [?], and finally Aries. This divine title is found in a Greek inscription placed on the ancient Priapus of the museum of Cardinal Albani[27].

An ass was sacrificed to Priapus, he was offered flowers, fruits, milk, and honey; libations were made to him by pouring milk or wine over the salient part which distinguished this deity; wreaths, and even little Phalli as *ex-votos*, were hung from it, and finally, the devotees came religiously to kiss the consecrated Phallus.

The introduction and progress of Christianity in Greece became disastrous to the cult of the *Phallus* and Priapus, but did not destroy it. From the very time that many Christian writers began to declaim against it, cried out against its indecencies, described, and perhaps even exaggerated its abuses, a sect favorable to the *Phallus* was established under a new form. This was the one that celebrated the fêtes called *Orphic*, a species of *Dionysia* regenerated under different names. The deity who was the object of them was named *Phanes*, a surname of the sun: he was figured with a very evident Phallus, which, according to some authors, was placed in a reverse direction[28]. To the violent and repeated declamations of the Church Fathers against the *Phallus*, the partisans of this cult responded that it was a symbol of the sun, of the regenerative action of this luminary on all nature. The sect of the *Orphics* was at first distinguished by its austere principles and pure morals, but it later degenerated into debauchery[29].

A Platonic philosopher, Iamblichus, who lived under the reign of Constantine, said that the institution of the *Phallus* was the symbol of the generative force; that this symbol promoted the generation of beings. "Truly," he added," it is because a great number of Phalli are consecrated that the gods shed fecundity over the earth[30]."

In spite of the blows of Christianity, the cult of the *Phallus* still maintained itself for a long while among the Greeks. The women of that nation continued to wear ithyphallic amulets of various forms around their necks as powerful charms, as the Indian women wore the *Tali*. Sometimes they even placed them lower than the breast. Arnobius and his disciple Lactantius, who lived under the reign of Diocletian, that is to say, around the beginning of the third century of the Christian era, prove by their declamations that this cult was then in full vigor in Greece. "I am ashamed," says Arnobius, "to speak of the mysteries where the *Phallus* is consecrated, and to say that there is no district in Greece where images of the part characteristic of virility are not to be found[31]." Lactantius turns the figure and fable of Priapus into ridicule[32]; and several Church Fathers who lived after them take the same tone and attest to the continuation of this cult.

The historian Evagrius, who wrote at the end of the sixth century, testifies that all the ceremonies of the cult of the *Phallus* still existed at his time. He derides the *Ithyphalli*, the *Phallogonia*, Priapus, remarkable for the gigantic dimensions of his characteristic sign, and the sacred basket which contained the Phallus[33]. Nicephorus Callistus, another more recent ecclesiastical historian, who died in the seventh century[34], also speaks of the *Phalli* and *Ithyphalli*, as well as of the cult of Pan and Priapus, as ridiculous objects which, nevertheless, still received religious homage from the Greeks[35].

The examples I shall report later of several peoples which, after embracing Christianity, still preserve many practices of idolatry and the cult of the *Phallus*, lead me to believe that it is thus with the Greeks. After becoming Christians, the Greeks nevertheless remained attached to an infinitude of pagan superstitions, and there ought still to remain traces of it among them.

Chapter 9

THE CULT OF THE PHALLUS AMONG THE ROMANS

T HIS people, whose unbridled ambition was the scourge of the world; who acquired its glory at the expense of the happiness of so many nations; who, always the conqueror by arms, was in the end conquered by its vices; who, raising itself to the highest degree of power, fell with the greater crash; and who, aftter having wearied humankind with the burden of its grandeur, became the object of its scorn; these Romans, so proud, so turbulent, so dominating, did they know how, even at the time when they were filling the subjugated world with the noise of their exploits, to resist the blows of shameful prejudices? Did they know how to defend themselves against ridiculous superstitions, children of ignorance, which insult reason, degrade man, and lead the way back toward barbarism? No. Their weakness, their blind credulity, their absolute submission to their priests, form, along with their courage and their independent and imperious character, a striking contrast. Some slight formalities forgotten during the ceremony of the sacrifices, some shadings in the color of the victims' entrails, some unforeseen encounter, the flight of a bird directed a certain way, chickens that ate little or did not eat, and a thousand other puerilities, sufficed to throw terror into the soul of these great men, to arrest an army ready to give battle, to change great resolutions, to suspend important enterprises, and to rule the destiny of the empire. These proud conquerors of the world trembled before a miserable soothsayer.

With this pusillanimity of reason, one feels that the Romans should have been enthralled by the most absurd cults. They even embellished their religion with all the superstitions of the peoples they had conquered. The Etruscans, the Egyptians, the Greeks, the Persians, the Thracians, the Phrygians, the Phœnicians, even the Gauls furnished their share. An infinitude of objects were gods

109

for the Romans. History does not offer any other nation which enslaved itself with as great a quantity of superstitions, nor which paid honor to a greater number of deities. The city of Rome alone contained more gods than inhabitants, although the number of these latter, it is said, amounted to several million[1].

Clement of Alexandria informs us how and by whom this cult was introduced among the Romans. "It was the *Corybantes* who, as Heraclitus tells, carried the cult of the *Phallus* and Bacchus into Italy. These *Corybantes*[2], also named *Cabiri*, who proclaimed to the people the death of the *Cabiri* gods, having become guilty of two fratricides in their country, stole the cist (or sacred basket) in which the Phallus of Bacchus was placed. After having committed this crime, they carried the cist into Etruria, where they made the most of this merchandise. Driven out of their country, they fixed their dwelling among the Etruscans, preached their venerable doctrine, and recommended the adoration of the Phallus and the sacred basket to these people[3]." The Etruscans, neighbors to the Romans, soon communicated this new institution to them, as well as the religious ceremonies and practices which went with it.

The period of the introduction of this cult into Italy does not seem to go back very far. The Romans, at the time of their kings, were not acquainted with the cult of Venus; that of Bacchus and Priapus ought then to have been equally unknown. All the Greek and oriental deities did not exist at the time of Numa.

The Romans designated Bacchus rather generally under the name of *Liber* or *Pater liber*, just as they often gave Venus the name of *Libera*: it is believed that this denomination came to him from the liberty which reigned at his fêtes. It is said that the sun bore an equivalent name among the Indians. "The sexual part of man," says Saint Augustine, "is consecrated in the temple of *Liber*; that of woman in the sanctuaries of *Libera*, the same goddess as Venus; and these deities are named the *Father* and the *Mother*, because they preside over the act of generation[4]."

The fêtes of the sun-god had two names among the Romans, which corresponded to those of Bacchus and Liber: the *Bacchanalia* and the *Liberalia*. The fête of the *Liberalia* took place on March 17, six days after the Greeks celebrated their Dionysia, in honor of the same god, and three days earlier than the Egyptians fêted Osiris and his Phallus, in the ceremony of the *Pamyles*. The Phallus figured with distinction in the fête of the *Liberalia*. The Romans named this image of virility *Mutinus*. It is of this symbol that Saint Augustine often speaks, in order to emphasize its indecency. He says, according to Varro, that at certain places in Italy the sacred ceremonies of the god *Liber* were celebrated with so much licence that there was no shame in their adoration of that which best characterizes virility in man; that decency was not respected enough to practice this cult in secret, but was entirely public, as if it were desired to honor libertinage; for this shameful image, placed in a little chariot, was promenaded with great honor during the days consecrated to the fête of the god *Liber*, first in the fields, then in the cross-roads, and finally through the city. He adds, still according to Varro, that at Lavinium the fête of the god *Liber* lasted a month, during which the people gave themselves up to rejoicing, license, and debauchery. Lascivious songs and the freest of talk corresponded to their actions. A magnificent chariot carried an enormous Phallus, and slowly advanced to the middle of the public square. There it was stationed; and the mother of the most respectable family of the city would place a wreath of flowers on this obscene figure[5].

In the indignation with which this indecent ceremony inspired him, Saint Augustine, informing us of the reasons for it, exclaims: "Thus, in order to appease the god *Liber*, in order to obtain an abundant harvest, in order to remove bewitchments from the fields, a venerable woman is obliged in the face of the multitude to do that which it would not

permit to a prostitute in the theatre! With what shame,
with what confusion should not the husband of this woman
be seized if by chance he were present at this crowning[6]!"

Some days later, toward the last of March and the first
of April, the fête of Venus was celebrated; and this deity,
at Rome, as in Greece, Syria, and Egypt, was associated
with the image of virility. During this fête the Roman
ladies ceremonially ascended the Quirinal, where the chapel
of the *Phallus* was erected, took possession of this sacred
object, and carried it in procession to the temple of Venus
Erycina, situated outside the Porta Collina. Having arrived in the temple of the Mother of the Loves, these ladies
themselves placed the Phallus in the bosom of Venus[7].

An antique stone comes to our aid and gives us the explanation of this ceremony. It is an engraved carnelian
which represents the phallic ceremony. A triumphal chariot carries a sort of altar on which the Phallus, of colossal
size, reposes. A genius hovers above the image and holds
a wreath suspended over it. The chariot as well as the figure
of the genius are entirely sheltered by a canopy or large
square drapery, supported at the four corners by lances,
each of which is carried by a half-naked woman. This chariot is drawn by goats and bulls, on which winged children
are mounted. It is preceded by a group of women blowing
trumpets. Farther ahead, and facing the chariot, is a form
characteristic of the feminine sex, representing the *Sinus
Veneris*. This form, proportioned to the Phallus elevated
on the chariot, is supported by two geniuses who seem to
point out to the Phallus the place it should occupy[8]. This
ceremony ended, the Roman ladies devoutly conducted
the Phallus back into its chapel; which later became famous through the edifice which the emperor Heliogabalus
had erected nearby, where he established a senate of women
charged with deciding upon questions of gallantry and debauchery. These assemblies were held at the time of the
fête of the *Phallus*[9].

The fêtes of autumn, consecrated to Bacchus, were called the *Bacchanalia;* they lasted from October 23rd to the 29th. There almost all the ceremonies practiced by the Greeks in their Dionysia were observed[10].

The Romans named the isolated Phallus *Mutinus* or *Tutinus*[11], and the Phallus adhering to a Hermes or Terminus, *Priapus*. When it was under one or the other form, this sacred object, or this deity, was considered as presiding over the fecundity of women, the vigor of husbands, and capable of turning away charms injurious to the marital act or the pregnancy of wives[12].

In consequence of these supposed virtues, the young brides, before being delivered to the embraces of their husbands, were religiously conducted by their parents to the idol of Priapus, and, their heads covered with a veil, they seated themselves on the very salient form which this figure presented. A certain contact doubtless sufficed to render the ceremony complete, to assure fecundity, and to neutralize enchantments. "It is a custom considered among the Roman women as quite proper and very religious," says Saint Augustine, "of obliging the newly married girls to come and seat themselves on the monstrous and excessive masculinity of Priapus[13]." Shall I speak of that *Mutunus*," says Lactantius, "on whose extremity the newly married girls come to seat themselves, so that the god appears to have been the first to receive the sacrifice of their modesty[14]?" By these last words, Lactantius seems to recall what young brides practice in some districts of India, where the god, of wood or iron, effects the sacrifice entirely. One would believe that the formality carried out by the young Roman women with this sacred object was only a modification, a diminutive of the Indian custom, and that the jealousy of the Roman husbands had placed limits on the devotion of their wives.

Married women also submitted themselves to this practice, doubtless in order to destroy the charm which was holding them in a state of sterility; but, more inured than the young brides, their devotion went farther. "Do you not lead, even with eagerness," says Arnobius to the husbands, "your wives to *Tutunus;* and in order to destroy supposed bewitchments, do you not make them bestride the horrible and immense Phallus of that idol[15]?"

A figure of the god *Tutunus* or *Mutinus* was discovered at Rome, on the Viminal, in the rubbish of an ancient temple. It is still to be seen today in that city: it is of white marble, and of a height of about three hands[16]. But one antique group, of which Meursius has given us the engraving, presents us with the faithful picture of this superstitious ceremony. This group, which is to be found in the gallery of Florence, offers an upright woman whose head, entirely covered by a sort of cap, presents a very unnatural position. Her hands, which reach below her haunches, seem to hold her clothing raised in order to allow a part of her body to be discovered. An enormous Phallus rises from the earth as far as the sexual parts of this figure, which, grandly proportioned, appear to be in contact with the upper extremity of the Phallus[17].

The *Phallus*, called *Mutinus* or *Tutunus* by the Romans, also received other homages. People prostrated themselves devoutly before it; they addressed prayers to it. "Because we do not address our prayers to *Mutinus* and *Tutunus*," says Arnobius, "and because we do not prostrate ourselves to the ground before their idols, does it not seem, to listen to you, that great calamities are going to descend on us, and that the order of Nature will be upset[18]?"

The chapel of *Mutinus* and *Tutunus* was situated, according to Festus, in the quarter of Rome called *Velia*, at the place where the thermæ of Domitian are. This chapel, having been destroyed under Augustus, was reëstablished at some distance from the city. "A holy and religious cult," says Festus, "was rendered these idols; and the Roman women came, heads veiled, to offer them sacrifices[19]."

114

Considered as an amulet, as a portable fetish, the *Phallus* received the name of *Fascinum*, and was of quite common use among the Romans, who knew of no more powerful preservative against charms, misfortunes, and the baleful glances of envy. It was ordinarily a little figure of the Phallus in alto-relievo, of various materials; sometimes it was a medal which carried the image of the Phallus. They were hung on the neck of children, and even elsewhere[20]. They were placed over the doors of houses, gardens[21], and public buildings. The emperors, on the report of Pliny, placed some on the front of their triumphal chariots[22]. The Vestals, when sacrifices were celebrated at Rome, rendered it a cult.

The forms of these ithyphallic amulets were varied to infinity. Some presented the Phallus combined with the *mullos* or the figure of the feminine sex. Cabinets of antiquities and one in the Bibliothèque Royale contain many of this variety. Others present a simple Phallus, but furnished with two wings and two bird's legs, and sometimes with little bells. This last peculiarity recalls the ancient custom of sometimes representing the figure of the god Priapus holding a little bell in his hand[23], and the modern custom of Hindu monks who go quite naked through the streets of India and call, by the sound of a little bell, the devotees, who come to kiss the living original of the *Phallus*. Other ithyphallic amulets have the form of a recumbent dog, or of human thighs and legs, bent but without a body. The most decent imitate the figure of a closed hand, the thumb of which is placed between the two following fingers. It is this figure which the antiquarians name the *ithyphallic hand*[24]. These kinds of amulets are still in use in the kingdom of Naples, as shall be described later.

There were double and triple *Fascina*, two or three branches coming out of the same center. The triple Phalli were much in use in antiquity. It has already been remarked from the report of Plutarch that Osiris figured in the fête of the *Pamyles* in Egypt with a triple Phallus, in order to signify the multiplication of his productive faculty[25]. Double or triple Phalli are still to be found on many ancient monuments, isolated or adhering to a human body. Some exist in France, at the Pont du Gard and at the amphitheatre of Nîmes, which are isolated: I shall refer to them soon. An infinitude of other monuments has preserved the image of these doubly and triply branched Phalli for us; but they are rarer when they are joined to a human figure. In the kingdom of Naples and in the province of Peucetia, engraven stones have been found, however, which represent the figure of Priapus furnished with a double Phallus. Near to him is a shepherd who seems to plant a staff of *lituus* in the ground. Perhaps this *lituus* signified the staff which the *phallophori* carried in the religious ceremonies. In the city of Trani, a votive picture in terra cotta has been discovered which represents Priapus with a triple Phallus[26]. That is how the ancients represented the *Diphallus* or *Triphallus*, and not by double or triple crosses, as has been thought by some authorities previously referred to.[27].

The urns, the utensils, the furniture in general, often received the imprint of the *Facinum* or Phallus. There were, and some are still preserved, ithyphallic rings, seals, medals, and engraven stones[28]. The collections of antique monuments present us with lamps formed thusly. The Romans, at the example of the *Baptæ* of Athens, or the initiates to the mysteries of Cotytto, employed drinking vessels of glass which had the shape of the Phallus[29]. Pliny, on two occasions in his *Natural History*, speaks of vessels on which were engraven libidinous scenes which were intended simultaneously to intoxicate the drinkers with wine and voluptuous desires[30]. Lampridius also makes mention of vessels in use by the emperor Heliogabalus which were laden with obscene figures[31]; but in the inventory of the furnishings of the emperor Commodus, which Pertinax had sold, there were found vessels similar to those which the *Baptæ* had used: these were of glass and had the shape of the Phallus. The historian Capitolinus names them *phallovitroboli*, a name which at the same time indicates their destination, their shape, and their material[32].

The Phallus, adhering to a stone called Terminus, or to a tree trunk often fashioned as a herma, received, along with the body of which it was part, the name of Priapus among the Romans, as among the Egyptians and Greeks. This idol was represented with the head of Pan or the Fauns, that is to say with the horns and ears of a goat. When he was given arms, for he was not always provided with them, Priapus held a scythe in one hand; and sometimes with his left hand he grasped, like Osiris, the characteristic feature of his divinity, which was always colossal and threatening, and painted a red color[33]. His head was crowned with vine branches or laurels, and his face shaded by a dense beard.

Just like the idol of Osiris carried in procession by the Egyptians during the solemnity of the *Pamyles*, that of Priapus was ordinarily of the wood of the fig tree; a great many of them were also to be seen of willow wood. Sometimes this god was only a tree trunk, a branch of which figured, by chance, as the characteristic sign which the hand of art had scarcely carved at all: such is the Priapus that Columella advises farmers to place in the middle of their gardens: "Have no labyrinths, no statues of the heroes of Greece; but in the midst of the garden let the trunk of an ancient tree, scarcely carved at all, present and have venerated the ithyphallic deity; let that formidable branch which characterizes it frighten the children, and the sickle with which it is armed, the robbers[34]."

All the figures of Priapus were not so crude: some were worked with great care, as well as the Terminus [herma?] which made up their lower portion. Whatever part of the human body this figure had was entirely naked and colored

117

red[35]. The Priapi, as well as the isolated Phalli, offered a great number of variations in their shape: some were represented as Termini [hermæ?], which had only a human head and the Phallus; others had half the human body, without arms, or with arms usually laden with attributes of this deity: attributes relative to agriculture. There were also some examples of Priapi represented under the complete figure of a man, but such were rare. Sometimes the image of this god was pictured holding a sickle or long scythe in his hand, as Columella describes.

In order to characterize the abundance of which he was believed in part to be the author, in order to keep off the sterility against which he was the preserver, Priapus was often portrayed carrying a long Horn of Plenty under his right arm, the large opening of which offered an assemblage of flowers and fruits: products and attributes of the garden, over which, particularly among the Romans, this deity especially presided. Sometimes also a long pole was raised behind and above his head; this served, as Horace says, as a scarecrow for the birds[36].

Such is the faithful portrait of this deity, the tutelary idol of whom was placed, in Italy, in vineyards, orchards, and especially in gardens. This idol was often seen, along with his indecent attributes, placed along the roads: it was thus that Priapus was confused with Mercury and Terminus. Scaliger asserts that he saw such a Terminus whose Phallus pointed out the road. This phallic Hermes was to be found at Rome in the palace of a cardinal[37]. The location at which the Terminus was placed, the addition or absence of the Phallus on this Terminus, whether made of wood or of stone, comprised the only difference which exists between the deities Mercury, Pan, Priapus, etc[38]. The Phallus joined to a way-marker was supposed to preserve travellers from accidents, just as the Phallus joined to a tree trunk was supposed to ward off accidents injurious to harvests from neighboring fields. This was the unvarying opinion of the ancients, and the sole cause for the erection of such a great number of idols to Priapus.

His fêtes were named *Priapeia*, as well as the verses that were sung in his praise. They recalled, in certain respects, the *Pamyles* of the Egyptians and the *Phallophoria* of the Greeks. Several antique monuments, preserved to our day, present the details of these orgies, which were often highly indecent. Among those which Boissart has had engraved, there is to be found a bas-relief which offers a picture of the principal fête of this god: it is women who figure there as ministers of the cult. One among them anoints the characteristic feature of Priapus, whilst the others bring as offerings baskets full of fruits and urns filled with wine. There are groups of dancing girls and female musicians, among whom is to be distinguished one who shakes the Egyptian sistrum. Here is a Bacchante, carrying a child upon her shoulders. Farther on, four priestesses are occupied with sacrificing an ass, the victim consecrated to Priapus.

Priapus had temples. If Petronius is to be believed, they were served by priestesses, who celebrated nocturnal mysteries in honor of this deity; here is the only information that this satirist has preserved for us: "We were wandering at random through the most retired streets, when we encountered two fairly pretty women. We followed them slowly as far as the door of a little temple which they entered; we heard voices come from this place as from the depths of a cavern. Our curiosity aroused, we descended after them. We found several women who, frenzied as Bacchantes, had figures of Priapus in their hands. We were unable to see more." Quartilla, the priestess of this temple, then sent her attendant to these curious strangers, who told them: "You have disturbed the mysteries that Quartilla was celebrating in the grotto[39]."

Besides honey and milk, this god was offered myrtle branches, the symbol of happy loves. The inhabitants of the country covered his head with roses in the spring, with clusters of wheat in summer, with sections of vine in autumn, and with branches of the olive tree in winter. In the cities Priapus had public chapels where the devotees, afflicted with certain maladies which fell within his province, came to hang up *ex-votos*: simple images of the sick part. These *ex-votos* were painted pictures or figures of wax, wood, or sometimes of marble[40].

Women, as devout as lubricious, were seen publicly to offer to Priapus as many wreaths as their lovers had made sacrifices to their charms. They hung them on the enormous Phallus of that idol; and this salient part was sometimes completely trimmed with them[41]. It was thus that Messalina, wife of the emperor Claudius, famous for her extreme lubricity, and quite worthy in this matter of figuring beside the throne of the Cæsars, after having come off victorious with fourteen vigorous athletes, had herself proclaimed *Invincible*. She took the title as a surname, and in commemoration of these fourteen successes made the god Priapus an offering of fourteen wreaths. Others paid homage to this god with as many Phalli of willow wood as the number of men they had vanquished in one night[42].

The different points I have just drawn together prove that among the Romans the cult of Priapus had degenerated a great deal; that these people had lost sight of the object symbolized in order to seize upon the symbol alone, in order to see in it only the indecent. Thus, by this degeneration of principle, religion became the pretext for libertinage. The *Phallus* was no longer that sacred object of veneration of the oriental peoples, that adored symbol of the sun, the regenerator of all nature, that god, the *Saviour of the World*, whose presence assured the preservation and propagation of all living or growing beings. He was invoked, in truth, in order to remove charms unfavorable to the fecundity of women; but in this case, far from being considered as a sun-god, he was no more than a simple talisman. He presided over the legitimate pleasures of marriage, but still more over the excesses of debauchery. Though some married persons were to be seen among his adorers, their greatest number was of libertines and prostitutes. His idol was still placed in vineyards, orchards, and gardens, but it no longer represented there the symbol of the sun fecundating the earth in the spring and giving new life to all plants. The mean guardian of an orchard or garden, it served solely as a scarecrow for superstitious thieves, for children, and for birds[43]. This degraded god was reduced to a menial state. Such were, at the time of the Roman emperors, the only functions of the *Phallus*, and the restricted and humiliating powers of Priapus.

Respected, whilst Roman manners still preserved their ancient simplicity; debased, by reason of the progress of their corruption, Priapus finally became an object of ridicule: he was the butt of the jokes, of the sarcasms of all writers. Horace was able to disparage this deity more ingeniously, which he does in the first verses of one of his satires. "I was a trunk of the fig tree, a quite useless log, when a workman, uncertain whether he would make a god or a Priapus of it, finally made up his mind, and preferred to make a god of me[44]." He was insulted even in his sanctuary, the walls of which often offered inscriptions of scant respect to the deity of this cult, and verses which provoked the laughter of the readers at his expense[45]. The Romans, then, having lost sight of the ancient motive, saw in him only a symbol of debauchery, only a ridiculous deity.

Christian writers came later to add their declamations to the insults of the Latin poets, to heap ridicule and scorn on this already vanquished deity, joyfully to seize that place abandoned by the partisans of the ancient religion of the Romans, and to obtain an easy victory. The cult of Priapus would have been irreparably annihilated, his idols and altars pulled down forever, if superstition and custom, the most indestructible of all human passions, had not come to his rescue. These two powerful springs of the conduct of nations triumphed over reason and Christianity, and contrived, in spite of the latter's continual efforts, to maintain in some manner the cult of this obscene and ancient deity. This is what I shall establish in the following chapters.

Chapter 10

THE CULT OF VENUS. OTHER RELIGIOUS CUSTOMS CONNECTED WITH THE CULT OF THE PHALLUS

AMONG nations where abundance of children is a means of wealth and a title to glory for their fathers; where a numerous progeny draws consideration and respect, and where, consequently, impotence in men and sterility in women become an opprobrium and are regarded as a sign of divine malediction, the act by which man reproduces his kind, and the objects which serve in this reproduction, ought to be held in great honor. Continence, indeed, far from being placed in the ranks of the virtues, is there considered a crime against society. It was evidently the necessity of increasing population which gave birth to this opinion, which ought to have been altered when this necessity was less obvious, and which then became a source of debauchery and superstition when time had effaced its primitive cause from the memory of man.

Under a climate where clothes are often useless and troublesome, the habit of seeing nakedness rendered people indifferent to it. It caused little or no emotion and excited no more desire than do those parts of the body which civilized nations today leave uncovered. Thus, it becomes obvious that shame of nudity is native only to regions where cold has rendered clothing indispensable.

The custom of honoring the act of generation and that of becoming accustomed to nakedness are two causes which have had a powerful influence on the manners of nations. When these causes have acted together in the same region of the earth, their influence has been more marked and has produced civil and religious institutions which bore all the characteristics of their double origin. When, in other countries, one of these two causes acted alone, its influence, less powerful, produced institutions less strongly characterized. Finally, among peoples where these two causes have not existed at all, there have resulted opinions, customs, and institutions absolutely contrary to those of peoples who lived under their influence.

Hence that strange diversity of manners and customs, those striking contrasts, those total differences which exist between the opinions and institutions of the nations which people or which have peopled the earth. At first glance, one would be led to believe that the nature of the man of the South is not the same as that of the man of the North, or to doubt the veracity of writers who have offered such different pictures of their respective manners. It is true that time, intercourse between nations, distant migrations, and political and religious revolutions have in many regions effaced, completely or in part, the native characteristics of the people, and have lessened the sharp distinctions between their inhabitants. But these events have not been active everywhere; and, at the places where their action was felt, it has not always been powerful enough to dispel the ancient character entirely. History, morover, as well as the attachment of nations for their old customs, has preserved from complete ruin numerous monuments characteristic of primitive societies. Strongly pronounced traits still exist and suffice to indicate the causes which originated them.

These moulding causes, in which the spirit of nations, so to speak, has come, like a fusible material, to be cast, take form, and harden, have acted together and with considerable force in certain regions. Vast deserts, waste and flood lands, peopled with deadly and ferocious animals, called on the genius, courage, and labor of men. Population was all the more desirable there as it assured power and wealth. Also the laws, precepts, and civil and religious institutions of ancient times, which tradition has preserved for us, tend toward this sole end: all favor and even facilitate an increase of population.

Circumcision, one of the most ancient rites, which the Egyptians and Ethiopians practiced before the Hebrews, evidently had as its end only that of rendering more convenient the act of the reproduction and of doing away with even the slightest obstacles to it. The first precept that God, in Genesis, addresses to man after the Deluge is this: *Be fruitful and multiply, and replenish the earth.* The precept is repeated in the same discourse, and this repetition makes its importance felt[1]. Also, among the Hebrews concubinage was not a crime: it was customary; and marriage did not preclude it.

Sarah, the wife of Abraham, herself furnished her husband with a concubine: she gave up her maid-servant Hagar to him, by whom the patriach had some children[2]. Nahor, the brother of Abraham, also had several children of a concubine called Reumah[3]. Lot, in order to appease the impetuous desires of the inhabitants of Sodom, offered them his two virgin daughters[4]. These same daughters shortly afterwards got their father drunk, gave themselves over to his caresses, and had children by him[5].

Jacob simultaneously married the two sisters Rachel and Leah; and when both became sterile, they had themselves replaced by their servant women. Rachel furnished her husband with her maid-servant Bilhah, and Leah her maid-servant Zilpah[6]. Bilhah, who *slept* with Jacob, also *slept* with Reuben, the son of that patriarch[7]. Tamar married in succession the two brothers Er and Onan, sons of Judah. Having had no children by them, and fearing to be accused of sterility, she went, disguised as a prostitute, to place herself by a road where her father-in-law passed. He, not knowing her, bargained for her favors, set a price on them, obtained them, and had two children by her[8].

These fornications, these adulteries, these incests, and many others which it is useless to report, are not presented in the books of the Bible as crimes but as ordinary actions. Those who are the authors of them receive no reproach, undergo neither blame nor punishment.

If the Bible complains of Solomon, who it asserts *surpassed in wisdom all the kings of the earth*[9], it is not because having married the Egyptian Pharaoh's daughter, and having had a transient affair with the Queen of Sheba, he also lived with seven hundred women qualified as *queens*, and three hundred qualified as concubines; but because this numerous seraglio, destined for the loves and pleasures of this *wise* king, was made up of foreign women, of Moabites, Ammonites, Edomites, Sidonians, and women of the country of the Hittites: nations from which the law of Moses forbade Hebrews to take wives, and which professed a religion different from theirs. Solomon was perverted by them: he erected altars, temples, and idols in honor of the deities adored by these foreigners[10]. Thus it is not the exorbitant quantity of women comprising Solomon's seraglio that the Bible reproves in this king, but their quality as foreigners and idolatresses.

When, on the contrary, it was a question of infamous sexual acts and sterile pleasures injurious to population, then Biblical opinion is declared strongly against them. The action of Onan excited indignation; and the corrupt morals of the inhabitants of Sodom and Gomorrah drew down on their cities an exemplary and terrible punishment. Finally, virginity, for nubile girls, was among the Hebrews, as it still is among the Indians, a species of opprobrium. Jephthah[11], before letting herself be scrupulously sacrificed by her father, says to him: "Allow me to go bewail my virginity in the mountains for two months." She went with her companions to bewail that she was to die virgin[12].

Young Indian women, according to Mendes Pinto, believe themselves unable to be received into Paradise with their virginity. "The Indians," says Sonnerat, "are so well persuaded that the gods have granted them existence only to reproduce themselves, that they regard sterility as a curse[13]."

If we cast our eyes on the institutions and customs of some other nations of the Orient, we shall see there under various forms, a similar motive: that of honoring the act of generation and of favoring population.

The cult of Venus, so wide-spread in the Orient, and which was later introduced into Greece and Italy, had for its object the veneration of the fecundating faculty of nature. Its origin was more ancient than and different from that of Priapus; but the cults of both had the same end: to increase population. In the ceremonies of the cult of Venus the act of generation was sanctified. The youth of both sexes came solemnly to offer their first-fruits to this goddess: just as elsewhere other deities were offered the firstlings of the flowers and fruits, and the newly born of domestic animals[14]. Policy founded this ceremony; superstition consecrated it; and the attachment for old customs, especially among those which cling to religion, maintained it until a time when advanced civilization and altered manners began to render it humiliating for the persons who were forced to submit to it.

"The cult that is rendered this deity," says Montesquieu, "is rather a profanation than a religion. She has temples where all girls of the city prostitute themselves in her honor, and make themselves a dowry from the profits of their devotion. She has some where every married woman goes, once in her life, to give herself to the one who choses her, and throws the money she has received into the sanctuary. There are some others where the courtesans of all countries, more honored than the matrons, go to carry their offerings. There are some, finally, where men make eunuchs of themselves and dress as women in order to serve in the sanctuary consecrated to the goddess and to the sex which they no longer are, and which they cannot be[15]." This is not poetic fiction. It is the truth which the illustrious author whom I have just cited has drawn from the history of various nations.

Many writers of antiquity testify that these devout and voluptuous ceremonies were practised in various countries of the Orient, and notably at Babylon. The prophet Jeremiah, in his letter addressed to the Jews destined to be led captive into that city, informs them of the existence of this custom[16]. The geographer Strabo also makes mention of it[17]; but Herodotus is the one who describes it in most detail.

"The Babylonians," he says, "have a law indeed shameful: every woman born in the country is obliged to go once in her life to the temple of Venus in order there to give herself up to a stranger. Many among them, disdaining to see themselves confused with the others, because of the pride inspired by their wealth, have themselves carried before the temple in covered carriages. There they remain seated, having behind them a great number of servants who accompanied them; but the majority of the others seat themselves in the precincts of the temple of Venus with a wreath of string around their heads. Some come, others go. At all times lanes were seen marked out by stretched cords. The strangers walk about in these lanes and choose the women who most please them. When a woman has taken her place here she cannot return home until some stranger has thrown silver on her knees and has had commerce with her outside the sacred place. In throwing the silver the stranger must say to her: *I invoke the goddess Mylitta*. The Assyrians give the name of Mylitta to Venus. However moderate may be the sum, it will meet no refusal: the law forbids it, for this money becomes sacred. She follows the first to throw her silver; and it is not permitted her to repulse anyone. Finally, when she has acquitted herself of what she owes the goddess by abandoning herself to a stranger, she returns home. After this, whatever sum might be given her, it is not possible to seduce her. Those who have beauty and an elegant stature for their share do not stay long in the temple; but the ugly ones remain there longer, because they cannot satisfy the law. There are even some who remain there three or four years[18]."

The same historian adds: "A quite similar custom is observed in several places on the island of Cyprus." This practice was in effect in full force at Paphus, a city of this island. Justinus also reports the causes for the foundation of Carthage: "Elissa, fleeing Tyre where her brother Pygmalion had assassinated her husband Acerbas in order to seize his treasures, landed with some Tyrians, companions of her flight, on the coast of the island of Cyprus. She disembarked there just at the time the Cyprians were celebrating the fête of Venus. The young girls of Paphus presented themselves to the strangers and offered them the enjoyment of their charms, the price of which was intended to form their dowry."

Elissa chose eighty of these gallant Cyprian girls, embarked them in her fleet, and united them with the young Tyrians who accompanied her, in order to people the city she proposed to build. She arrived in Africa and there founded Carthage[19]. The Tyrians and the Cyprian girls transported the manners and religion of their country into this new region. The custom which obliged the young girls to earn their dowry at the seashore was instituted there. At some distance from the new city there was a place consecrated to Venus, called *Sicca Veneria*. A similar place, consecrated to the same deity and intended for the same cult, existed among the Phœnicians under the name of *Succoth-Benoth* or *Siccoth-Venoth*. These words signify *tents of the girls*. It is believed, with very much reason, that the name *Venus* is derived from them[20]. Valerius Maximus informs us that the young Carthaginian girls came to this place and under the auspices of the goddess religiously gave themselves up to the brutality of strangers, and acquired, as the price of their virginity, a sum which served to marry them[21].

This religious and gallant custom was established throughout Phœnicia. The goddess who presided over generation was there named *Astarte*, and the place which was consecrated to her, *Succoth-Benoth*. At Byblus the young girls had the alternative of prostituting themselves for an entire day to strangers, or of sacrificing their hair to the goddess[22]. If one judges by the vigorous declamations made by various writers against the cult of Venus at Byblus and against its indecencies, he will be convinced that the girls of this city preferred to keep their hair. In this last case, the price of the prostitution did not serve as their dowry but was intended to meet the expenses of the cult. It is Saint Augustine who informs us of this particular, in telling us that in his time religious prostitution was the custom all over Phœnicia[23].

It even existed there for a long time afterwards, until under the reign of Constantine. According to Eusebius and Theodoretus, the temple of Heliopolis, in Phœnicia, and that of the *Aphacians*, located on the Libanus mountains between Heliopolis and Byblus, were dedicated to deities who demanded similar sacrifices. These two writers inform us that this emperor had these temples destroyed and abolished the indecent cult that was celebrated there[24].

The Hebrews, neighbors to the Phœnicians, could not resist the attraction of the example these latter offered them. Moses had foreseen the danger by positively forbidding these impure religious practices to his people. His words even proclaim that the Phœnicians and Canaanites had at his time corrupted the spirit of the primitive institution and had let themselves fall into still more revolting disorders: "There shall be," he says, "no whore of the daughters of Israel, nor a sodomite of the sons of Israel. Thou shalt not bring the hire of a whore, or the price of a dog, into the house of the Lord thy God[25]." In this passage the practices of the cult of Astarte or Mylitta are seen well designated: the prostitution of the young people of both sexes, and the price of this prostitution offered to the deity. The author of *Deuteronomy* employs in the Hebrew text, in place of the coarse words of *meretrix* and *scortator* which are found in the Vulgate, expressions which correspond to those of *consacrées, consacrés* [*consecrated* (masculine and feminine forms)], or *efféminés* [*effeminates* or *sodomites*]: names serving to characterize the boys and girls who pretended to honor the deity by such acts of impurity[26].

In spite of these prohibitions, the Israelites fornicated with the *consacrées* and even with the *effémines;* and they fornicated with so much enthusiasm that Asa, King of Judah, drove these *efféminés* from the country of his dominion. His son Jehoshaphat, who succeeded him, did still more: he exterminated a large number of them. The effects of these terrible examples were not of long duration. Religious prostitution again took favor among the Israelites, and they exercised it even in the place consecrated to the Lord. "Josiah," says the author of the fourth book of *Kings*, "knocked down the huts of the *efféminés* or *consacres*, which were in the house of the Lord, for which the women worked to make hangings in honor of *Asherah* or *Astarte*[27]."

The goddess of generation of the Armenians was named *Diana Anaïtis*. Strabo informs us that these people rendered her a particular cult. They consecrated to her the first-fruits of their slaves and girls, even of the girls of the highest quality. These girls prostituted themselves in the temple of the goddess: then only were they worthy of marriage, and the men were honored to marry them[28].

"It was a common practice among the Lydians for the newly married girls to prostitute themselves before living with their husbands; but, the marriage once consummated, they owed their spouses an inviolable fidelity. There was no mercy for those who would deviate from it[29]." "All the girls in the Lydian country," says Herodotus, "give themselves up to prostitution. They earn their dowry by it, and continue this commerce until they marry[30]."

Pomponius Mela says the same thing of the girls of the

Augilæ, a people of Africa[31]. They received all men who offered themselves with a present and the greater the number of men who sacrificed to their private charms, the more were they honored. The Nasamones, a people of Libya, observed the same custom: "When one of them," says Herodotus, "marries, the bride accords her favors on the first night of the nuptials to all the guests; and each one makes her a present, which he has brought from his house[32]." Prostitution was in honor at Naucratis in Egypt: the girls of this city passed for the most beautiful courtesans of the country; some have made themselves famous, such as Rhodôpis and Archidice[33].

This prostitution of girls before their marriage seems, at first glance, foreign to the cult; but when it is compared with the custom of religious prostitution, an intimate relationship is noticed, and it becomes evident that it derives from it. Similarly with the courtesans of antiquity. One would believe that libertinage and the profits which could result from it were the only motives for their profession; but it should be known that these courtesans, so numerous and so celebrated in Greece, officiated in the temple of Venus and that they were the only priestesses of this deity. Besides, it is certain that the same religious prostitution which took place at Babylon, in all of Phœnicia, and in other parts of the Orient, was, in principle, in force at Paphus, on the island of Cyprus, at Samos, Corinth, Amathus, and Hermione, where several temples of Venus were built.

Among the various honors that the inhabitants rendered this deity, says Pausanias, there is to be remarked a custom which obliges the girls who are marrying, and widows who wish to contract a new bond, to sacrifice to Venus before their nuptials[34]. The same ceremony was practiced in all the places where this goddess received a particular cult; but soon the progress of civilization made the impropriety of this cult felt in many cities. Wise laws brought reform. The daughters and wives of citizens were freed from this indecent servitude; and the prostitution demanded by Venus became the function of the titular courtesans who, through duty, sacrificed themselves to the deity, and, through taste or avarice, lavished their favors or sold them in public. The courtesan priestesses of Venus were numerous in the principal cities of Greece: more than a thousand of them were counted at Corinth. The honor of having abolished religious prostitution at Samos is attributed to a certain Dexicreonte.

The cult of Venus maintained itself for a long time in Greece in its primitive indecency. Besides custom, which among the vulgar is one of the strongest supports of ancient institutions, the people had another motive for preserving this cult: they were persuaded that those who scorned it drew down on themselves the ill-will and vengeance of the deity. Young girls feared the fury of Venus; and fear made them devout. The priests would relate the fable of the Propætides who, rejecting the cult of this goddess, were cruelly punished for it. They felt the fires of lust in their veins, and were, says Ovid, the first women who prostituted themselves to all comers. *Elège* and *Célène*[35], daughters of Proetus, were punished for the same fault. "They were to be seen," says Ælianus, "running about completely naked, like madwomen, through a part of Peloponnesus and some other regions of Greece[36]."

The Romans honored many gods of generation. Venus had four temples at Rome, and was honored there, under different surnames, by various fêtes, celebrated in the month of April. *Flora* appears to be one of the most ancient gods of generation that the Romans have worshipped; Venus is much more modern. The 1st, 22nd, and 28th of April were consecrated to honoring, under various names, the Mother of the generation of beings. The ceremonies of these fêtes recall the religious prostitution of the Orientals. The hymn entitled *Pervigilium Veneris*, or the Vigil of Venus, offers points of conformity. There it is seen that the Romans, after the example of the Phœnicians and Greeks, set up tents or huts of leafy branches dedicated to the mysteries of love. The obscurity coming on at the end of the day, the shadow of the trees, the shelter of those tents formed by myrtle branches, the symbol of happy loves, emboldened desire and screened various modest alarms.

"Tomorrow," one reads in this poem, "under the verdant shelter of the myrtle, set up in the shadow of the trees, the Mother of Loves will dictate her laws to youth." Diana is too chaste, according to the poet, to be invited to this fête. "If your modest glances could linger on these sports," he says to this goddess, " you would see groups of young boys and maidens, crowned with flowers, wandering about for three nights in your groves, or reposing deliciously under the shelter of the myrtle[37]."

The Church Fathers, and especially Saint Augustine in his *City of God*, loudly cried out against the indecencies of these fêtes; but they did not succeed in having them abolished entirely.

In countries where religious prostitution was unknown, ceremonies were practiced which resembled it. In the temple of Belus, at Babylon, a chosen woman was each night conducted by a priest and installed on a magnificent bed situated in the sanctuary. Here is the explanation Herodotus gives in speaking of this temple: "No one passes the night there, unless it be a native woman whom the *god* has chosen, as is told by the Chaldæans, who are the priests of this god. These same priests add that the *god* himself comes into the chapel, and that he sleeps on the bed. That does not seem credible to me. The same thing," Herodotus further says, "occurs at Thebes in Egypt, if one must believe the Egyptians, for a woman is there put to bed in the temple of the Theban Jupiter; and it is said that these women have commerce with no men. The same thing is also observed at Patara, in Lycia, when the god honors this city with his presence: then the high priestess is shut up for the night in the temple[38]."

At Jagannath, a city of India, the priests of Vishnu, for the week that the fête of this god lasted, also conducted a virgin into the vast temple which is dedicated to him, and she passed the night there in order to espouse the god and to consult him on the meagerness or abundance of the coming harvest[39]. It was at Babylon, Thebes, and Patara, as it is today at Jagannath, not the god, but the priests who, under cover of the shadows of night, espoused the young mortal. What is remarkable is that there is worshipped at Jagannath, as was worshipped at Babylon, a deity who presides over generation, and that the young girls of Jagannath come before marrying to make an offering to their Venus as those of Babylon made to theirs. Another point of resemblance exists in the form of these deities, the Mothers of generation: they were represented in Assyria, Phœnicia, and Paphus as they are in India, at Jagannath, Benares, Kesscrech, and elsewhere, under the form of a landmark, a pyramidal stone[40].

The dissoluteness of the mysteries celebrated among the Greeks of Alexandria in honor of Isis is known, and of those at Athens, celebrated by the sect of the *Baptæ* in honor of *Cotytto* or the *popular Venus*. To these can be added the mysteries of Flora, Bacchus, and the Bona Dea among the Romans. *Do not shun*, says Ovid in addressing the men, *do not shun the temple of Memphis where the heifer of the Nile is worshipped. There everything is done that Jupiter formerly did*[41]. And elsewhere the same poet says to his mistress's guardian: *Do not look into what goes on in the temple of the Egyptian Isis.* Juvenal confirms the custom of prostitution in the temple of Isis; and, at this place, he gives that Egyptian deity a highly injurious epithet[42]. In his ninth Satire the same poet again comes back to the prostitution practiced in the temple of Isis; he even informs us that Venus was there often replaced by Ganymedes[43].

This prostitution in the temples was so universal that Herodotus did not hesitate to say: "Almost all other peoples, if the Egyptians and Greeks are excepted, have commerce with women in the holy places[44]." Even these exceptions appear to arise from the complaisance of the author, and what he says elsewhere on the same subject proves that they are scarcely admissible, as we have already seen and as we shall see hereafter. Juvenal does not make any such exceptions, and he expresses himself more clearly than Herodotus on this custom where, after having spoken of many places consecrated to this religous libertinage, he adds: *What temple is there where the women do not prostitute themselves[45]?*

The Dionysia of the Greeks were highly indecent; but it appears that the Bacchanalia of the Romans even surpassed them. Civilization adds its vices to the vicious institutions already dedicated. Livy has left us a revolting picture of the disorders which were practiced in those nocturnal religious assemblies. The mysteries of Bacchus were celebrated at Rome in the temple of that god, and in the sacred woods called *Simila*, situated near the Tiber. At first only women were admitted to them; and the light of day illumined all the ceremonies. Respectable, married ladies were by turn invested with the dignity of priestesses. No scandalous talk had been raised against these mysterious assemblies at the time when a woman of Campania, named Pacculla Minia, obtained the priesthood of the mysteries of Bacchus. She changed the institution entirely by initiating her two sons into them. This example was followed: men were introduced, and along with them disorders. By order of the same priestess, the mysteries were no longer celebrated except at night. Before her, they took place but three days a year; she had them celebrated every month, and for five days. The young boys that were admitted to them were never more than twenty years old. At a more advanced age they would have had less passion for pleasure, a less inflammable imagination, and a mind less credulous and less suited to receive vicious impressions, that it was desired to give them.

Introduced by the priests into subterranean places, the young initiate found himself given over to their brutality. Frightful howlings and the noise of many instruments, such as cymbals and drums, served to stifle his cries from the violence he suffered. Excesses of the table, where wine flowed in abundance, excited other excesses favored by the shadows of the night. Age, sex, all were confused. Each one satisfied the taste to which he was inclined; all shame was banished; all varieties of lewdness, even those which nature reproves, stained the temple of the deity. If any of the young initiates evinced shame at so much horror, opposed any resistance to the pursuits of the libertine priests, or even if they acquitted themselves negligently of what was required of them, they were sacrificed; and, for fear of their indiscretion, their lives were taken. They were firmly tied to certain machines with which they were suddenly raised and then plunged into a deep cavern. The priests publicly justified these disappearances by saying that the angry god authorized them.

Dances, running about, cries of men and women said to be moved by a divine fury, but who were moved only by the fumes of wine, formed a principal episode of these ceremonies and introduced another diversion among the disorders. Women with dishevelled hair and holding flaming torches in their hands, were seen to plunge them in the waters of the Tiber without extinguishing them. This pretended miracle worked, says Livy, through the inflammable material of the torches which were composed of sulphur and chalk. Crimes of another sort were hatched in these nocturnal assemblies. Poisons were prepared; accusations and false testimony were drawn up; wills were forged; murders were planned. Initiates from all classes were found there, even Roman men and women of the first rank: their number was immense. It was no longer a society, it was a whole nation which shared in these abominable disorders, and even plotted against the State. It was on this score that the consul Postumius had this aggregation looked into, and denounced it in the Senate at Rome. And it was perhaps solely this consideration which determined that superstitious Senate to permit any attack upon religion by abolishing these abominable assemblies: they were dissolved in the Roman year 564[46].

If the Romans for some time abolished the Bacchanalia, they allowed the cult of the Bona Dea to go on. Men, in truth, were banished from these mysteries, but not excesses. "The secret practices of the cult of the Bona Dea are known to us," says Juvenal. "Excited by the noise of trumpets, drunk with wine, those lustful Mænads run about dishevelled, calling, by howls, Priapus to their aid. Who could express the libidinous ardor which devours them? Who could paint their lascivious dances, mingled with cries, and the torrents of old wine with which they are drenched? See Saufeia who, a wreath of flowers in her hand, provokes even the maid-servants of the meanest courtesans, and carries off the prize for debauchery; but Medullina surpasses her in the art of lascivious movements and postures. Here the greatest excesses draw the most glory: nothing is pretended, everything in their actions is real. Old men of the coldest sort through age, as Priam and Nestor, would be inflamed at the sight of their lubricity, if they could support the spectacle of it without being revolted. Soon these Furies, excited by the progress of their desires whose violence is unbearable to them, fill their den with these cries: *Let the men be brought in, it is time for them! Would he be sleeping, my lover? Let him be awakened.* The lover does not come. *Have some slaves come; if none can be found, a water-carrier.* If men are lacking, they are reduced to asking the assistance of a vile quadruped[47]."

The Romans transplanted the cult of Venus among the

138

Gauls. The gate of *Vendres* or of Venus, *portus Veneris*, was dedicated to this goddess; for Vendres was, by contraction, the name which the Gauls gave to the Mother of Loves. We have proof of it in the word *vendre-di* [Friday], day of Venus. Many places in France are still called *Vendre, Ventre, Vendœuvre*, etc., which would imply that they owe their names to the cult which this deity received there.

If a legend in verse of Saint Romain, Bishop of Rouen, can be believed, the cult of Venus existed in that city even in the seventh century. Within the walls of Rouen was a fortified château; there, in shadowy vaults, sectarians of the goddess gave themselves over to the excesses of the table, and then to the wildest debauchery. In the center of the château there was reared an edifice called the *Temple of Venus*. An idol of this goddess was adored there, and her priestesses, to whom our impolite legendist gives the title with which the crude common man addressed the lowest courtesans, shockingly fulfilled their indecent office. Saint Romain destroyed all these haunts of prostitution, overthrew the temple, broke the idol, and set the priestesses and their partisans to flight[48].

It is to such depths of depravation that a cult whose motives were originally pure, will degenerate; a cult, in truth, highly susceptible of abuse, which was not able to preserve itself, but whose first founders had praiseworthy intentions. They doubtless believed it necessary for the propagation of humankind and for its prosperity; proper for the uniting of families, for the tightening of social bonds, for the maintenance of peace and union among nations, for increasing the population, and perhaps for destroying vicious customs which were contrary to it. It would be necessary to have lived in the time and place of the origin of such institutions in order to judge them properly[49].

It can be believed that if the act of generation was honored as religious, the members of it, the principal coöperators in this act ought to have enjoyed at least the same prerogatives. Also, the organs of generation, far from being an object of ridicule or shame, were highly considered and honorably qualified. Their exposure to public view caused no scandal, nor wounded either morality or convention. These objects were even religiously invoked in the most solemn oaths. To swear while holding the hand on the genitals was a practice as holy as that of swearing while holding the hand on the altar; this was to give the strongest guarantee of the inviolability of a promise.

Sesostris, a king of Egypt, during the course of his vast conquests, had pillars erected in almost all the nations he had subdued, bearing this inscription: *Sesostris, King of Kings, Lord of Lords, has conquered this country by his arms.* Among brave and warlike peoples, these pillars offered the symbol of virility; and on those raised among a craven and unenergetic people there was on the contrary to be seen the mark of the feminine sex. These representations suggested nothing of the indecent about them; and the historians of antiquity who tell us about them do not give them that reproach[50].

Psammitichus, another king of Egypt, wishing to hold in their country some Egyptian soldiers who, dissatisfied, were going to Ethiopia, spoke to them of their fatherland, their wives, and their children. These soldiers then raised their tunics and, showing the sign of their virility, answered that they should lack neither wives nor children. This fact is cited by Diodorus Siculus as bravado, and not as an action contrary to decency[51].

The manners of the Hebrews, especially before the laws of Moses, scarcely differed from those of the peoples who surrounded them. Noah, being drunk, exhibited his nakedness: he is not blamed for it; but his son Ham, who had made game of him about it, was cursed along with all his posterity. David, in dancing before the ark with *all his might*, raised his linen ephod too high, allowing that to be seen which he ought to have hidden, and making the servant girls of Jerusalem laugh. His wife Michal later reproached him with this. David, piqued, answered: "I will play before the Lord, and I will yet be more vile than thus, and will be base in mine own sight: and of the maid-servants which thou hast spoken of, of them shall I be had in honor[52]." David is not blamed for having committted an indecency during a public and religious ceremony and having shown his nakedness: on the contrary it is his wife Michal who is punished for having reproached him with it; she was smitten with sterility.

These two examples prove the great respect of the Hebrews for the instruments of generation; but we have on this head many other proofs. They placed their hand there during solemn oaths; and then the oath was held to be inviolable[53]. When Abraham is made to say, in addressing Eliezer: *Place your hand on my thigh and promise me that you will not marry my son to a Canaanite woman;* when this speech, by the dying Jacob, is addressed to Joseph: *Touch my thigh, my son, and swear to me that you will not bury me in Egypt,* the Hebraic text has been inexactly translated. It is not the *thigh* that is here in question, say the most learned commentators; and the rabbis believe that such contact was instituted in order to honor circumcision.

This custom is preserved in that country up to our time. The Arabs, according to many travellers, either for greeting, or for engaging their promises in the most solemn form, place their hand at the genitals. Here is a recent example of it, reported in a letter of Adjutant-general Julien to a member of the *Institut d'Egypte*: "When the Mamelukes appeared for the first time at Rahmanyéh, our outposts arrested an inhabitant of the country who was crossing the plain. The volunteers who were leading him pretended to have seen him leave the enemy's ranks, and treated him harshly enough, regarding him as a spy. Finding myself in his path, I ordered that he be conducted to headquarters without harm. This unfortunate fellow, reassured by the manner in which he saw me speak, sought to prove that he was not a partisan of the Mamelukes. . . . He readily saw that I was unable to understand him; then he raised his blue shirt and, taking his *Phallus* in hand, remained a moment in the theatrical attitude of a god swearing by the Styx. His countenance seemed to say to me: *After the terrible oath I have sworn to prove my innocence to you, dare you doubt it?* His gestures recalled to me that in the time of Abraham people swore to truth by placing their hand on the organs of generation[54]."

A practice which bears much relation to this manner of swearing existed in the north of Europe, and there is a law which attests to its existence. An article of the laws that Olaf the Good made in the tenth century, for the province of Wales in England, states that if a violated woman wished to prosecute before the law the one who has done her the outrage, she must, in offering the oath declaring the crime and criminal, place her right hand on relics of the saints, and with her left hold the virile member of the accused[55].

Moses, whose principal object was to establish laws absolutely opposed to the customs of the Egyptians and the Canaanites or Phœnicians, prescribed to the Hebrews not to imitate those peoples, and not to display the private parts of their relatives or kinswomen. "After the doings of the land of Egypt," he tells them, "wherein ye dwelt, shall ye not do; and after the doings of the land of Canaan, whither I bring you, shall ye not do; neither shall ye walk in their ordinances. . . . None of you shall approach to any that is near of kin to him, to uncover their nakedness[56]." Moses then specifies all the degrees of relationship in which such indecency toward women should be prohibited. He also speaks of still graver offences, and adds: "Defile not ye yourselves in any of these things: for in all these the nations are defiled which I cast out before you: and the land is defiled: therefore I do visit the inquity thereof upon it, and the land itself vomiteth out her inhabitants[57]." Thus it can be concluded from these words that the indecencies prohibited by Moses were common to the Egyptians, whose country the Hebrews had just fled, and to the Canaanites or Phœnicians, into whose country they were going to establish themselves.

Indeed, it is clear from many aspects of history that shame was not the principal virtue of the Egyptian women. It has already been remarked that, for forty days, they went to present themselves to the bull Apis and exposed themselves in an extremely indecent manner before that animal-god, and that they gave themselves up to similar or yet graver indecencies toward the sacred goat. In various other circumstances they showed themselves no more reserved. When, each year, they went by water to Bubastis in order there to celebrate the fête of Diana, the men and women, mingled together in the same boat, occupied themselves with singing and dancing, accompanied by the sound of the flute and the noise of the castanets. "When they pass near a city," says Herodotus, "they make the boat come near the bank. Some of the women continue to sing, to play the castanets; others shout with all their might and cry insults to those of the city. These latter begin to dance; and the former, standing up, indecently tuck up their dresses. The same thing took place at each city they encounter along the length of the river[58]."

In the war which Cyrus, King of Persia, had to support against Astyages, King of the Medes, a similar act of indecency may be observed. The historians of antiquity describe it as an act of patriotism and courage. Astyages, after having harangued his troops, fell vigorously upon the Persian army. These latter, astonished, gave way and fell back by slow degrees. Their mothers and wives hastened out to them, begged them to return to the charge, and, seeing them hesitate, uncovered themselves before their eyes, presented them the wombs which had borne them, and asked them *if they wanted to hide themselves in the breast*

143

of their mothers or wives[59]. This sight and this reproach made them turn; they were victorious. Plutarch ranks this act among the courageous actions of women. He adds, after having reported it, that Cyrus, full of gratitude and admiration for this act of indecency and patriotism, made a law stating that every time the king of Persia should enter the city, each woman would receive a piece of gold[60].

Tacitus says, describing the death of Agrippina, who was murdered by her son Nero, that this Princess uncovered herself before her executioners and cried out to them: *Strike me in the belly*. "*Uterum protendens, ventrem feri exclamavit*[61]." During the civil war between Vitellius and Otho, some of the troops of this latter emperor penetrated into the province of the Maritime Alps and there committed a great deal of disorder. A Ligurian woman hid her son, whom the soldiers were pursuing; torments, even death could not make her confess his hiding place; but she answered: *It is there that he is hidden*, uncovering the womb which had borne him. *Uterum ostendens*, says Tacitus, who reports this fact not as an indecency, but as a remarkable example of maternal affection and courage[62].

The face was and still is the shameful part of the fair sex in oriental countries; a long veil shields it from the eyes of lovers. These women hide what our European women uncover, and without difficulty show what these latter scrupulously cover[63].

The Greeks were all as indifferent to nakedness as the other peoples of the Orient. They made use of it as a politic means proper for drawing one sex toward the other, for exciting desires which should turn to the profit of the population. These were the views of Lycurgus when he instituted exercises and dances at Sparta in which young girls and boys participated in public entirely naked. "In order to prevent the softness of a sedentary education," says Plutarch, " he accustomed the young girls to appear naked in public, like the young men; to dancing, to singing, to certain solemnities in the presence of those at whom, in their songs, they cast timely sharp little darts of raillery when they had made some mistakes, just as they gave them praise when they had merited it. . . . The nakedness of the girls had nothing shameful about it, because virtue served them as a veil and removed all idea of intemperance. This custom made them contract simple manners, inspired a lively emulation of vigor and strength among them, and gave them elevated sentiments by showing them that they could share the prize of glory and virtue with the men. . . . This was also a bait for marriage, these dances and exercises which the girls did in this condition before the young men, who felt themselves attracted, not by that geometrical necessity of which Plato speaks, but by a necessity yet stronger: that of love. Not content with that, Lycurgus attached a note of infamy to celibacy. Bachelors were excluded from the gymnastic contests with these girls; and the magistrates obliged them to make a circuit of the place during winter completely naked, singing a song made against them which said that they were justly punished for having disobeyed the law[64]."

This last provision plainly demonstrates the aim of the legislator: he wanted to people his republic; he wanted to people it with strong and robust citizens capable of defending it with zeal and vigor. Knowing the influence of women on men, he formed these in such a manner that they in their turn might be able to form men morally and physically fitted for fulfilling his wise intentions. The success he obtained proves his great genius and the excellence of his institutions.

Plato adopted these same ideas, which doubtless were not contrary to his time and country. He wished that the girls, before the age of puberty, might enter the race-ground naked, and that the young people of both sexes might dance naked together in order mutually to become acquainted with each other.[65].

145

THE GODS OF GENERATION:

There should here be added the description of the gymnastic exercises, of the indecent scenes which accompanied the religious ceremonies and the fêtes of various deities, of the lascivious dances of the Greeks and Romans in which nakedness and even lubricious gestures did not wound decency at all, and often called up only religious ideas. But my object is not to offer these additional pictures. The judicious reader will easily conclude from the exposition of the opinions, manners, and institutions which I have just elaborated, that these opinions, manners, and institutions derive from the warmth of the climate and from the necessity of favoring population. He will conclude that shame, that seemly virtue, is such only for peoples who have made a custom of it; that this custom ordinarily results from the temperature of the country they inhabit and from the necessity of clothing themselves; and that shame differs from chastity.

He will conclude that the difference of climates produces the difference of opinions on what seems decent and what does not; that the same influences have acted on religious practices; that what, in religious as in civil customs, seems shocking in one age and country, is not shocking in another age and country. Finally, he will conclude that the cult of the *Phallus*, of Priapus, the various ceremonies of which I have disclosed in this chapter, did not wound modesty at all and did not go against the prejudices of the nations where they were in force. In fact, among the writers of antiquity there is found no complaint, no declamation against this cult. It was only in a corrupt age that they made sport of Priapus and his Phallus, as of the majority of other deities. The Christians were the first to rise seriously and forcibly against this god and his images[66].

Chapter 11

BEFORE the establishment of the Romans in Gaul, and as long as the religion of the Druids remained pure and unmixed with foreign practices, the worship of human figures or animals was completely excluded from it. This truth is established by many historians of antiquity, and is not contradicted by any monument prior to the introduction of Roman idolatry. The cult of Priapus, which was part of it, was consequently unknown to the Gauls and the Celts. It might have been possible, however, that the Phœnicians, who had commerce with these peoples long before the conquests of Cæsar, had, attempted to establish this cult among them. But a strongly constituted religion, protected by priests vested with great authority, and indisposed to let themselves be stripped of a cult which was profitable to them for another which went contrary to the dogmas and rites of which they were the guardians, would not permit the Phœnicians to succeed.

Besides, the Gauls, although they had not the reputation for being chaste, were nevertheless modest; and when, through bravado, they presented themselves naked in battle, they took care to cover that which among civilized nations decency forbids placing in evidence. The climate of Gaul, modern France colder than that of Italy and the Orient, had accustomed the inhabitants to clothing themselves. It was the custom of hiding certain parts of the body, and not Nature, as is commonly said, that gave birth to modesty among them.

This modest character of the Gauls is further noticed in the earliest human figures they set up after they had admitted the practices and worship of the Romans. A statue of a woman, which appears to be very ancient, preserved at the Château of Quénipili, in Brittany, is represented with a stole the two parts of which descend from the neck to

147

the middle of the figure, and cover the sex. A statue of Hercules, which exists in the same province, is represented with the waist amply covered by a lion's skin. Several statues of Mercury, found on the top of Mount Donon, situated between Lorraine and Alsace, although naked offer certain singularities which it would be difficult to find among purely Roman monuments. The sexual mark is there completely hidden or disguised. Instead,one of these statues presents a large button in the form of a nailhead; another wears a little band which encircles its loins and covers the spot which characterizes masculinity; finally, three other Mercurys, equally naked, exhibit in place of their sex two large rings passed one through the other[1].

This aloofness which the Gauls at first evinced for complete nakedness and for the representation of the sexual parts was not of long duration, and could not resist the example of the Romans, their conquerors. Nevertheless it is certain that the cult of the *Phallus* or Priapus was not admitted into Gaul before the conquests of Cæsar[2].

The peoples of the north of Europe did not offer the same obstacles to the introduction of the cult of the *Phallus*. Whether the Phœnicians, who transported their merchandise and gods everywhere, had transplanted this cult there, or whether the cult had come to them from the northern parts of Asia, it is certain that it existed there before the establishment of the Roman domination in Germania.

The Saxons, the Suevi, and other peoples of the North, worshipped deities which certainly did not come to them from the Romans. Such were the three gods[3], often joined together, called *Odin* or *Woden*, *Thor*, and *Frikko*. Odin was the father[3], Thor his son[4], and Frikko was the same deity or the same symbol as the *Phallus*, or Priapus. Adam of Bremen, in his *Ecclesiastical History of the North*, reports that in the capital of the Swedes, called Uppsala, and near the city of Sietonia, there was to be seen a gold covered temple in which the statues of these three gods were exposed to the adoration of the people. Thor, placed on a throne, occupied the center, as the most powerful; at his sides were Woden and Frikko. This last was figured with an enormous Phallus. Before the Romans had introduced among the Germans the custom of representing gods by human figures, Frikko was only a large isolated Phallus.

Among the Saxons, where he was named *Frisco,* he was adored under this latter form. Sometimes there was substituted for the god Frikko a deity called *Frigga*; this was the goddess of voluptuousness, the Germanic and Scandinavian Venus. She was represented holding a Phallus in her hand. Phalli are still to be seen on the *batons ramiques,* at the points corresponding to the beginning of the year. This fact leads Olaf Rudbeck to believe that the phallic cult took birth in Scandinavia, and thence it was propagated among the Orientals. This cult had the same motif in the North as in the Orient. "If the women," says Olaf Rudbeck, "so religiously honored the sun under the symbol of the Phallus, it was not only in hope of seeing fecundity spread over the earth, but also over themselves. They were led to it less by debauchery than by the honor attached to maternity; for nothing was more scorned among them than a sterile beauty[5]."

Here are to be seen the symbols of both sexes, adored under names almost alike, *Frikko* and *Frigga,* and joined with the sun-god Thor. The same connections are found in the *Phallus* of the Orientals and the *Lingam* of the Indians. Such was the deity equivalent to the *Phallus,* which I believe was introduced into ancient Germania by the Phœnicians, or by the peoples of northern Asia.

When the Romans had put Gaul under their dominion, they introduced their worship among its inhabitants. At first they meddled with the religion of the Gauls only in order to abolish the human sacrifices in it; then, drawn to Gaul by commerce, war, and public business, they there naturalized their persons and their worship. The Romans dominated: the Druids, stripped of a great part of their authority, had lost their influence over the people; and the religion of the vanquishers became that of the vanquished. The gods of the Capitol established themselves in Gaul, mingled with the Celtic deities, soon dominated them, left them only the rural inhabitants for worshippers, and penetrated to the heart of Germania.

Priapus, although fallen into contempt among the Romans, followed the celestial band in this migration, established himself in Gaul, in Germania, and left evidences in these different countries of the existence and long duration of this cult. The Gauls, the Bretons, and the Germans erected altars to him, worshipped his images, confided the guardianship of the gardens to him, and invoked him against charms contrary to the fecundity of the fields, cattle, and women.

In Spain, Bacchus was worshipped along with his *Phallus* under the name of *Hortanes;* and his cult was established in ancient Nebrissa, today Lebrija, a city of Andalusia. "The inhabitants of Nebrissa," says Silius Italicus, "celebrate the orgies of Bacchus. There one sees nimble Satyrs and Mænads, covered with the sacred skin, carrying the figure of Bacchus *Hortanes* during the nocturnal ceremonies[6]." This Bacchus Hortanes was no different from Priapus. In France, many ancient monuments of this cult still exist. Cabinets of curiosities contain *Fascina*, Phalli, and Priapi of all shapes. The enormous Phallus of white marble found at Aix in Provence, and which is to be seen near the hot springs of that city, is decorated with wreaths. It was certainly an *ex-voto* offered to the deity of the springs by a cured invalid, or one hoping to be.

The bas-reliefs of the Pont du Gard and of the amphitheatre at Nîmes offer singular varieties in forms of the Phallus. There one sees simple ones, double ones with a leash, and triple ones, the three branches of which are pecked by birds, and are furnished with wings, animal legs, and little bells. One of these triple Phalli is bridled and mounted by a woman who holds the reins[7]. In the city of Saint-Bertrand, in what was formerly Comminge, there has been discovered an entire Priapus, terminating in a herma, on the subject of which President d'Orbessan in 1770 read a dissertation to the *Académie* of Toulouse. The idol is characterized by a Horn of Plenty filled with fruits, and still further by his usual sign[8]. A chapel dedicated to the same deity formerly existed at Autun, on the mountain of Couard; the majority of the historians of that city make mention of it.

In an ancient cemetery, situated near Bordeaux in a place called *Belaire,* or *Terre nègre,* there was discovered in 1807 a phallic arm in bronze. The fingers of the hand were disposed in such a manner that the thumb was placed between the index and middle fingers. The Phalli seemed to go out from this arm, one in repose and the other in its state of vigor. On the arm, whch was an inch and a half in length, was a ring by which this phallic amulet could be suspended[9].

Many Phalli of bronze have been discovered in the excavations made on the little mountain of the Châtelet in Champagne, where a Roman city was built. Here is how Grignon, who presided over these excavations, speaks of them: "Three Phalli to hang about the neck. These Phallus-amulets prove that the ladies solicited the protection of the god Priapus. One of these Phalli is triple: the middle attribute is in repose; the two collateral ones are in a state of the greatest degree of power. Two others, provided with their appendices and hair, are simple[10]." In the same excavations Grignon has further discovered the fragments of a colossal Priapus: these fragments consisted of one hand, with part of the forearm, and the characteristic sign of this deity. The gigantic proportions of this last piece so astonished Grignon that he applied to it the epithets which Virgil employed to depict the giant Polyphemus: *Monstrum horrendum, informe, ingens*, etc[11].

In the excavations made at *Labatie-Mont-Saléon*, the location of a Roman city, called *Mons Seleucas*, in the department of the Hautes-Alpes, a great number of antiquities has been discovered, among which were several Priapi. One only has been described: his chin is bearded; his head is covered with a cap; his arms are bent, and his hands supported on his hips[12]. One of the most singular monuments of this cult is the one which was found in an ancient tomb near Amiens. It is of bronze and represents a human figure in the exercise of its functions and with its head covered with a cowl called *Bardocuculus*. This figure is in the attitude of a man walking. It is made up of two pieces, the upper of which, comprising the head, arms, and trunk, detached from the lower part, allows the Phallus hidden in its hollow to be seen: then this Phallus is supported by human legs. The chapter-house of the cathedral of Amiens preserved this antiquity in its archives up to the Revolution[13].

At Antwerp Priapus enjoyed great veneration, and his cult was so solidly established there that it maintained itself, in spite of Christianity, up to the seventeenth century, as I shall prove later in this work. Many antique vases carry paintings or bas-reliefs offering the picture of the fêtes of the same god, called *Priapeia*. They have been discovered in France and are preserved in cabinets of curiosities. "I have seen in the sacristy of the church of Saint-Ouen, at Rouen," says Millin, "a ciborium ornamented with antique medallions representing *Priapeia* and scenes of Sicilian shepherds with their she-goats[14]." Grivaud published many priapic figures and amulets in his *Recueil d' antiquités*. He informs us that he has the designs of a great many other figures found at Arles, Moissac, and elsewhere, but that he refused to publish them because of their extreme obscenity. These citations are sufficient to prove that

the cult of the *Phallus* and Priapus was introduced into
Gaul by the Romans, and that it triumphed there over the
repugnance which the inhabitants at first evinced for its
indecencies.

The cult of Priapus had the same success in Germany,
and maintained itself there until the twelfth century. Even
the name of this god had undergone scarcely any alteration
there. Only the cult had received the imprint of the barbarous and warlike manners of the people among whom it
was transplanted. It was no longer the deity which presided over the fecundation of plants and animals, over the
prosperity of all living beings, over the pleasures of lovers,
of married people. It became a tutelary god of the country,
a ferocious god, like the character of the inhabitants who,
instead of offering him flowers or making honey and milk
flow on his altars, steeped them in human blood. This cult
resembled an exotic plant which an unfriendly soil had
degenerated.

The inhabitants of Sclavonia, still given over in the
twelfth century to the practices of paganism, had a horror
for the name Christian. They rendered a cult to Priapus,
whom they named *Pripe-Gala*. These people, enemies to
their neighbors, who had embraced Christianity, made frequent incursions on the dioceses of Magdeburg and Saxony.
The treatment they practiced on the vanquished was all the
more cruel because the motive of their animosity was sacred. Many prelates and princes of Saxony joined together,
about the year 1110, to implore the aid of some powerful
neighbors. They wrote to the prelates of Germany, Lorraine, and France, setting forth the deplorable situation into
which the hatred of these idolaters had sunk them. Their
letter, the expressions of which seem dictated by despair
and eagerness for vengeance, solicited a special crusade
against them. Some slight details are to be found in this
letter on the cult of this Priapus. "Every time," it reads,
"that these fanatics assemble together to celebrate their

religious ceremonies, they proclaim that their god *Pripe-Gala* demands human heads as offerings. *Pripe-Gala*, according to them, is the same as Priapus, or as the lewd Baal-Peor. When they have cut off the head of several Christians before the profane altar of this god, they begin to give vent to terrible howlings, and cry out: *Let us rejoice today: Christ is vanquished; and our invincible* PRIPE-GALA *is his vanquisher*[15]*."*

The facts contained in the following chapters, by proving the continuance of the cult of the Phallus among the Christians, will leave no further doubt of its ancient existence in Gaul and Germania.

Chapter 12

THE CULT OF THE PHALLUS AMONG THE CHRISTIANS, THE
FASCINA OR FESNES, THE MANDRAGORAS, ETC.

OF all human affections, custom is the most dangerous to combat and the most difficult to destroy. Reason never succeeds against it; and violence triumphs over it only when it is constantly sustained and long prolonged. Therefore it is not surprising that the cult of the *Phallus* maintained itself in the countries where Christianity was established, that it braved the austere dogmas of that religion, and that for more than fifteen centuries it successfully resisted the efforts of Christian priests, often fortified by civil authority. But, it must be admitted, this triumph was not complete. The cult yielded to circumstances. It was obliged to disguise itself, to adopt forms and denominations belonging to Christianity. This disguise favored its preservation and assured its duration.

Priapus received the name and costume of a *Saint*; but his attributes were retained by him, his preservative and fecundating powers, and that salient and monstrous member which is the symbol of it. Priapus, metamorphosed into a Saint, was honorably placed in churches and invoked by sterile Christian women who, making offerings, bought the hope of being heard. Christian priests often fulfilled toward him the ministry of the priests of Lampsacus. It was not only in the early days of Christianity that the cult of Priapus existed among the peoples who had embraced that religion. This mingling would have had nothing extraordinary about it, for ignorant peoples given to routine, uncertain between two religions, one of which succeeds the other, could easily preserve the practices and ceremonies of the old while adopting the dogmas of the new. But this cult has maintained itself in France up to the seventeenth century, and still exists in some parts of Italy.

The *fascinum*, that species of phallic amulet that women, and especially children, wore about their neck or shoulders, was in use among the French for many centuries. From *fascinum* they made, by contraction, the word *fesne*. They also named these amulets *mandragoras*, the name of a plant whose root resembles the masculine sex, and to which in consequence was attributed occult and preservative powers against charms. Incantations and prayers were made in honor of these phallic amulets; magic verses were addressed to them in order to obtain their aid.

A piece entitled *Sacerdotal Judgments on Crimes*, which appears to have been written at the end of the eighth century, carries this article: "If anyone has made enchantments or other incantations with the *fascinum*, let him do penance on bread and water for three Lents[1]." The Council of Châlons, held in the ninth century, prohibits this practice, pronounces penalties against those who lend themselves to it, and testifies to its existence at this period. Burchard, who lived in the twelfth century, reproduces the article of this council containing the prohibition. Here is the translation of it: "If anyone makes incantations with the *fascinum*, he shall do penance on bread and water for three Lents[2]." The synodical statutes of the church of Mans, which are of the year 1247, carry the same penalty against any one who "has sinned with the *fascinum*, who has made enchantments, or who has recited any formula, provided that it be not the Creed, the Lord's prayer, or any other canonical prayer[3]." In the fourteenth century, the synodical statutes of the church of Tours, of the year 1396, renew the same prohibition. These statutes were then translated into French, and the word *fascinum* is expressed there by *fesne*: "If anyone recites any enchantments to *fesne*, etc[4]."

It will be observed from these citations that it was the custom to address chants, prayers, and magic formulæ to the *fascinum*. This *fascinum* was none of those amulets whose small size permitted their being worn hung about the neck, but it was a Phallus of wood or stone similar to the Phalli sculptured over the doors of private houses and public buildings. It must be remarked that it was not forbidden to address the Apostolic Creed, the Lord's prayer, or other canonical prayers to this indecent image. The custom of placing Phalli on the exterior of public buildings, in order to preserve them against witchcraft, is verified by existing monuments; some are to be seen on the public buildings of the ancients. What is more remarkable is that the Christians, moved by their old superstitions, have even placed them on their churches. An artist who had gone through France and given himself over to sketching Christian monuments, has reported many examples of the existence of this custom[5]. Sonnerat, in his *Voyage aux Indes et à la Chine*, says that the figure of the *Lingam* is to be seen over the portals of our old churches, over that of the cathedral of Toulouse, and of several churches of Bordeaux[6].

Another amulet, more portable and of similar figure, was in vogue in the fifteenth century. It was named *mandragora*. It was supposed to ward off charms and procure wealth and happiness for those who wore them on their persons, properly wrapped up. The use of mandragoras, as amulets, is very ancient. Genesis reports that Reuben, found mandragoras in the fields and brought them to his mother Leah. Doubtless to them were ascribed the faculty of procuring fecundity, for which the Hebrew women were so eager. Rachel, who, like Leah her sister, was a wife of Jacob, earnestly asked for these mandragoras. Leah at first refused, but when Rachel declared that she would permit her to pass the following night with Jacob if Leah would grant them to her, she conceded to this price; and in order to lie with the patriarch, she gave away her mandragoras[7].

The cult of the mandragoras and the superstitious ideas which were imputed to it were in vogue throughout Europe. The Templars were even accused of worshipping in Palestine a figure called *mandragora*; this is expressed in

a manuscript interrogatory of the monks of that Order[8].
A Franciscan friar, named Brother Richard, in April 1229
made a vigorous sermon against the mandragora amulet. He
convinced the men and women of its inutility, and had
many of them burned which were voluntarily turned over
to him. "The Parisians," says a writer of the time, "had
such great faith in this filth that, in truth, they firmly believed that so long as they had it, if only it was quite properly wrapped up in fine silk or linen cloths, they would
never a day of their life be poor." The author says further
that these mandragoras had been placed in fashion "by
the advice of some old women who are too dense to recognize, when they run into such wickedness, authentic sor-
ceries and heresies[9]."

Nature was not alone responsible for this phallic composition. Art came to its aid to form images resembling
human figures of both sexes. The mandragora itself, in the
opinion of the ancients, possessed magic properties only in
so far as it was prepared by mysterious ceremonies[10]. Phallic figures were even applied to articles of food. The Romans had set this example and the French imitated it. In many
parts of France breads are made which have the figure of
the Phallus. Some in this form are to be found in what formerly was Bas-Limousin, and especially at Brives. Sometimes these breads or *miches* [round loaves] have the form
of the feminine sex: such are those which are made at Clermont in Auvergne, and elsewhere[11]. These phallic breads
were and still are, in the cities of Saintes and Saint Jean
d'Angély, considered as sacred objects. I shall speak of
them soon.

The ancient Romans placed the *fascinum* around the
neck or shoulders of children in order to ward off glances
of envy, which, they believed, injured their growth and
health. The Neapolitans still follow the same custom:
around the shoulders of children they attach with a rib-
bon a *fascinum* such as the ancients employed. Martin

d'Arles informs us that also in his time superstitious women, in order to ward off the baneful effects of the glances of certain old women, placed fragments of mirror, bits of fox-skin, and various tufts of hair around the shoulders of small children[12]. Such fetishes ought to be ranked in the class of *fascina*; they occupied the same place, they had the same motive, and certainly they have a common origin. A little univalvular shell, set in silver and worn about the neck as a preservative, ought also to be ranked with the numerous superstitions that the inhabitants of France have borrowed from the Romans. The figure and name of this preservative, still in use, leaves no doubt as to the obscene object it represents.

There existed some centuries ago, and perhaps still exist, some souvenirs, some traces of the *Phallus* among the absurd old wives' tales. These were very seriously published as edifying truths by pious monks and doctors of theology. Here is one of these tales, which I find in the work of Brother Jacques Sprenger, Inquisitor of the Faith: "What is to be thought of those sorceresses who enclose in a bird's nest, or in various boxes, twenty or thirty virile members, which move about as if they were alive and live on barley and oats? However, this is what everybody relates, and what has been seen by many persons. It ought to be said that an illusion of the devil has fascinated the eyes of those who believe to have seen them[13]."

Phallic forms have also been employed even in the head-dress of women. Montaigne, after having spoken of the customs established among various nations having connection with the cult of Priapus, and of the different methods of honoring the *Phallus*, adds that married women of a country adjoining the one he lived in still wear this image on their forehead, and that when they have become widows they wear it behind their head. "The married women near-by," he says, "make a figure on the forehead of their head-covering, in order to glory in the enjoyment they have of

it; and coming to be widows, place it in the rear and bury
it under their coiffure[14]." The same author, speaking of the
ceremony practiced at Lavinium in which the Roman ladies came to crown the image of the masculine sex in a public square, seems to recall having seen a similar custom practiced in his time. "Still I know not," he says, "if in my days
I have seen any air of similar devotion[15]."

I have spoken of the Indian and Roman girls and women
who, in order to obtain a desired fecundity and ward off
witchcraft, pay homage to the *Phallus* with the first-fruits
of marriage by limiting themselves to a mysterious touching, or by completing the sacrifice. I have also spoken of
the women of Israel, who fabricated Phalli in order to abuse
themselves with them. It behooves me now to show how
Christian women have imitated, up to a certain point, these
ancient examples.

One is at first led to believe that the violent need of satisfying pent-up desires alone suggested to Christian women
the use of the figure in default of the object figured; but
that would be incorrect. This shameful practice certainly
belongs to the religion of the ancients: it formed, as has
been said, an integral part of the cult of the *Phallus*. It was
the religious and obscene ceremony which has furnished
the example; a depraved passion later imitated it. Besides,
it is clear that superstition, which is only an abuse of the
religions of antiquity, induced the same women to stimulate
the passions of their lovers or husbands, even if it killed the
latter, and to give themselves over to other practices quite
as monstrous and obscene. The most disordered imagination
can conceive of nothing worse[16].

It is therefore presumable that if Christian women abandoned themselves, with superstitious purposes, to the disgusting practices I have just referred to by Burchard[17],
they could, with the same purposes, fabricate Phalli and
misuse them. Libertinism continued a custom that a superstitious motive had instituted. Acts of religion which touch

so closely upon debauchery easily became confused with
it. Time made the religious intention forgottten; disordered
passions replaced it. Be that as it may, some penitential canons of the eighth century, in prohibiting this practice, testify that it was in usage at that period. Here is what the
article entitled *de Machina mulierum* carries: "A woman
who, by herself or with the help of another woman, fornicates with any instrument whatsoever, shall do penance for
three years, one year of which on bread and water. If this
variety of fornication takes place with a nun," the following article states, "the penance shall be for seven years,
two years of which on bread and water[18]." A penitential
manuscript, cited in the glossary of Du Cange, verifies the
same offense. This item is to be found there: that if a nun,
by means of this instrument, fornicates with another nun,
the delinquents shall be condemned to seven years of penance[19]. The same Burchard, Bishop of Worms, who in the
twelfth century composed a collection of canonical ordinances and regulations on penances, further attests to the
existence of the same vice. But his expressions are so grossly
naïve and the details so indecently set forth, that he leaves
me unwilling to translate them. It belonged only to the
casuists of bygone times to describe with impunity these
filthy mysteries[20].

This excess, which insults nature, which dishonors the
age, societies, and institutions in which it was manifested,
if it is not an imitation of the ceremonies practiced toward
the *Phallus*, *Lingam*, and *Mutinus*, is at least one of the scandalous results of forced continence, one of the usual effects
of those absurd and always powerless laws which pretend
to reform nature, which seem to accuse the work of the
Deity of imperfection, and which foolishly forbid the custom instead of forbidding the abuse. These inconsiderate
laws, dictated by a blind zeal, have produced a great many
more sexual vices than they have blocked. The impetuosity of pent-up senses, it is known, is like a torrent which

overtops the dam that constrains it and bursts forth with all the more violence and havoc; or like saltpetre compressed in a tube, whose explosion has all the more force because of its contracture.

It is true that if the priests desired the cause, they condemned the effects. If they instituted absolute continence, they blamed and punished the sexual vices which it brought on. They opposed themselves as much as they could to the superstitious and obscene practices which I have just described; but they did not act the same toward other practices no less indecent. Less severe and more adroit, they turned to their profit the ancient cult established by the Romans, and which long custom had strengthened. They appropriated to themselves what they could not destroy; and in order to draw the worshippers of Priapus to them, they converted that deity to the Christian religion.

Chapter 13

THE CULT OF PRIAPUS UNDER THE NAMES OF SAINT FOUTIN,
SAINT RENE, SAINT GUERLICHON, SAINT GUIGNOLE, ETC.

THE ancient god of Lampsacus was given the names of various Saints of legend. These names bore a relation to the action over which this god presided, or with his most characteristic attributes.

In Provence, Languedoc, and the Lyonnais, the first bishop of Lyon, called *Pothin*, *Photin*, or *Fotin*, was honored as a Saint. This name was commonly pronounced *Foutin*. In Grégoire de Tours, this name is written *Fotin*: he says that he was entombed in the vault which is under the altar of the Basilica of Saint-Jean, and that the dust which came from the scraping of his tomb, taken together with faith, was an assured remedy against many maladies. It will soon be seen that the scrapings yielded, not by his tomb, but by a certain part of the idol of the same *Saint Fotin*, were later much in use as a powerful remedy.

The people said *Foutin*; and as they often judge things according to their names, they judged that *Saint Foutin* was worthy of replacing *Saint Priapus*[1]: all the prerogatives were conferred on him. *Saint Foutin de Varages* was held in great veneration in Provence. To him was attributed the power of rendering sterile women fecund, of reviving listless men, and of curing their secret maladies. Consequently, it was the custom to offer him, as was formerly offered the god Priapus, *ex-votos* in wax which represented the weak or afflicted parts. "To this Saint are offered," one reads in the *Confession de Sancy*, "the shameful parts of both sexes, formed in wax. The ceiling of the chapel is well decorated with them, and when the wind makes them knock together, it somewhat disturbs the devotions in honor of this Saint. I was highly scandalized when I passed through there to hear of plenty of men who had the name *Foutin*. The daughter of my host had a spinster named *Foutine* for a godmother[2]."

163

The same Saint was similarly honored at Embrun. When in 1585 the Protestants took this city, they found amongst the relics of the principal church the Phallus of Saint Foutin. The devotees of this city, in imitation of the devotees of paganism, made libations to that obscene idol. They poured wine over the end of the Phallus, which was quite reddened from it. This wine, received into a vessel, soured there: it was then named *saint vinaigre* [holy vinegar]. "And the women," says the author who furnished me these details, "employed it in a strange enough fashion." He gives no other enlightenment on this matter. I leave it to be guessed[3].

At Orange there existed a Phallus which formed an object for the veneration of the people of that city. Larger than the one at Embrun, it was made of wood, covered with leather, and furnished with its appendices. When in 1562 the Protestants laid ruin to the church of Saint Eutrope, they seized the enormous Phallus and had it burned in the public square. A fountain, situated near Orange, whose waters, according to what superstitious old women believed, had prolific powers, perhaps gave rise to the idea of setting up in the city an image which had the same power and produced the same effects. Thus Priapus found himself in rivalry with the Naiad of the fountain whose waters were drunk by sterile women. According to the same author, there was a *Saint Foutin* at Poligny of whom the women went to ask assistance for having children. There was another called *Saint Foutin de Cruas*, in the diocese of Viviers. Others were to be found in Bourbonnais, in the little city of Vendre, on the banks of the Allier. At Auxerre, this Saint miraculously impregnated all the women who invoked him[4].

In Auvergne, four leagues from Clermont, near the old road from this city to Limoges and on the eastern part of the mountain called Tracros, is a rock which seems a separate being. From a distance this isolated rock presents the form of a statue. The inhabitants name it *Saint Foutin*. This rock, thus termed, would have no connection with our subject and could not be taken for the image of *Saint Photin*, if its shape were not characterized so as to leave no doubt as to its identity. Standing in the plain which is to the north or northwest of the mountain of Tracros, one perceives that *Saint Foutin* has strongly pronounced phallic forms. It is beyond any doubt that the inhabitants of the district have rendered a cult to this figure. His denomination as *Saint* proves it; and there has been preserved the tradition of superstitious ceremonies which were formerly practiced there.

The inhabitants of Puy-en-Velay still speak of their *Saint Foutin*, honored in their city at a period quite close to our own, and whom sterile women came to supplicate. They made scrapings from the enormous phallic branch that the statue of the Saint presented. They believed that the scrapings, infused in a drink, would render them fecund. This was, as we shall soon notice, the means most generally employed for obtaining from these Saints with enormous Phalli the fecundity that was asked of them. It is doubtless one of these Saints that Court de Gébelin refers to when he says, regarding the goat of Mendes: "I have read somewhere or I have heard it said that in a corner of southern France there existed, not so long ago, a custom analogous to this: the women of this district went in devotion to a temple in which there was a statue of a Saint, which they kissed in the hope of becoming pregnant[5]." In a little monastery of hermits living under the order of Saint Augustine, situated at Gironet near Sampigny, was a *Saint Foutin*, invoked by sterile women, who enjoyed a great reputation. Not far from this monastery was located, on the heights of a mountain, a monastery of the Minims, under the invocation of *Sainte Lucie*, whom sterile women also invoked in order to become fecund. Anne of Austria, the wife of Louis XIII, went there in pilgrimage[6].

Traces of the cult of *Saint Foutin* are to be found even

in Germany. A writer of that country speaks of him as a Saint well-known in the seventeenth century, and to whom girls, ready to become wives, paid homage with their virginal robe. This author relates how a young bride, the first night of her marriage, sought through a deceit to remove the suspicions of her husband from her past conduct; and in order to suggest that this woman's honor had already received some injuries, he says that *she had long since placed her robe of virginity on the altar of* Saint Foutin[7].

Saint Foutin is not the only name that Priapus bore among the Christians; but his other names, like this one, always had some connection with the supposed powers of the Saint. One of these idols existed, doubtless since the time of the Romans, in the place of Bourg-Dieu, diocese of Bourges. The inhabitants, who had a great deal of faith, continued to render him a cult even after they had become Christians. The monks of the monastery dared not destroy religious practices consecrated by time; and Priapus was adored in the abbey of this place under the name of *Saint Guerlichon* or *Saint Greluchon*[8]. Sterile women came to implore his prolific powers, and there held a neuvaine. On each of the nine days, they stretched themselves over the figure of the Saint, which was placed horizontally. Then they scraped a certain part of *Saint Guerlichon*, which was as much in evidence as that of Priapus. These scrapings, diluted in water, formed a miraculous beverage. Henri Estienne, from whom I borrow this fact, adds: "I do not know if this Saint is still in such favor today, for those who have seen him say that he had that part quite used up about twelve years ago because of scraping it[9]." Pastureaud informs me that at Bourges, faubourg du Château, rue Chevrière, there exists a little statue placed in the wall of a house, the form of the sex of which is worn away from being scraped by women who swallowed the scrapings in the hope of becoming pregnant. In this country this statue is named the good *Saint Greluchon*[10].

A History of Phallic Cults

The same author places a *Saint Gilles* in the ranks of the Saints of this sort. In the country of Cotentin, in Brittany, he also bore the reputation of procuring the fecundity that the women solicited with similar ceremonies[11]. He also speaks of a Saint René, in Anjou. The feature which characterized his fertilizing powers appeared in the greatest evidence. The ceremonies that the women practiced to render the Saint favorable were of such indecency that Henri Estienne, elsewhere quite free in his expressions, dares not describe them. "I should be ashamed," he says, "to write of it; also, my readers would be ashamed to read of it!"

Saint Regnaud, like *Saint René*[12], and perhaps because of the resemblance of names, a Saint with Phallus, was formerly highly honored by the Burgundians[13]. *Saint Arnaud*, another Saint of the same character, was less indecent than *Saint René*, or rather he was so only at intervals. A mysterious apron ordinarily veiled the symbol of fecundity, and was raised only in behalf of sterile devotees. The inspection of the objects opened to view sufficed, along with faith, to work miracles[14].

In the neighborhood of Brest, at the end of the valley through which the river Penfel runs, was the chapel of the famous *Saint Guignolé* or *Guingalais*[15]. The phallic sign of this Saint consisted of a long wooden peg which ran through his statue from one side to the other, and showed itself in front in a quite salient manner. The devotees of the country acted toward *Saint Guignolé* like those of Puy towards *Saint Foutin* and those of Bourg-Dieu toward *Saint Guerlichon*. They devoutly scraped the extremity of this miraculous peg; and these scrapings, mixed with water, made a powerful antidote against sterility. When, by this often repeated ceremony, the peg was worn down, a blow with a mallet from behind the Saint, readily made it come out again in front. Thus, though always scraped, it did not appear to diminish. The mallet blow performed the miracle.

Here is what I read in the account of a trip made to Brest

in 1794: "To the rear of the port of Brest, beyond the for-
tifications, going up the river, a little chapel existed near
a fountain and the woods which cover the hill. In this chapel was a statue of stone honored with the name of *Saint*. If
decency permitted describing Priapus with his indecent
attributes, I should depict this statue. When I saw it, the
chapel was half demolished and exposed, and the statue was
outside, stretched on the ground, and unbroken; so that it
existed entire, and even with recent repairs, which made it
appear still more scandalous to me. Sterile women, or those
who feared being so, went to this statue; and after having
scratched or scraped that which I dare not name, and drunk
this powder infused in a glass of water from the fountain,
these women would return home with the hope of becoming fertile[16]."

"Let us not forget," says a modern writer, who has described one of the departments included in the former province of Bretagne, "Let us not forget to speak of the famous
Saint Guignolet, and that eternal peg, so favorable to im-
pregnation. Since the Catholic religion made Saints of the
gods of paganism, could Priapus be forgotten? The wood
of that threadbare peg was swallowed by the unfruitful
women; and after some time they conceived. Evil people
pretended that some nearby monks aided a great deal in
this miracle." The author[17] charitably adds: "I don't believe
the monks had anything to do with it." It is certain that the
cult of this Saint existed in Bretagne up to the middle of
the eighteenth century. His chapel was closed about the
year 1740 and when it was opened, after some years, *Saint
Guignolet* with his miraculous peg was to be discovered
there[18].

This same *Saint Guignolet* was honored in a chapel of
the village of Chatellette, in the commune of Alichamp, in
Berry, at present the canton of Saint Amand, department
of the Cher. There sterile women came to hold neuvaines,
invoked the fecundating Saint, scraped his phallic branch,

and the powder which resulted from this, infused in wine, was swallowed by these devotees anxious for the miracle. The curé took care of providing that the Phallus, often scraped, preserved itself in a state worthy of the great Saint Guignolet. An archbishop of Bourges suppressed the Saint, and interdicted the curé to whom it was so profitable; but the devotion of the sterile women continued up to the Revolution, as was further asserted, in 1806, by Pajonnet, an antiquarian scholar and the curé of Alichamp[19].

Antwerp was the Lampsacus of Belguim, and Priapus the tutelary god of that city. The inhabitants named him *Ters;* and the female inhabitants had the greatest veneration for this deity. They were accustomed to invoke him even in the least accidents of life; and this devotion still existed in the sixteenth century, as Jean Goropius informs us. "If they allowed," says he, "an earthen vessel to escape their hands, if they hurt their feet, or finally, if some unforseen accident angered them, the women, even the most respectable, loudly called Priapus to their aid. This superstition was formerly so rooted in their minds that Godefroy de Bouillon, a marquis of that city, in order to make it disappear, or to lead it over to the ceremonies of Christianity, sent to the city of Antwerp from Jerusalem as an inestimable present, *the foreskin of Jesus Christ.* He believed by this to turn the inhabitants away from a cult so shameful; but this present profited little with the women and did not make them forget the sacred *Fascinum*[20]."

Goropius finds in the anagram of the word *Ters* which is the name of Priapus at Antwerp, a word which in the idiom of the country expresses the action over which this god presides. "There is still shown," he says elsewhere, "a little statue, formerly furnished with a Phallus, which decency has done away with." He adds that this statue is placed over the neighboring gate of the public prison. He informs us that Priapus had a very celebrated temple at Antwerp, where all the people of the neighborhood flocked together in great devotion to offer their homage to that deity. On this matter he reports an opinion which derives the name of the city of Antwerp (Anvers) from the Latin word *Verpum*, which expresses that of which the Phallus is the figure; but he does not adopt this etymology because he has never heard this word pronounced by the women, but rather the word *Ters*, which in that city is synonymous with *Fascinum*.

Some authors have thought that the temple of *Saint Walburge* was consecrated to Priapus; that this Saint is suppositious; that her name signifies *citadel*; and that this was the one which the ancient inhabitants of Antwerp took as the tutelary deity of that city. Goropius quite believes that *Walburge* signifies citadel, and that this was the name of a protective deity of the city. But he does not believe that the temple of *Sainte Walburge* had been that of Priapus. "Perhaps" he says, "this god was worshipped in a place situated to the left of the city, where the ruins of an ancient temple are still to be seen[21]." The Romans did not erect any temple to the deity of Priapus. They limited themselves to setting up statues, altars, and chapels to him. If the inhabitants of Antwerp built him a temple, the city of Lampsacus alone must have furnished the example.

Various other writers have spoken of the Priapus of Antwerp. Abraham Golnitz says that the figure of this god is to be seen at the entrance of the precincts of the temple of *Saint Walburge*, in the Rue des Pêcheurs, and below the gate of the public prison. It is a little statue of stone, about a foot high, represented with raised hands and spread legs, and whose sexual sign has entirely disappeared: "A great many tales," he says, "are told about the cause of this disappearance; and there is also talk of the custom employed by sterile women of scraping the part which is lacking on this statue, and of taking the resulting powder in a potion in order to conceive[22]." Another contemporary traveler, speaking of Antwerp, says: "There is to be seen an idol of

stone there, placed over an ancient gateway. Many believe
that the powder from the scraping of the sexual parts of
this figure, drunk in a potion by women, preserved them
from sterility[23]."

I have spoken of the *Phallophori* who, among the Greeks,
formed a group in the processions made in honor of Bacchus[24]. I have described his religious ceremonies which the
Egyptians, Greeks, and Romans celebrated at the approach
of the spring equinox. Curiously enough, some remnants of
this practice are preserved up to our day. The *Phallophori*
among the Greeks were men who in the procession of Bacchus carried long staffs, from the top of which hung *Phalli*.
At the fête of the Thargelia, young men also carried olive
branches to which were attached breads, vegetables, acorns,
figs, and Phalli. In the city of Saintes a similar custom was
practiced on Palm Sunday: women, even the most devout,
and children of both sexes, carried in procession, at the end
of a consecrated branch or bough, a hollow bread in the
form of a Phallus. The name of this bread agrees with its
shape in betraying its origin, and leaves no doubt as to the
indecent object it represents[25]. The priest blessed these
phallic breads, and the women kept them throughout the
entire year as an amulet. At Saint-Jean d'Angély, on Cor-
pus Christi day, little breads were carried in procession
named *fateux*, which had the shape of Phalli. This custom
still existed when Maillard was sub-prefect of that city.
He had it suppressed.

These religious and indecent practices would perhaps
still exist in France if knowledge, ever growing since the
fifteenth century, had not brought the light of day on their
turpitude and manifested how much they were opposed to
the principles of Christianity. They would still exist if
Protestant writers had not launched sarcasm and mockery
against them, and caused laughter at the expense of those
who believed in them. Then, ashamed of the rôle they
had played, and wishing to snatch from their antagonists

171

this means of ridiculing and disgracing them in the opinion of the people, Catholic priests gradually reformed these Priapic Saints, or substituted for their cult one which resembled it, but those forms did not so overtly wound decency.

Thus the sterile women, instead of scraping the phallic branch of a statue, or contemplating it with devotion, were reduced: some to drinking the prolific waters of a fountain consecrated to a Saint; others, as at Rocamadour in the Rouergue, to kissing the bolt of the church, or a bar of iron called the *Bracquemart de Roland*; or to making neuvaines to various fecundating female Saints, as *Sainte Foy* of the city of Conques, also in Rouergue, or the Holy Virgin of Orcival in Auvergne, in whose church was a pillar which the sterile women kissed[26].

In the little city of Saint-Fiacre, a league from Mouceaux, in the corner to the right of the chapel, is a stone named *le Fauteuil de Saint Fiacre* [*Saint Fiacre's armchair*]. This stone has the power of rendering sterile women pregnant. They come to seat themselves there; but in order for the miracle to operate, it is necessary that there be no clothing between the body of the woman and the stone. Elsewhere, women remain lying for a certain time on the tomb of some Saint renowned for his prolific powers. This is especially practiced in the city of Saragossa in Spain, in the monastery of Saint-Antoine-de-Paule, and in the chapel which is dedicated to him[27].

On the extreme frontier of the department of Allier, in the arrondissement of Mont-Lucon, is the oratory of Saint-Jean and Saint-Remi, in the midst of an immense moor situated in the comune of Saint-Janvier. On the 20th of June, barren women and young people of both sexes gather together there from three or four leagues all around. They pass the night there pell-mell in the desert. The next day they make offerings, and drink the *saint-vinage* [*holy wine mixture*]. This beverage, composed of the water of a fountain surnamed of *Saint-Jean*, and a little wine, passes for a powerful preservative against sterility and the charms of the *fasciniers*, sorcerers who *nouent l'aiguillette* [tie up or knot the point][28], and render young husbands impotent[29].

These changes have not been brought about everywhere. There are peoples who, favored by a dense superstition and the ancient shadows of ignorance, have remained continually sheltered from the rays of light which have enlightened other nations. Without bothering themselves with the strange contradiction of their conduct, they have continued to mingle paganism with the Christian religion, to confuse the cult of Priapus with that of the Saints, and have preciously preserved even to our own day the absurd practices of the barbarous ages.

Chapter 14

THE CULT OF THE PHALLUS AMONG THE CHRISTIANS IN ITALY
AND AT NAPLES

AMONG the numerous antiquities dug up from excavations made at Tuscany in the Roman country, in
the Kingdom of Naples, and elsewhere in Italy, a great
quantity of Phalli and Priapi of all varieties, proportions,
and shapes are to be found. In order to be convinced of this,
it suffices to go through the different galleries of antiquities which these places contain, and the large collections of
engravings which represent the principal objects among
them. These figures, to which the Italians are accustomed,
do not wound their eyes. Besides, complete nakedness in
statues and pictures is to be seen everywhere at Rome and
Naples, in the gardens, vineyards, villas, public squares, and
even in the churches[1]. This consideration lessens somewhat
any possible astonishment at the discovery of the actual existence in these localities of a cult similar to the one that
the ancients rendered Priapus. Here is what I have been
able to gather on the state of this cult.

The *Fascinum* is still in use in Apulia; and the modern
inhabitants of this province in following this superstition
of the ancients have also followed the motive which led
them to it. It is to ward off charms and the baneful glances
of envy that they hang *fascina* of coral with ribbons from
the shoulders of children. These often have the form of
ithyphallic hands, which the Italians call *fica*[2].

The preservative jewels which in the Kingdom of Naples
the children wear around the shoulders, the women and
children of Sicily wear around the neck. This is a custom
which has been observed by many travelers. But it is not
to these amulets that the cult of Priapus is limited in Italy.
Suidas, a Greek monk who wrote in the eleventh century,
says that in Italy the god of generation is named *Priapus*;
that the shepherds render him a cult; and that his idol rep-

resents a child whose sexual member is remarkable for its length and state of energy: *Qui penem habet magnum et intentum*[3].

There still remained in the eighteenth century manifest traces of this cult in the Kingdom of Naples. In the city of Trani, capital of the province of that name, there was promenaded in procession during the carnival an old wooden statue which represented Priapus quite completely, and in his ancient proportions: that is to say, the feature which distinguishes this god was highly disproportionate with the rest of the idol's body. It rose up to the height of his chin. The inhabitants of the country named this figure *il santo Membro*, the holy Member. Joseph Davanzati, Archbishop of this city, who lived at the beginning of the eighteenth century, abolished this ancient ceremony[4]. It was evidently a remnant of the ancient fêtes of Bacchus, called *Dionysia* among the Greeks, *Liberalia* among the Romans, and which were celebrated about the middle of the month of March. We have already noted that the *Phallus* figured with distinction in these religious ceremonies.

A similar cult existed in the same kingdom in 1780; and perhaps it still exists there. The details I am going to give are extracted from an account written in Italian by an individual living at the spot where this cult is in fashion. This account, addressed to Sir William Hamilton, Ambassador of the King of England to the Court of Naples, was later transmitted by this minister to Joseph Banks, president of the Royal Society of London.

At Isernia, a city of the county of Molise, there is held every year on September 17[5] a fair of the sort that is named *Perdonanze* (Indulgence) in Italy. The place of the fair is on a little hill situated between two rivers, a scant quarter of a league from the city. On the most elevated part of this hill there is an ancient church, with a vestibule, which is said to have belonged to the Order of Saint Benedict. It is dedicated to Saint Cosmus and Saint Damianus. During the fair, which lasts for three days, a procession is held in which the relics of these Saints are carried. The inhabitants of the surrounding country, attracted by devotion and pleasure, flock together there in a crowd. Those of each village have a particular costume; moreover, the young girls, the married women, and the *daughters-of-joy* (*donne di piacere*), each wear clothing which distinguishes their various conditions. This concourse offers a highly varied spectacle.

They are to be seen in the city of Isernia, as well as at the place where the fair is held, men who sell wax figures of which the Christians make offerings to their Saints, just as the pagans made them to their gods. These figures are called *vows* or *ex-votos*. These waxen vows have the form of the afflicted member, for the cure of which the devotees come to intercede with the Saint. Homage is paid him with this image; it is hung up in his chapel, doubtless in order that the Saint, having it ceaselessly before his eyes, does not forget what is asked of him, or rather for fear that he be mistaken and his powers affect a healthy part instead of the sick one. Human legs, arms, and faces of wax are to be seen there; but this variety of vow is not the most numerous (*ma poche sono queste*). Those which most abound among the venders and those for which the devotees have the preference, I shall name, like the ancient Greeks, *Phalli*. The author whom I quote calls them *Membri virili di cera*. They are to be seen of all ages, in all conditions, and of all sizes. Those who retail this merchandise hold a basket and a plate: the basket contains the waxen Phalli, and the plate serves to collect the alms of the devotee purchasers. These venders go crying: *Saint Cosmo, Saint Damiano!* If they are asked how much they are selling them for, they answer: *The more you give, the more you will merit.*

In the vestibule of the church are two tables. Near each of them is seated a canon. One, who is ordinarily the Dean, cries to those who enter the church: *Here money is received for Masses and Litanies.* The other, who is the Archpriest, also cries from his side: *It is here that vows are received.* This latter receives in a basin the waxen *vows* that

the devotees have bought at the fair, and receives some
coins that each of them does not fail to give him in depositing his *vow*. One sees scarcely anything but women at this
fête. It is they who make almost all the outlay for it. It is
they who pray with the most fervor to the two Saints who
enjoy here in common the rôle of Priapus. It is they, above
all, who contribute the most to decorating their chapel with
numerous waxen Phalli. The Italian author adds a remarkable item: when they present the waxen image to the Archpriest, they usually pronounce such phrases: *Saint Cosmo,
I recommend myself to you. Saint Cosmo, I thank you.* Or
better: *Good Saint Cosmo, it is thus that I want it.* In saying
these words, or some other similar ones, each of them never
fails, before depositing the Phallus, to kiss it devoutly.

This does not suffice to effect miraculous cures, to fer-
tilize sterile women. Another ceremony is necessary, which
doubtless is the most efficacious. The persons who gather at
this fair sleep, for two nights, some in the church of the
Capuchin fathers, others in that of the Cordeliers. When
these two churches are insufficient to hold every woman,
the church of the *Hermitage of Saint Cosmus* receives the
overflow. In these three edifices the women are, during
these two nights, separated from the men. These latter sleep
in the vestibule, and the women in the church. They are
kept there, either in the church of the Capuchins or in that
of the Cordeliers, by the vicar and a trustworthy monk. In
the Hermitage, it is the hermit himself who watches over
them. One now conceives how the miracle can come about
which the sterile women come to ask for. The power of
Saint Cosmo and Damiano extends even over the young
girls and the widows[6]. The author of this account appears
to me to be a frank unbeliever; he seems convinced that
the women are impregnated on this occasion without the
blessed Saint Cosmo and Saint Damiano troubling themselves about it.

This fête is followed by other ceremonies. In the church,
near the great altar, holy unction is given with the oil of

Saint Cosmo. The recipe for this oil is the same as that which is indicated in the Roman Ritual; only the prayer of the holy martyrs, Cosmus and Damianus, is added to it. Those who are afflicted with any complaints present themselves at this altar and without shame uncover the affected part, which is always the original of the wax figure they have offered. The canon, in administering the unction, recites this prayer: *Per intercessionem beati Cosmi, liberet te ab omni malo. Amen.* This holy oil serves not only in the unction administered by the canons, but it is also distributed in small flasks so that it can be used to anoint the loins of those who are afflicted in that part. In the present year, 1780, adds our Italian observer, fourteen hundred of these flasks were sold to the devotees of these countries[7].

There is to be found in England, and the corps of naval officers offer an example of it, some remains of this cult or these customs in a mysterious society named *The Very Ancient and Very Powerful Order of Beggars Benison and Merryland,* of which Sir Louis Chamber was the Grandmaster in 1761. The seal of this society offers as its principal figure a well characterized Phallus: above is an anchor and below is a fortress. No one knows why this society, a diploma of which I have before my eyes, and which contains only resolutions on the prosperity of industry, commerce, manufacture, and exemptions from customs and other rights, takes for its symbol a figure formerly sacred but today so indecent. It is the secret of the initiates.

Thus the Christians, like the Greeks and Romans, have at various places observed all aspects of the cult of the *Phallus* or Priapus. They have adored it under the name of *Fascinum*, as a preservative, a powerful amulet; they have adored it under the names of different saints, as the dispenser of fecundity to women. They have made libations to it, addressed prayers to it, promenaded its effigy in procession, and hung *ex-votos* in its chapels, images of the virile sex. With the exception of the custom of scraping the Phallus and swallowing these scrapings with water, a custom of which I know no example in antiquity, all the other practices belong to the cult which the ancients rendered Priapus.

The Christians in preserving this cult so foreign to their dogmas, had not the excusable motives of the peoples who professed Sabeanism or the religions which are derived from it. These latter worshipped in the *Phallus* the symbol of the regenerating sun. The Christians, who were attached to this cult only through routine, saw in it only a sort of talisman. It can be said that if the Phallus was a sacred object for the ancients, it could be only an object of ridicule and indecency in the modern religions of Europe, which are based on entirely different principles.

Chapter 15

CIVIL AND RELIGIOUS CUSTOMS OF PAST CENTURIES, WHOSE
INDECENCY SURPASSES THE CULT OF THE PHALLUS

THE cult of the *Phallus* or Priapus among the Christians of Europe in the centuries that have preceded ours, today appears so strange to us, so improbable, so incompatible with our manners, that we are tempted to question the copious evidence which proves its existence. It is therefore necessary, in order to do away with these doubts, to examine whether the manners of the time and countries where this cult maintained itself were as contrary to it as is ordinarily thought, whether this cult contrasted too strongly with the spirit and customs, and whether its indecency equalled or surpassed that of certain practices and institutions which existed at the same period.

I shall not here draw up a complete history of the absurd and barbarous manners which stained the whole of Europe for many centuries. The material, very abundant, would exceed the confines to which our subject is restricted. I shall not occupy myself even summarily with all the customs and institutions, nor with all that which characterizes manners in general. The picture of them would be hideous, and would become as humiliating as instructive for humankind. I must limit myself to painting, in quite a narrow frame, only a few of these customs and institutions which have direct relation with chastity and modesty, and consequently with the cult of the *Phallus*. Further, I shall only touch upon that delicate subject, only sketch in rapidly the bulk of the picture, and gather together only the most salient features that characterize the almost unknown manners of the thirteenth, fourteenth, and fifteenth centuries.

But what I shall expose will suffice to convict of ignorance those perpetual declaimers who drag themselves along in the old, deep ruts of routine, resembling the old man of whom Horace speaks, and who ignorantly praise the past ages at the expense of the present[1]. We shall soon observe that the indecencies practiced by our good ancestors are scarcely second to those of the ancient Greeks and Romans. I shall first speak of the customs which belong to civil life, and then pass on to those which relate to religion.

Conjugal faith was formerly so easily violated, the conduct of the women inspired such distrust, that husbands found themselves obliged to imprison their wives and daughters, to subject them to a continual surveillance, and what is still worse, to think up a mechanical enclosure which in spite of them preserved their honor intact and shut off all access to voluptuousness. The invention of the *girdles of chastity* is attributed to Francesco da Carrara, Imperial Provost of Padua, who lived toward the end of the fourteenth century. He had thus padlocked all the women comprising his seraglio. His acts of cruelty brought him to the scaffold, and he was strangled in the year 1405 by decree of the Senate of Venice. One of the chief accusations against him was the use of *girdles of chastity* for his mistresses[2]; and, according to Misson, there was long preserved in Venice, in the palace of St. Mark, a chest filled with these girdles and padlocks, as bits of convincing proof in the trial of this monster[3]. But I believe this custom to be very much older.

Since that time, it is said, the style was adopted in Italy. Here is how Voltaire expresses the consequences of this evil example:

> *And since that time in Venice and in Rome,*
> *There is, to guard the honor of his home,*
> *Neither townsman, pedant, nor nobleman,*
> *Who hasn't his supply of padlocks laid in:*
> *There, so jealous, fearless of any blame,*
> *Holds under lock and key his wife's good name.*

This style failed to find its way into France under the reign of Henri 11. Brantôme says that "in the time of King Henry there was a certain pedlar who brought to the fair of Saint-Germain a dozen of certain tools for bridling women's affairs. They were made of iron and went around the waist like a girdle and branched down to be caught at the bottom and locked. They were made with so much art that it was not possible for the woman, once she was bridled with one, ever to be able to avail herself of it for sweet pleasure. ... They say that there were some five or six peevish jealous husbands who bought some of them and bridled their wives with them in such a fashion that they might well say: Farewell merry times! ... They say, moreover, that there were many honest, gallant gentlemen who threatened the pedlar in such a fashion that if he ever meddled in carrying such trumperies, he would be killed; that he should not go there again; and that he should throw all the others which still remained into the privy, which he did[4]."

In the early times of Christianity, the girls and nuns accused of lewdness were submitted to a scrupulous examination, from which was supposed to result proof of the innocence of the accused or proof of the offence. Syagrius, Bishop of Verona, who lived at the end of the fourth century, sentenced a nun to undergo this outrageous examination. Saint Ambrose, his archbishop, disapproved the sentence of the bishop, classed this examination as indecent, and by this testifies to its existence. The sentiment manifested by this prelate and various others did not prevent the maintenance of the custom for a very long time. The ecclesiastical and civil tribunals often ordered this proof; and Venette reports the proceedings of a similar examination made by order of the Provost of Paris, in the year 1672, on a woman who complained of having undergone violence by a libertine[5].

The *congress*[6], which formed part of our old jurisprudence, the formalities of which are still more indecent, is only an extension of this custom. Here is what the procedure of it was: When two married persons asked their separation or the annulment of their marriage on account of impotence or some bodily imperfection, the official or judge of the Church (for it was always the priests who meddled in such affairs) began by ordering the complete examina-

tion of the bodies of the two litigant parties. Doctors, surgeons, and matrons proceeded with this examination; and
after their report, which was never decisive, the official
ordered the *congress*. Some experts were named anew; they
and the parties in question came together in a room. There,
the husband and wife were again very minutely examined,
naked from the top of the head to the soles of the feet, says
a jurisconsult, from whom I borrow these details. "This
done," he adds, "and after the woman has taken a half-bath,
the man and woman lie together on a bed in full view with
the experts present, who remain in the room, or retire (if
one or both of the parties require it) to some nearby closet
or gallery, but with the door half-open nevertheless. As for
the matrons, they keep close to the bed. The curtains being
drawn, it is for the man to set about making proof of his
potency, in which ridiculous disputes and altercations often
arise[7]."

One can surmise the nature of the altercations which
would arise between a hostile man and wife forced to act
as lovers. I spare the reader these as well as many other licentious details, all the less attractive since they are the sad
effects of hatred and constraint. I shall add only this particular, which offers a new aspect of the indecency of these
proceedings. "What is still more shameful," says a writer
of the seventeenth century, "is that in some trials the men
have examined the woman, and, contrarily, the women
have been permitted to examine the man. This has caused
so much derision and mockery that such procedures have
served for merry tales and sportive talk in a great many
places[8]." Nor shall I speak further of the report, full of ob-
scenities, from which the judge of the Church pronounced
his sentence. I shall only say that the description of the liti-
gious objects was the principal matter in it, and that the evidence of the congress was repeated as much as three times.
This procedure was not abolished until February 18, 1677,
by decree of the Parliament of Paris.

Indecency was no less extreme in the penalties placed

against adulterers. The guilty of both sexes were sentenced to walk stark naked through the streets of the city, or even to follow, in the same condition, the most solemn processions. Women convicted of having spoken insults to other women underwent a similar penalty. Sometimes they were permitted to keep on a chemise; but the guilty woman was forced to raise it very high in order to hold in it some large stones which she was obliged to carry throughout the course of the procession or her walk through the streets of the city; and the insulted woman pricked the naked buttocks of the culprit with a needle[9]. In some countries an additional circumstance rendered the ceremony still more indecent. The adulterers were likewise promenaded stark naked through the city. The woman walked ahead, and held in her hand the end of a cord whose other end was attached to the sexual parts of the man. This last custom existed in France in the little city of Martel in Limosin, in that of Clermont-Soubiran in Languedoc, and in many other places, especially in Sweden[10].

Public women guilty of any excess were punished quite as indecently. They were condemned to go through the streets of the city, *stark naked* and mounted on an ass, with their faces turned toward the tail-end of the animal. It was to this punishment that the Duc d'Orléans, brother of Louis xiii, had *la Neveu* condemned, after having debauched her many times. This famous courtesan, immortalized by two verses of Boileau, traversed the streets of Paris mounted stark naked on an ass[11]. All these customs, attested to by the charters of communes, the most authentic and the most curious monuments on the history of the manners of our ancestors, appear generally to have been tolerated in France as well as in various other countries of Europe.

We must now speak of that odious privilege which has existed in France and other countries for many centuries, by which the secular and ecclesiastical lords stole from husbands the first-fruits of marriage, and came to stain the nuptial couch with their impure presence. This privilege was known in Scotland, in England, under the names of *marchet* and *prelibation;* in Piedmont, under that of *cazzagio;* and in France, under those of *cullage, culliage,* or *jus cunni*[12].

The monks of *Saint-Théodard* enjoyed this privilege over the inhabitants of Mont-Auriol, a town which adjoined their monastery. "In the feudal privileges," says the historian of Quercy, "they had the *jus cunni,* a remnant of ancient barbarism, a privilege as dishonoring for those who exercised it as for those who were subjected to it[13]." The inhabitants, so deeply outraged, addressed themselves to the over-lord, the Comte de Toulouse, who permitted them to establish themselves near one of his châteaux, situated in the neighborhood of the abbey. They repaired there in haste. Freer, and secure from monkish tyranny, they prospered, and their new habitation received the name of *Montauban.* Such was the event which gave birth to this considerable city of Quercy.

This privilege, taken over by the kings of Scotland, had excited many uprisings there. The lords of Persanni and Presly, in Piedmont, having refused to replace it with a tax, their subjects threw off the yoke and went over to Amedeus IV, Count of Savoy. The Lord of Bargone, in the States of Parma, today the department of Taro, enjoyed the same privilege. It is related that a young bride, wishing to escape it, threw herself from the window of his room. This tragic occurrence resulted in the abrogation of this atrocious privilege[14]. The canons of the cathedral of Lyon also pretended to have the right to sleep, the first night of the marriage, with the brides of their serfs or *hommes de corps*[15]. The bishops of Amiens and the monks of Saint Etienne de Nevers had the same privilege, and boldly prosecuted it.

"I have seen," says Bœrius on this subject, "at the court of Bourges, a trial carried by appeal before the Archbishop in which a parish curé pretended to have the privilege of sleeping with the new bride the first night of the marriage.

The court abolished this pretended privilege, and sentenced the curé to a fine[16]." He adds that many lords of Gascony have the same privilege, but that they confine themselves only to introducing a leg or thigh into the bed of the new bride, unless the vassals make a settlement with their lord and pay what he asks them. This privilege is named *cuissage* or *droit de cuisse* [thigh privilege].

"A lord, who possessed a considerable estate in Vexin Normand," says Saint-Foy, "assembled in the month of June all his serfs of both sexes of marriageable age and had them given the nuptial blessing. Then they were served with meat and wine. He placed himself at table, drank, ate, and rejoiced with them. But he never failed to impose on the couples that seemed most amorous, various conditions which he found humorous. He prescribed to some *to pass the night of their nuptials in the top of a tree, and there to consummate their marriage*; to others, *to consummate it in the river Andelle, where they should bathe for two hours naked to a chemise, etc*[17]."

Let us now report some features of the old state of prostitution in the cities; but first of all let us pause a bit on its causes. In civilized States, the primary cause of the corruption of morals consists in the over concentration of people in one place. The secondary causes, which give a baneful activity to the moral miasmas, are the laxness of the police, the inequality of wealth, and the abundance of celibates. A police which does not suppress, converts particular vices into general habits, authorizes them, and strengthens them. The great disproportion of wealth divides the population into two classes: the one, idle, in order to ease the burden of ennui, conceiving successive and always more stimulating tastes, artifical or refined enjoyments, finds need of immorality; the other, tormented by necessity, finds need of being debased in order to receive the price of corruption. The celibates cannot long hold their vow against nature, because laws that go contrary to it are always powerless. They are therefore reduced to transgressing them and augmenting the number of agents of public corruption. Thus it is not the fault of the celibate priests, as is commonly thought, but it is their passions and great number which contribute to bring on the depravation of morals. It is unfailing that the country of Europe where morals are most depraved is the one where priests are most abundant: this is a proven fact, indisputable according to statistics, and against which all contrary sophisms are quickly shattered.

Now, in the centuries whose manners I am sketching, the over-crowding of cities, the primary cause of their corruption, did not exist as prominently as it does today. The capitals of the provinces were much less inhabited than many a village at present, and Paris was less peopled than are certain provincial cities today. Nevertheless, although religious ceremonies and credulity were not lacking, corruption in the thirteenth, fourteenth, and fifteenth centuries was, through the laxness of the police and the abundance of celibates, much greater than it is now. I am going to furnish some proofs of it.

In many other cities of France the places of debauchery were qualified by *abbey*; and those who presided over them carried the title of *abbess*[18]. At the beginning of the twelfth century, Guillaume VII, Duc d'Aquitaine and Comte de Poitou, had a building similar to a monastery constructed in the little city of Niort, in which he gathered all the prostitutes. He wished to make of it an *abbey* for debauched women, says Guillaume, a monk of Malmesbury. He there created the dignities of abbess, prioress, and others, with which he gratified those most distinguished in their infamous commerce[19].

There had long existed at Toulouse a very celebrated place of debauchery, to which several of our kings gave privileges; it likewise carried the name of *abbey*. Charles VI wrote some letters in its favor, of which here are some passages. He begins thus: "Hear, the supplication which has been made us on the part of the daughters-of-joy of the brothel of Toulouse, called *Great Abbey*, etc." He then orders the Senechal, Royal Provost, and other officers to have the said suppliants, and those who in time to come shall dwell in the aforementioned *abbey, enjoy and use it peaceably and perpetually, without molesting them or suffering them to be molested, now or in the future*. These letters are of the month of December, 1389[20]. Charles VII, in 1425, also granted letters of safeguard in favor of the same house of the *Great Abbey*, occupied by public women, at the request of the *Capitouls* and the Syndic of the city. "It is to be seen from these letters," say the historians of Languedoc, "that the city of Toulouse drew some profit from this place of prostitution: so careless were they in those times in preserving the least propriety[21]."

At Paris the prostitute women formed a professional body. "They were," says Saint-Foy, "assessed with taxes, and had their own judges and statutes. They were called *femmes amoureuses, filles folles de leurs corps* [amorous women, girls mad over their bodies]. Every year they held a solemn procession on St. Magdalen's day. For their commerce they were appointed Rues Froimentel, Pavée, Glatigny, Tyron, Chapon, Tire-Boudin, Brise-Miche, du Renard, du Hurleur, de la Vieille-Bouclerie, l'Abreuvoir, Macon, and Champ-Fleuri. In these streets they had a hutch which they tried to keep clean and comfortable. They were obliged to return there at ten o'clock in the morning, and to leave it when the curfew was rung, that is to say, at six o'clock in the evening in winter, and between eight and nine in summer. They were absolutely forbidden to go about elsewhere, even to their homes. *Those who followed the Court*, say du Tillet and Pasquier, *were obliged for the duration of the month of May, to make up the King's bed with ribbons*[22]."

It was in the same century that the kings Charles VI and Charles VII granted privileges to the houses of debauchery at Toulouse, and made regulations to assure the condition of those at Paris. In this century also Joanna I, Queen of Naples and Countess of Provence, organized a place of pros-

titution at Avignon. She wanted the mother superior, qualified as abbess, to be renewed each year by the city council,
and that the latter should decide the quarrels which came
up between the women of her convent. The spirit of religion, or rather of fanaticism, arose in this shameful institution. Queen Joanna wanted this place of prostitution open
every day, except Good Friday and Saturday, as well as
Easter Day. She prescribed to the abbess to allow no Jew
to enter there. If one contrived to get in by stealth, and
had commerce with one of the girls, he was to be impris-
oned and publicly flogged[23]. This house was established at
Avignon, Rue du Pont-Troué, near the monastery of the
Augustines.

Pope Julius 11, in order to avoid greater evils, issued a
papal bull on July 2, 1510, which authorized the establishment of a similar house in a designated quarter. Popes Leo
x and Clement vii confirmed this establishment, on condition that a quarter of the goods and chattels of the courtesans who lived there should belong, after their death, to the
convent of the nuns of Sainte-Marie-Madeleine.

The charter of exemption of the little city of Villa-
franche, in Beaujolais, granted in 1373 by Edouard 11, *Sire
de Beaujeu*, offers some features too remarkable to pass over
here. I shall not describe the article which permits husbands
to beat their wives, nor of the one by which adulterers are
condemned to make a tour of the city *completely naked*;
these things are to be found in the majority of the com-
munal charters of the cities of France. But I shall pause at
the one which states "that if a man or woman, both ministers to public debauchery, that if a boy devoted to prostitution, or if a girl devoted to prostitution, happens to speak
insults to a townsman of Villefranche or to one of his
friends, he may strike them with a slap in the face, a punch,
or a kick, without incurring fine[24]." Thus a city, peopled
by scarcely three or four hundred souls, contained within
its precincts places of prostitution for both sexes. Do our
manners offer these examples[25]?

The Gods of Generation:

The fêtes and both private and public ceremonies serve also to characterize the manners. Let us examine some of them. The famous Castruccio Castracani, a General of the Luccese, after the battle of Servalle, which he won from the Florentines, gave brilliant fêtes under his enemies' eyes. He had prostitute women, stark naked, run the races of the *palio*. The prize of this race was a rich piece of cloth, from which this exercise draws its name[26].

Under the reign of Henri III, fêtes were to be seen in France accompanied by similar circumstances. "On Wednesday, May 15, 1577, the King, at Plessis-les-Tours, gave a feast to Monsieur le Duc his brother, and to the Lords and Captains who had been with him at the siege and capture of La Charité; at which ladies clothed in green, dressed as men, half-naked, and having their hair dishevelled like brides, were employed for the service. The Queen-mother gave her banquet at Chenonceau[27]."

The entry of the Kings or Princes into various cities were often accompanied by spectacles which would to-day wound the eyes of the least chaste. When Louis XI in 1461 made his entry into Paris, there were placed before the Ponceau Fountain, says the author of the Chronicle of that King, "three beautiful girls playing the parts of entirely naked sirens. One could see their beautiful breasts, straight, separated, round, and firm, which was a thing indeed pleasing. They sang little motets and *bergerettes*[28]."

During the entry into Angers of King François I and Queen Claude, daughter of Louis XII, which took place in 1516, a Bacchus was represented on the top of a vine-stock, having in each hand a bunch of grapes which he was pressing. White wine came from one in great quantities, and red wine from the other. At the foot of this vine-stock "was represented," says Bourdigné, "the patriarch Noah, asleep and showing his shameful parts." Near him were written these verses:

A History of Phallic Cults

Despite Bacchus, horned master to you,
His verjuice now seems to me so new
That straight to my brain its flavor flew,
And put me to sleep, my c— in view[29].

Charles le Téméraire, duc de Bourgogne, made his entry
into Lille in 1468. Among the fêtes that the inhabitants gave
him, there was to be remarked the representation of the
Judgment of Paris. Three Flemish women took upon themselves the rôles of the three goddesses. She who figured as
Venus was of tall stature, and of a plumpness which typi-
fies the beauties of that country. Juno, quite as tall, offered
a lean, spare body. Pallas was represented by a small woman, big-bellied, humped in front and rear, and whose body
was supported by thin, gaunt legs. These three goddesses
appeared before Paris, their judge, and before the public,
naked as a hand. After the description of their shapes and
various attractions, one presumes that the Flemish Paris did
not hesitate to give the apple to Venus[30].

The shows were also highly indecent. We should not today dare read in private the plays that were given in public
under Henri IV: *The new and recreative farce of the Doctor
who cured all sorts of diseases, and also made a nose for a
big woman's child, etc. The joyous and recreative farce of
a woman who asks arrears of her husband. The new farce,
containing the altercation of a young monk and an old
gendarme before the god Cupid, for a girl.* These pieces
are of an extremely shocking indecency of word and intention[31]. With such manners and practices, one would
think that decency was to be found neither in clothing,
speech, nor even in writing.

Dante speaks of the immodesty of the women of Florence
who appeared in public with their breasts entirely uncovered[32]. This poet lived in the thirteenth century. Petrarch
paints for us the extreme corruption and wild debauchery

which reigned at Avignon the residence of the Popes there. Philelphus, who lived in the fifteenth century, speaks with truly cynical freedom of the excessive and improbable debauches he was witness to in the city of Genoa, and complains of the scant respect held in that city for public shame[33].

The preachers declaimed still more vigorously than the poets against the nakedness of the female bosom; but the declamations of both were, as is known, almost always without effect. Let us listen to a preacher of the fifteenth century, whose name is unknown. "How rare it is, shame among men of this century!" he says. "They do not blush when in public they blaspheme, gamble, steal, take usury, perjure themselves, utter unseemly words, or even sing them. And the women leave their arms, neck, and breasts uncovered, and exhibit themselves thus before men in order to excite them to the horrible crimes of adultery, fornication, rape, sacrilege, and sodomy[34]."

In the fifteenth century, the elegant courtesans were named *Gores, Gaures,* or *Gaurières* [words pertaining to throat or breast], and low-necked dresses, *les robes à la grant Gore* [fancy whore dresses]. That is why a poor preacher, famous for the coarseness of his speech and for his buffooneries, Brother Maillard, often cries out against *Mesdames les bourgeoises* who wear dresses *à la grant Gore*[35]. He says elsewhere: "And you, women, who show your fine breasts, your neck, your throat, would you wish to die in that condition? Tell me, foolish women, do you not have lovers who give you bouquets and do you not, for love of them, place these bouquets in your bosom? Very well, your names are inscribed in the book of the Devil[36]."

Michel Menot, another preacher of the same time, likewise cries out against the nakedness of women's bosoms. He speaks of those who, not content with wearing clothing above their condition, cover themselves with wordly ornaments, follow the style of large sleeves, take on a saucy air, and uncover their breasts as far as their belly, in order to attract the glances of lovers[37]. "It is to you whom I address myself, Mesdames" says the same preacher. "When you come to church, it seems from your pompous, indecent, and *openbreasted* clothing, that you are at a ball. When you go to a dance, to a feast, or to the baths, *dress as you please*. But when you come to church, I beg you, make some difference between the house of God and that of the Devil[38]."

Another preacher cites an example of the punishment experienced in the other world by ladies who bare their bosoms. "A certain priest," says he, "weeping for his dead mother and desiring to know the condition of her soul, made prayers that God heard. Being near the altar, he saw his mother tied in a sack, between two demons. Her hair, which during her life she had taken care to ornament, was then made up of flaming serpents; her breast, neck, and throat, which she ordinarily left uncovered, were occupied by a toad which vomited forth torrents of fire[39]." These predictions, this terrifying example, in no wise changed the habits of the ladies; and the natural desire of pleasing and arousing men triumphed formerly, as it triumphs today, over the fear of eternal punishment and the fire-vomiting toad.

Women, in the time of Montaigne, had the same habits. After having spoken of the men who, before his age, dressed with the stomach uncovered, he adds: "And our ladies, as soft and delicate as they are, they go about open as far as the naval[40]." The men, besides the custom of uncovering their stomach, followed a much more indecent one at the same time. That which in the sixteenth century was called the *braguette* was a species of clothing which, in covering them, outlined the hidden parts of virility exactly as a glove shows that of the hand. Old portraits offer us examples of this singular style. The custom began to die out in the time of Montaigne. "What did that ridiculous piece of footwear of our fathers mean, that is still to be seen in our

Switzerland?" he asks. "What is the purpose of that monstrosity that we to this day have shaped on our trousers; and often, which is worse, beyond its natural size, through falseness and imposture[41]?"

The indecency in speech and writing was no less than that which existed in clothing. The sermon writers furnish numerous examples, not from the books directed against them, but from their own works. The partisans of preachers ought to thank me for this moderation, which deprives this chapter of many singular and piquant features.

"Poor sinners," Maillard cries out, "the blessed Anselme, who was a monk, did not live like you; he did not eat meat; he did not have, like you, daughters-of-joy in his room at all times[42].—We have many mothers who sell their daughters, who prostitute them themselves; they make them earn their marriage by the labor and sweat of their body[43]."—— "Isn't it a fine thing to see the wife of a barrister, who has bought an office and who has not ten francs income, clothed like a princess? Her head, neck, and waist are covered with gold. And you say that she is dressed according to her condition! All the devils take the condition, you, the wife, and you also, Messire Jacques, who so lightly gives them absolution! they say, doubtless: Our husbands do not give us such clothing; but we earn them by the labor of our body. Thirty thousand devils take such labor[44]!"

In anger, he sends the following word to a woman: "Go, infamous whore, you hold brothel in your house[45]!" He addresses himself thusly to the women of Paris: "You are *p—* [whores] who keep places of debauchery; you have made your daughters *p—* like yourselves, and your sons *macquer....*[46]" A few more citations from this coarse preacher and his strange eloquence. They offer us a faithful picture of the manners of the fifteenth century. Here is what he says to the women of Paris who go to the baths: "Sainte Suzanne, when she washed her feet in her garden, had her maid-servants move away for fear of being seen by them.

And you, on the contrary, you stay stark naked in the baths, and show others that which you ought to hide[47]."—— "And you, women," says Maillard, "who make amorous signs to your lovers while saying your Hours; and you, *Madame la Bourgeoise*, who are filled with lewdness, but who have an exterior of devotion when someone speaks to you, you say: *Let us not speak of that*, and you spit on the ground and say: *Fie, fie, let us hush up*. I say that it is a mortal sin, etc[48]." Elsewhere he reproaches married people who give themselves up to the pleasures of marriage in the presence of their servants and children[49].

I should not finish if I reported all the characteristic traits of immodesty and debauchery of the fifteenth century that the sermons of Maillard and the other preachers present. They repeat the same reproaches endlessly, and especially those which they address to mothers who prostitute their daughters in order to make them earn their marriage *by the sweat of their body*: which makes it credible that the custom then was general enough. Maillard likewise reproaches the debauchery of the prelates, canons, and monks who publicly have concubines with whom they live intimately. Maillard always presents them as the principal corrupters of youth. He even goes so far as to say that girls twelve years old were already trained to the courtesan's profession, and followed it quite proficiently.

The preacher Menot, who, like Maillard, preached for a long time in Paris, paints the same manners in the same colors, and with expressions equally as vulgar and as little restrained. Barlette, another preacher, is no less indecent. Of his sermons I shall report only a single passage, in which, speaking of carnal love, he introduces a young girl who addresses these words to him, which I am forced to paraphrase. "O father! my lover loves me very much. He has given me some very pretty red sleeves; he has made me many other presents. He loves me with a true love; I readily see it by the evident ardor he experiences near me[50]."

If the preachers were so licentious, it should be presumed

that the poets, story-tellers, and other writers were more so. The *fabliaux*, and especially those contained in the third volume of them published by Barbazan; the Tales of Boccaccio, those of the Queen of Navarre, the *Cent Nouvelles* related at the court of the Duke of Burgundy, the *Pantagruel* of Rabelais, and a thousand other works of this type offer proof of it.

The historians were not exempt from this indecency, or rather heedlessness in their manner of describing certain objects. Froissart, historiagrapher and canon, in speaking of the torture of Messire Hugues le Despencier le fils, reports a circumstance of it with expressions of the grossest debauchery[51]. Jean d'Auton, priest and historiographer of Louis XII, referring in the history of this monarch to a monstrous birth, employs the same expressions as Froissart. He repeats them without repugnance; and they are to be found at full length in the edition given by Theodore Godefroy[52].

The monk Gaguin, also a historiographer of France, composed a poem on the Immaculate Conception of the Virgin. "One finds there," says a modern, "the filthiest and even the most libertine ideas. They are such that one cannot render them into French without offending the chastity of our language." The same writer informs us that to his poem of the Immaculate Conception, Gaguin joined the praise of one of his mistresses, *cabaretière de Vernon* [tavern hostess of Vernon]. In this piece he praises the pretty ways of this belle, her *bons mots*, the comfort of her chairs, the quality of her wine and beds, and above all the hidden beauties of the lady herself, with which our good monk seems to have been perfectly acquainted[53].

In many of the writings of that time it was not only the expression but the matter that was indecent; and this indecency is much more shocking when it is allied with religious subjects. Here is another example of it in a fable given, as a true happening, by the priest who relates it for public edification. It is such that, out of respect for my readers, I shall carefully guard against translating it literally.

A priest, strongly suspected of having fornicated with a very high lady, and fearing to be arrested, took to flight. Having arrived in a forest, he encountered a man whose exterior proclaimed him a holy monk. "You are sad," the latter said to him, "what is the cause of it? Tell me your trouble." The priest confessed everything. "If you are deprived entirely of that part which has been the most guilty," the monk added to him, "you could return in security to the city, and convict of calumny those who accuse you. Let us see." He sees, he touches; and *the most guilty part* disappears. It must be said that this man, under the guise of a holy monk, was the Devil in person. The priest, overjoyed, returns to the city in order to offer his accusers this irrefragable proof of his innocence.He arrives in his church, has the bells rung, and convokes the people. There, in the presence of the multitude, mounted on high, he confidently produces his proof. But, O miracle! O deception of the devil! he bares to the spectators' eyes a quite contrary proof, and that proof is monstrously evident[54].

If this tale, in its literal, original form, does not equal in obscenity the lewd works of Pietro Aretino, and the *Capitolo del Forno*, composed by Giovanni della Casa, Archbishop of Benevento, it is on a par with those of Ariosto, Boccaccio, Coquillart, an official of Reims, of Beroalde de Verville, a canon of Tours, of Rabelais, a curé of Meudon, of Abbé Grécourt, and of many other story-tellers of this sort; all works whose indecent material ought to enter to some extent into the composition of a moral history of the past centuries.

Ought I to forget here the picture of the dissolute manners of the sixteenth century that Brantôme has left us in his volume of *Dames galantes*? What corruption! and what gross colors this author employs to paint it for us, to extol it, to render it pleasing! There one finds everything that the most studied genius of lewdness, favored by opulence, idleness, and example, can imagine. The persons whose behavior he describes were, through their rank and wealth, secure from the vices which ordinarilly follow the drawbacks of a poor education and poverty; thus their conduct is less excusable. It is Kings, Princes, great Lords, Queens, and great Ladies whom he continually calls *honorable*, even when he proves that they were not; it is to the persons of a class whose actions most commonly serve as a model for the other classes of society. The deceits employed by wives to fool their husbands, by girls to trick their mothers and guardians, in order to satisfy forbidden thrills, are exalted as virtuous actions. The assurance with which he praises these vices strikes present-day readers with astonishment, and depicts truly the opinions and morality of his contemporaries. It is thus that Machiavelli publicly advised political crimes, that Cardinal de Retz boasted of those he had committed, that the old and sanguinary Montluc glorified himself for his acts of cruelty, and that, a long time before them, Pierce, Abbé of Vau-Cerney, made apology for the betrayals and perfidies of which his hero, the devout and cruel Simon de Montfort, had been guilty[55].

Everything felt the effects of this grossness, of this licence in manners. The paintings and tapestries that decorated the houses of the rich received the imprint of the age. I again invoke on this score the testimony of a preacher of the fifteenth century. "Often the pictures and tapestries," he says, "represent abominable subjects, full of dissoluteness, and capable of stirring and inflaming desire in the most insensible hearts. Some are ordinarily to be seen in palaces, in the chambers of the Princes; and please God that some may not be found in those of the prelates and ecclesiastics! I have seen," he adds, "and I do not lie, paintings similarly filthy in the interior of a very celebrated church, which had been decorated thus for the solemnity of Easter. I was horrified on seeing them. I had them taken up and carried elsewhere[56]."

The château of Fontainbleau, constructed and decorated

by Italian artists, which François 1 had brought to France, presented, according to the custom of the time, a great number of obscene paintings. "There one saw," says Sauval, "gods, men, women, and goddesses who outraged nature and plunged themselves into the most monstrous dissoluteness." in 1643, the Queen, having come into the regency, had a great many of these paintings destroyed, says the same writer. The loss amounted to more than a hundred thousand crowns[57]. The manuscript books intended for prayer, which were called *Hours*, were formerly ornamented with miniatures. Collectors of curiosities preserve some in which these miniatures offer some extremely scandalous scenes[58].

How many nude and semi-nude figures formerly ornamented, and still ornament the churches, and especially their exterior portals? How many male and female Saints, in statues and in pictures, leave uncovered that which it would be a crime for people of this century not to hide? Indecent images, paintings, and figures were quite common in the churches, for the provincial Council held at Paris in 1521 was forced to prohibit their use[59] I have seen an *Ecce homo* as naked as the Venus de Médicis, and who, like her and almost as clumsily, employed his hands to cover that which must not be shown. I have seen female Saints as negligently draped as the three Graces of Germain Pilon, and who, like them, were placed in a church[60]. The Last Judgment, painted by Michelangelo, in the chapel of the Vatican at Rome; the same subject, treated by Jean Cousin, in the picture that formerly was to be seen at the Minims' of the Bois de Vincennes, besides complete nakednesss, offer scenes which if not lewd, at least prove the licentious intention or misplaced gaity of their authors.

In the thirteenth and fourteenth centuries, and consequently in the sixteenth century, the imitative arts, adapted to manners, frequently produced many works for civil and religious monuments which today appear indecent or ridiculous to us. Legrand d'Aussy, in his *Voyage d'Auvergne*, noticed on the altar of Sainte-Chapelle de Vic-le-Comte figures of Adam and Eve, between which a Virgin Mary is to be seen. The bodies of the two first parents of mankind were represented in complete nakedness. "But what passes indecency," says our traveler, "and what becomes truly scandalous and worthy of the gravest reproaches, is the use that Adam is making of one of his hands. . . . Why indeed," he exclaims in indignation, "the most impudent debauchee would not dare show himself to the eyes of the public in such an attitude! And it is to be found on an altar[61]!"

There was still to be seen in Paris in 1660, in the chapel of Sainte-Marie l'Egyptienne, a part of a glass window which was there for more than three centuries, and which the curé of Saint-Germain-l'Auxerrois had removed about that time. It represented the Saint on the deck of a boat, tucked up above her knees before the boatman, with these words below: *How the Saint offered her body to the boatmen for her passage*[62].

This is only an artlessness in conformity with the custom of the time and the general indifference to nakedness held by people; but what I am about to relate offers definitely indecent intentions: An abbot of the monastery of Saint-Geraud d'Aurillac had had painted in the sixteenth century, in a garden cabinet intended for his debauches, nude figures representing the two sexes in the most indecent postures. This cabinet bore an obscene name which implied its purpose. The sexual vices reigning in this abbey were so excessive that, after complaint by the inhabitants of the city, it was secularized[63].

Chapter 16

THE FEAST OF THE FOOLS AND OF THE SUB-DEACONS. THE
PROCESSIONS OF PERSONS DRESSED IN CHEMISE OR ENTIRELY
NAKED. PUBLIC FLAGELLATIONS. THE CUSTOM OF GIVING
THE INNOCENTS, ETC.

THE feasts of the Fools, the Sub-Deacons, the Ass, etc., imitating the ancient Saturnalia were celebrated in almost all the churches of France, and deserves a long exposition here. Although their burlesque and indecent ceremonies are well known and have been described by a great number of authentic witnesses, I shall speak of them as succinctly as possible.

The priests of a church elected a *Bishop of the Fools*, who came, pompously escorted, to place himself in the choir on the bishop's seat. High mass then began; all the ecclesiastics attended it, their faces smeared with black or covered with a hideous or ridiculous mask. During the celebration, some, dressed as buffoons or as women, danced in the middle of the choir and there sang droll or obscene songs. Others came to eat sausages and *boudins*[1] on the altar, and to play cards or dice before the officiating priest. They perfumed the latter with a censer in which old shoes were burning, and made him breathe the smoke. After mass there were renewed acts of extravagance and impiety. The priests, mixed up with the inhabitants of both sexes, ran about, danced in the church, and excited each other to the most licentious act which an unbridled imagination could suggest. No longer any shame or modesty; no dam arrested the flood of folly and passion. In the midst of the tumult, blasphemies, and dissolute songs, some were seen to strip themselves entirely of their clothing, others abandoning themselves to the most shameful libertinage. The scene of action then moved out of the church, into the street. Less sacrilegious, it was no more decent. The actors, mounted on carts full of dung, amused themselves by throwing it at the

201

populace that surrounded them. They paused at intervals at
theatres expressly set up for their follies. There they renewed their sports in the face of the public. The most debauched among the seculars mingled with the clergy, and,
disguised as monks or nuns, performed lascivious movements and assumed all the postures of the most unbridled
profligacy. These scenes were always accompanied by
filthy and impious songs.

Such ceremonies, amazing for their mixture with religion, for the sacred place in which they partly took place,
and for the sacerdotal dignity with which the actors were
cloaked, existed for twelve to fifteen centuries. They found
apologists among the Doctors of the Church, and were abolished only with the greatest difficulty[2].

In the first centuries of Christianity, the prelates flogged
the penitents in order to reconcile them to the Church[3].
When, at the end of the twelfth century, confession was
generally established among the Christians, the confessors
themselves flogged their male and female penitents, in a
secret place of the church set aside for this performance.
Saint Louis, King of France, let himself be flogged quite
roughly by his confessors. One can imagine what sexual
vices must have resulted from such penances, better suited
to kindle than to extinguish passion[4].

Those who were excommunicated were publicly flogged
in order to obtain their absolution; and they were often
forced to follow, *stark naked*, the processions and to carry
the instrument of their punishment in their hands or hung
around their necks. Sometimes the culprit, man or woman,
entirely naked, received the whip during the whole course
of the procession. Almost all processions were accompanied
by a few individuals of one or the other sex, their body
completely exposed and reddened by blows of the whip.
This barbarous and indecent custom continued up to the
sixteenth century.

It was doubtless this custom of stark naked, flogged penitents following processions to obtain absolution for their sins, that inspired the idea of those crowds of naked men and women, those swarms of floggers who, roving in procession from city to city, offered during the course of three or four centuries the spectacle of their nakedness, their extravagant devotion, and their noble emulation in tearing their backs with heavy whip blows. Germany was, in 1257, the first stage for these sad and lamentable farces. Soon, in 1260, Italy imitated this fine example; she offered an entire people carried away by a holy fervor, armed with whips, marching in procession, and flagellating themselves with all their might. "Nobles and commoners, young and old, even children of five went about in the streets and public squares of the city and without shame showed themselves there *entirely naked*, with the exception of the sexual parts, which alone were covered. . . . They were to be seen in troups of a hundred, a thousand, ten thousand, preceded by priests and carrying the Cross and Banner, filling the cities and churches, and prostrating themselves before the altars. The towns and villages were not exempt from it. The plains and mountains seemed to resound with their lamentations[5]."

The women, noble or not, virgin or married, mixed in with them and flogged themselves without pity; no arm was there which did not flog, no back that was not flogged. But these flagellations were not to the taste of everybody. Pope Alexander IV refused to approve them, France to adopt them, and the King of Poland placed heavy penalties against the flagellants who attempted to come into his state. Nevertheless, in 1296, new troops of floggers appeared in Germany; and in 1349 the contagion was general. Germany was flooded with naked men and women who flogged themselves to the extreme. England also became the stage for their religious fervor. This time women were to be seen animated by a mad zeal, running about through the cities and country and exposing their bloody nakedness to public admiration. France alone preserved itself from the contagion[6]. This mania calmed down a bit only in the sixteenth century, when the floggers were organized into societies of *penitents* or *battus* [beaten ones], which lasted up to recent times. They had permission to tear their skin as much as they wished, but not to roam about flogging themselves[7].

Such examples were not without fruit; they brought about another institution, less cruel, but equally devout and indecent. From the thirteenth to the seventeenth century processions were to be seen made up of men, women, and children in chemise or absolutely naked. In order to obtain rain or fine weather from their gods, the Romans formerly held processions bare-footed, called *nudipedalia*. The early Christians made game of them[8]; but in later centuries the Christians no longer mocked them, imitated the *nudipedalia*, and through the same motives held processions bare-footed. Already in the seventh century the emperor Heraclius was seen leading a procession with head and feet bare. In the eighth, Charlemagne led a similar one before going to subdue the Huns. These examples were generally imitated. It is the tendency of abuses, when they were not suppressed in their origin, to keep on growing. This devotion was carried further: nakedness was not limited to the feet; the people stripped off their clothing and made the processions in chemise.

The thirteenth, fourteenth, and fifteenth centuries offer a great number of examples of processions made up of persons of all ages, all conditions, all sexes, and *nu-pieds et en langes* [bare-footed and in swaddling clothes], as it was then expressed, which is to say, having only a chemise for clothing. Also it was in such apparel that they made voluntary or forced pilgrimages. When in 1224 Louis VIII went to La Rochelle to drive out the English, Queen Isemburge, and other Princesses, led a large procession in Paris for the success of his armies, in which the inhabitants, and even foreigners, participated bare-footed and in chemise; some were even absolutely naked[9]. In 1241, because of a great drought, the inhabitants of Liège instituted a procession in which it was resolved that the clergy and people should march barefooted and in chemise for three consecutive days[10].

Joinville confesses that he himself, ready to leave for the Crusades, visited several monasteries in which there were *holy bodies*, and that he made this sort of pilgrimage barefooted and in swaddling cloth[11]. Saint Louis, being in Palestine, ordered a procession in which the Christians should come *bare-footed and in swaddling clothes*[12]. A young girl was cured at the tomb of Saint Louis. Her mother made a vow to go every year with her to that tomb, *bare-footed and in swaddling clothes*. An old commentary on the Psalter carries these words: *It is still customary in holy church for the penitents to go bare-footed and in swaddling clothes*[13].

It is useless to fatigue the reader with further citations about the custom of chemise processions, when I can demonstrate that people in such religious calvacades appeared stark naked and stripped of the last covering, and that the Christians, through excess of devotion, went to that excess of folly and indecency.

We have already seen, in the procession held at Paris for the success of the armies of Louis VIII, that among those who took part in chemise there were some more zealous who presented themselves there stark naked. One reads, in the book of the Miracles of Saint Dominick, that a man made a vow to visit the relics of this Saint, *barefooted and without chemise*[14]. Some letters of grace of the year 1354 condemn a guilty person to make a pilgrimage bare-footed, without clothes, and *without chemise*[15]. In 1315, abundant rains accompanied by frost in July made the harvest despaired of. In order to avoid this calamity, the people had recourse to processions. One was made, from Paris to Saint-Denis, famous for the great multitude of persons of both sexes who took part in it. It was followed by many private processions in which all the participants, except the women, *were entirely naked*[16]. It was doubtless at that time generally believed that women were less susceptible to sexual excitation at the sight of virile nudities than were men at feminine nudities.

Toward the end of the sixteenth century, a period in which reason was beginning to make definite progress, but which was almost neutralized by the contemporary progress of fanaticism, many processions were held in which men and women marched bare-footed and in chemise. Some writers of the time make mention of them, and mock them; prejudice may have directed their pens, may have led them to exaggerate the follies of their antagonists: they are therefore of questionable veracity. Thus it is not from their writings that I borrow my citations, but from that of a good and zealous Catholic, whose words I shall report scrupulously.

"The said day" (January 30, 1589) "of Monday, there also took place in the said city" (Paris) "many processions in which there were numerous children, both boys and girls, men and women, *who were all naked to the chemise,* such that there had never been seen so fine a thing, *thank God.* There were some parishes in which five or six hundred *stark naked* persons were to be seen, and in some others, eight to nine hundred, according to the size of the parish. The next day, Tuesday, the last day of the said month, *similar processions* took place, which grew from day to day in devotion, *thank God.* The said day" (February 3), "as on preceding days, some fine processions took place in which there were large numbers of people *stark naked* and carrying very beautiful crosses. Some of them who were *naked* in the said procession had attached Jerusalem crosses to their tapers or white wax torches that they carried; others, the coat-of-arms of the said defunct Cardinal and Dukes of Guise; also some of the said people who were in the procession had over their chemise or other white linen that they wore, large chaplets of paternosters. The next day, the fourth of the said month of February, *similar* processions were held. The said day of

Tuesday, fourteenth day of the said month of February, and the day of carnival-time, a day when one is accustomed to see masquerades and follies, the churches of the said city formed a great number of processions that went there in great devotion, even the parish of Saint-Nicolas-des-Champs, where there were more than a thousand persons, boys and girls as well as men and women, *stark naked*, and even all the monks of Saint-Martin-des-Champs, who were *all bare-footed*; and the priests of the said church of Saint-Nicolas, also *bare-footed*, and some of them *stark naked*; as was the curé named François Pigenat, who was more highly esteemed than any other, who was *stark naked*, and had only a *guilbe* of white linen on him[17]. The said day, Friday the twenty-fourth of the said month of February, there also was no end the whole day long of processions which had a great many persons, children as well as women and men, who were *stark naked*, and who carried and represented all the tools and instruments with which our Lord was tormented in his Passion, and among others the children of the Jesuits, joined with those who go there for study, who were *stark naked* and amounted to more than three hundred, two of whom carried a large cross of new wood weighing fifty, and even sixty pounds, and there were three choruses of music[18]."

The curé of Saint-Eustache, more reasonable than the other curés of Paris, wished to remonstrate against these pious indecencies; he was treated as a politician and a heretic. He was restrained, in order to avoid popular rage, from heading processions, "where," says l'Estoile, "men and women, boys and girls, marched pell-mell, and where everything partook of carnival-time; it is enough to say that the fruits of it were later seen[19]." Here are nakedness and religious indecencies well proved by eye-witnesses, and especially by a witness who apoligizes for it as for a holy and praiseworthy custom. This naïve apology is a necessary consequence of contemporary views. Nakedness was still not indecency and was definitely associated with religious acts.

The same judgment will be placed on another custom in vogue at the same period. Although ennobled by religious qualifications and ceremonies, it was more indecent and more susceptible of abuse than the one just described. The day of, the day before, or the day after various solemn church fêtes, the persons who arose earliest, whether secular or ecclesiastic, would go ceremoniously in the early morning to find in bed those men and women who were still asleep.

At Puy-en-Velay, on Easter Day and the six following days, some of the canons, after matins, accompanied by some choristers and preceded by the cross and holy water font, went processionally to the homes of their slothful brethern, entered their rooms furtively, surprised them in bed, gave them some holy water, and sang the anthem: *Hæc dies quam fecit Deus*, etc. The sleepy canon dressed forthwith, was led with ceremony to the church, and sentenced to pay a breakfast to those who had awakened him[20]. The same custom was practiced at Nevers. The canons and other members of the clergy, during the interval between Easter and Pentecost, would ceremoniously awaken their sleeping brethern. Doubtless this practice was accompanied at Nevers with indecent or criminal circumstances, for in 1246 it was prohibited under penalty of excommunication, and the statue which carried this prohibition called it a detestable custom[21].

The following facts reveal what the nature of these indecencies were, and what made this ceremony merit the term, *detestable*. In some cities, early in the morning on the day after Pentecost, the inhabitants went into the houses of those who were not yet awake, carried off whatever things they found at hand, and then went to have a meal at the inn. The one from whom they had taken these things was obliged to pay the reckoning in order to get his possessions back[22].

At Nantes a similar ceremony was customary on the day after Easter. Here is what is to be found in the Council held in this city in 1431, when this custom was prohibited: "The priests of the church and various other persons scatter through the houses of the city, enter rooms, seize those who are lying in their beds, lead them *stark naked* through the streets and public squares, then conduct them, giving vent to loud cries, into the churches, place them on the altars and elsewhere, and throw water on them. This disturbs divine service and brings about accidents, as lesions and sometimes mutilations of the member. Similarly, other persons, priests or laymen, early in the morning on the first day of the month of May, go into the homes of their neighbors. They carry off various things, and force those to whom they belong to pay in order to get them back[23]." At Angers the same custom prevailed: persons found in their bed in the morning were likewise carried into the church and placed on the altar, *entirely naked*. These are the expressions of the Council of Angers, which prohibited this practice in 1448.

In some cities it was named *Prisio*; but in other countries where it took place on the day of the Feast of Holy Innocents, it received its name from this holiday. People said *innocenter, donner les Innocents* [to innocentize, to give, or play, the Innocents], in order to express the action of going on the day of this fête to awaken some one, and at the same time giving him the whip. Flagellation on this day formed an essential part of the ceremony. It was the punishment inflicted on the slothful person. It is believed that Rabelais had this custom in mind when he has the judge *Grippeminaut* say: "*Or çà, vous autres gentils innocents, or çà, y serez bien innocentés*"—"Now then, you other innocent pretty fellows, now then, you shall indeed be innocentized[24]."

Gallantry of the old days contrived, in certain towns, to steal this ceremony from religion; it took it over entirely. It became the custom for young men to go early in the morning on this day to surprise their sweethearts in bed, and to act toward them as a schoolmaster acts toward his unruly pupils. The youth of the actors in this stimulating scene led them to extend this privilege beyond its limits, as the reader may well imagine.

It is related how a Seigneur du Rivau, taking leave of some ladies in order to go on a hunting trip far away, heard one of them say: "We are going to sleep at our ease, and we shall pass the Innocents without receiving them." These words struck du Rivau. He flew to his rendezvous, then hastily covered twenty leagues over the roads in order to arrive at the lady's home early in the morning on Innocents' Day, surprised her in bed, and made use of the privilege of the fête[25]. This custom existed at Dijon. Here is what is to be read in the *Escraignes Dijonnoises*: "You know that they of Dijon have that little custom of whipping girls on Innocents' Day, which is kept up by gallant lovers in order to have occasion for giving some sort of handsel to their sweethearts." It is on this subject that the author reports two erotic adventures which will not be recorded here[26].

Marot testifies to the existence of this custom, and especially to its abuse, in the following verses:

> *Dearest sister, if I knew where lay*
> *Your person, I'd to your pillow hasten*
> *In early morn on Innocents' Day*
> *That sweet form I love above the nation,*
> *To see. My hand (such fire is my ration)*
> *Unable simply itself contenting*
> *Save by touching, holding, feeling, trying;*
> *And if some one chanced in and we were seen,*
> *Seeming you to be innocentizing:*
> *Would not that make a virtuous screen?*

The sports of the *Innocents* did not always deserve this

qualification. Henri de Guise wrote, about the year 1556, to his father François, Duc de Guise: "I have been in great danger, for Innocents' Day gave us quite a fright. Madame Isabeau had come *to give the Innocents* to us, but I was already up, and the Duc de Bavière, who also came to give them to us, was quite provoked; and so I gave them to Monsieur de Lorraine in his bed. I shall keep good watch in the future for fear of blows[27]." This custom, if I may believe a person who is worthy of faith, was still practiced not so long ago on the first of May and the following days in German Lorraine. On these days people went early in the morning to their neighbors' homes. Such men and women as were found asleep were pitilessly whipped with nettles. I am assured that this same custom still exists in Piedmont.

How could manners not have been carried to the last degree of sexual corruption in such times of ignorance and crime, when even those appointed to direct them set the example of the most immoderate dissoluteness? How could modesty be respected when those who should have recommended it did not themselves observe it? I have already reported several proofs of this; here are some additional ones.

Concubinage for the priests was in this century, as in the preceding ones, universal and public. About the middle of the thirteenth century, the canons of the church of Saint Mary at Rome, in imitation of the religious prostitution of antiquity, had located the stage for their debauchery in the place consecrated to worship. It was in the subterranean chapel of the church of Saint Mary that they gathered together some public women; there, in the face of the most revered objects of Christianity, they fearlessly gave themselves over to the brutality of their passions. This fact is attested to by a letter of Pope Urban IV, who forcibly cries out against this sacrilegious debauchery[28].

Some prelates profited by this disorder and sold unmarried ecclesiastics the permission to have concubines. Every priest, even those who because of old age could not take advantage of it, were obliged, in some dioceses of Germany, to pay a tax for this privilege. The inhabitants of Strasbourg complained to Cardinal Campège that their Bishop opposed marriage of the priests of the diocese, whilst the unmarried clergymen led an infamous life and, to great public scandal, kept many libertine women in their houses. The Cardinal answered that he knew that the bishops of Germany were accustomed to compel the priests to pay for permission to live in debauchery; that perhaps these prelates had their reasons for acting thusly; that, for himself, he could not permit the priests to marry; and that he preferred they should keep several concubines in their house rather than one wife[29].

A preacher of the order of Saint Francis came, in 1455, to preach the Lenten sermons in the city of Liège. He began with a declamation against the concubines of the priests and canons. The magistrates, awakened to these disorders, gave out several ordinances. One of them stated that adulterers and concubines of priests should have a distinctive mark on the upper part of their garments. The indignant priests rose against the preacher who had provoked this police measure; after many altercations, they refused to acknowledge the preacher, and ended by having the ordinances annulled[30].

Elsewhere, country people were to be found who did not want to receive a curé unless he had a concubine, for fear that these curés might debauch their wives. Some Milanese priests murdered a certain Heribalde Corta chiefly because he wanted to proscribe marriage among them[31]. Indeed, priests were so scorned that a contemporary author, at the beginning of the thirteenth century, relates that lords no longer permitted the sons of their farmers, servants, or serfs to embrace the ecclesiastical life; that the priests themselves had so debased their calling that they no longer dared show themselves in public for what they were, and took care to hide their shaven crown or tonsure which would have made them known; that they were more scorned by the seculars than even the Jews, which is saying a great deal; and finally, that in order to express the worst of all conditions, people commonly employed this proverbial imprecation: *I should rather be a priest than to have to do such a thing*[32].

When the Council of Constance assembled in that city, there was to be seen, to the great scandal of the laity, an unbelievable number of prostitutes flocking there after the prelates who composed it[33]. The author of the book entitled *Speculum humanæ vitæ*, after having passed in review the manifold abuses which at his time existed in all classes of the clergy, speaks thusly of the canons: "The freer they are, the more licentious they are, giving themselves over to all vices. A single woman does not suffice for a canon; and besides the one who lives with them in their home as their wife, they further have a large number of young girls for concubines[34]."

Dietrich of Niem, secretary of Pope Urban VI, and later a bishop, informs us that it was an accepted custom among the prelates and priests of Iceland and Norway publicly to keep concubines. "When the bishops," he says, "go twice a year to pay visits to the inferior priests, to the curés, they take their mistresses with them. These women do not permit them to make these trips without them, because they are magnificently received by the curés and their concubines, because they receive presents from them, and because they fear that their bishops, finding the concubines of the priests visited more beautiful than they, may become amorous of them[35]."

Bishop Dietrich of Niem also refers, in lengthy detail, to the debaucheries of the nuns. According to him, they were a prey to the lust of bishops, monks, and lay brothers. The children born of this libertinage were placed in convents; sometimes the nuns practiced criminal abortion on themselves; or commonly, adding crime upon crime, with their maternal and villanous hands they plucked the life from the being to whom they had just given it. "If any secular women," he says, "were guilty of the foul deeds that these nuns commit, they would be condemned, according to the law, to the extreme penalty[36]."

Pierre d'Ailly, a Cardinal who lived in the fourteenth century, after having said, in his treatise on the reformation of the Church, that the corruption of the ecclesiastics was excessive; that their indolence, pride, wrath, gluttony, and lewdness scandalized the seculars, adds: "What is further scandalous is the abominable custom that many among them have today adopted; they are not ashamed to have concubines and publicly to acknowledge them[37]." Gerson, Chancellor of Paris and disciple of Cardinal Pierre d'Ailly, declaims no less vigorously against the concubinary priests and the sexual intemperance of the clergy. Both also speak of the convents for nuns, which they treat as places of debauchery and assemblages of prostitutes[38].

This recalls what the monk Matthew Paris, an English historian, reports of the Bishop of Lincoln who, under the reign of Henry III, in order to convince himself of the debauchery or chastity of the nuns, went through their convents and touched the breasts of each[39]. This further recalls the dissoluteness of the majority of the nuns of France before, during, and after the civil wars of the League. Their convents were called *places of pleasure*, and received more dishonoring names. Sauval informs us that the nuns of Montmarte, abandoned to prostitution, poisoned the Abbess who wished to reform them. The nuns of the abbey of Maubuisson, near Pontoise; those of the city of Saintes, of La Trinité, at Poitiers; of Villemur, in Albigeois; of the abbey of Lys, near Melun; those of Sainte-Catherine-les-Provins, famous for their gallantries with the Franciscan friars of that city, and an infinitude of others, may be ranked in the same class. These individuals, devoted to chastity, gave themselves over to the most excessive debauchery. The libertinage authorized among some priests of ancient religions was no greater than that of the priests of Christianity, although it was strictly proscribed by that religion. Iniquity was carried to the last extreme; society's laws and those of nature were horribly outraged[40].

Many other ecclesiastical writers, respected for their doctrine, and whose position ought to inspire the most complete confidence, have painted for us similar pictures of the clergy of past centuries. I could add their testimony to that which I have just reported. I could, to complete the picture, join to this the long series of laws which for almost twelve centuries have enjoined absolute continence on the priests: impotent laws, whose constant nullification attests either to their own flaws or to the continuance of the infraction. To these general features I could further add an infinitude of particular features scattered through various histories, annals of tribunals, or different archives, and which apply to individuals, even to those who are the most eminent in dignity in the sacerdotal order. The history of the Popes would yield an abundant harvest. I could further enrich this matter with the extremely manifold and virulent declamations of the majority of the preachers of the fifteenth century, and especially with those of the Protestant writers, which my impartiality has made it my duty to discard. But the little I have said suffices for my subject. What I have uncovered in raising only a corner of the veil ought to suggest what remains to be uncovered. Besides, I am weary of stirring up these ordures, and my reader, doubtless, experiences the same weariness.

Is it to the strange corruption of past centuries, to the law commanding continence, or is it to these two combined causes that the rampant sexuality of the clergy must be attributed? This question goes beyond my subject. I leave its solution to others; but I cannot forbear reporting here what the learned Pius II said: "Even if there were good reasons for forbidding marriage to the priests, it is better to permit it to them[41]." However, here is what those centuries were that are so extolled through that ineradicable habit of praising the past at the expense of the present; here is what those times were in which, it is commonly said, innocence and purity reigned; here are those men, those good ancestors, who are cited to us as models[42]. Indecency in the law, indecency in public manners and private life, indecency in games, indecency in art productions, indecency in civil ceremonies, in worship, and even in the most sacred places.

I now ask, was the cult of the *Phallus* or Priapus foreign to such manners? Could not its indecency have associated itself with such indecencies? Could not those who endured actual nakedness, burlesque and obscene actions even in religious ceremonies, even in holy places, even on the altars of the Deity, have put up with a factitious nakedness, a nakedness by representation? Could the cult of Priapus, qualified by the name of some Saint, presented under Christian forms, have shocked the minds of our good ancestors and not concurred with them? Were not such corrupt manners and abusive practices in harmony with the practices of ancient cults? Were those who rendered a cult to the pretended *navels*, to the pretended *fore-skins of Jesus Christ*, to the tail of the ass preserved at Genoa, so very far removed from the cult of the *Phallus*[43]?

As for me, I think, and many readers will share my sentiments, that the Christianized cult of Priapus is less derogatory to public decency, shocks reason less, and is less opposed to religion, less debasing for it, than the majority of the customs, ceremonies, abuses, and lascivious unrestraint I have just set forth. The manners of the time in which the cult of Priapus existed among the Christians being well known, there is nothing strange or improbable about the existence of that cult. It prospered through such manners as a plant prospers when placed in soil most suitable for it.

Chapter 17

GENERAL CONSIDERATIONS ON THE GODS OF GENERATION AND
THE CULT OF THE PHALLUS

IT seems that the union of the two sexes being amply
enjoined by nature and stimulated by the attraction of
pleasure, it should not be necessary for civil and religious
laws to intervene in order to procure its practice. However,
this is what happened among various nations of antiquity,
and what still endures among several modern nations. I have
furnished numerous proofs of it[1], and I should wish to dis-
cover the source or motive for an institution so foreign to
our manners, and which appears so contrary to the natural
course of the human mind.

Was man, then, in the infancy of society so assailed by
needs, so brutalized by savage life, so occupied and hard-
ened by the habit of struggling ceaselessly against ferocious
animals and his fellow-creatures, that he was insensible to
the delights of love? I cannot believe it. Savage man and the
brute, in spite of their isolation and ferocity, are tormented
by this imperious need of nature; and all their faculties are
put into action in order to assuage that devouring appetite.
Their instinct guides them with surety. A magnetic torrent,
whose violence is increased by obstacles, sweeps one sex
along toward the other; and their union, so passionately
desired, has no need of being commanded by law[2].

In order to determine its cause, one must go back to the
first ages of human society; one must represent to himself
their conditions and needs. The tribes existing today, which
we name savage, offer us a faithful picture of them; and
one may, without fear of deceiving himself, apply to the
most ancient human societies the traits that they preserve.
One must picture to himself isolated families, separated
from each other by vast mountain chains, rivers, forests, and
deserts, each of them living on the chase, on milk, on the
flesh of their domestic animals, or the fruits yielded by the
soil. In order to protect their harvests and flocks from the

teeth of voracious animals, from the rapacity and incursions of neighboring families; in order to be able to extend the territory they occupied in proportion to the progress of population and their needs; in order, finally, to enjoy complete security and assure the subsistence of each family, it required a population capable of surpassing that of the neighboring families whose attacks were to be feared. Strength, which results from a numerous population, alone could thus calm so much uneasiness and bring on abundance and prosperity. It was the first necessity of societies, and became the principal object of their mutual ambitions. Power, riches, happiness resulted from a great number of individuals; and everything that tended to increase them was eagerly seized upon; everything that could injure that increase was combatted with the same zeal. Thus it seems, according to the traditions left us of the ancient state of society, that minds were directed toward this sole end as toward their first needs. All institutions in the early days, as I have remarked, were guided by this exclusive motive. The brightest hopes of a father of a family consisted in a numerous posterity[3].

One cannot therefore be astonished by those ancient institutions favoring population, or that solemn prostitution consecrated by religion, which itself only presented the sanctified exercise of what made up the manners of the nations. One must not be astonished to find in antiquity so many deities favorable to generation and fecundity, it was the necessity of man that created the powers of the gods.

Some obstacles were prejudicial to population, and the resources employed to surmount them served only to give more stability to the institutions favorable to it. The males of a tribe, often taken up with expeditions of long duration, with hunts, or with almost continual wars in which the majority lost their lives, perhaps did not suffice for the fecundation of the women. Their long absence, their separation from their wives, the heat of the climate, the youth of these warriors or hunters, and consequently the impetuosity of their desires, doubtless led them to deviate from the aim of nature in order to assuage their natural passions. These supplementary enjoyments, useless and consequently prejudicial to population, justly abhorred in civilized societies, were only too frequent in primitive societies.

Such obstacles to the progress of population, especially the last, were additional motives for bringing the two sexes together, for commanding their union, for establishing express laws for this purpose, and favoring its execution by all possible stimulants. Each budding society had no more pressing interest. It was then that religion united itself with politics in order to repair what the long absences, the death of the men, and especially what their sterile habits caused the population to lose, by inviting even strangers to supply the default of the men of each tribe[4].

It was doubtless the tribes that were weak and small in number that, in order to increase themselves, strengthen themselves, and attach themselves to neighboring tribes by the attraction of pleasure and blood ties, first instituted those solemnities in which young girls were held to give themselves over to the caresses of strangers on one special day of each year; or rather those customs which obliged women and girls to go before travelers to offer them hospitality and half their bed. Individual pleasure and general interest being in accord, institutions founded on such bases flourished. Sanctified by religion and custom, they were lasting and respected. Also, they were in vogue among almost all the peoples of the earth, and had been maintained up to the time when the progress of population rendered them useless, and when the growth of civilization caused one to blush to submit to them[5].

It is known that religious prostitution still existed among many Oriental peoples shortly before the Christian era, that it continued in certain regions for some centuries after, and that it exists today in many districts of India. As for the custom which obliged women to share their beds with travelers, it was doubtless still more general; for in spite of the ravages of many centuries, numerous remains of it are preserved even up to the present[6].

I do not place in the rank of primitive religious prostitution the custom to which the women of many Oriental cities were subjected, which obliged them to give themselves up to the pretended will of a god and pass the night in a temple, in order to be fecundated by the deity himself. This is a result of the extreme credulity of the people, which the priesthood abused: a religious knavery which placed the libertinage of the priests to the account of the god, and brought the most beautiful women of the country to their lusting arms.

In these gallant solemnities in which strangers were, so to speak, invited to come to the aid of the nation, the stage chosen for them was a neutral ground, a frontier or cross-roads. Peoples who lived along the sea or on islands consecrated the shore to this ceremony. Boundary-markers, the limiting stones which were to be found there, regarded as protective talismans, were soon looked upon as tutelary deities of the territory. It was in the neighborhood of this variety of rustic deities that those voluptuous scenes, instituted by politics and consecrated by religion, took place. The boundary-markers, worshipped as protectors of territories, were so worshipped because of the proximity of this religious prostitution; as gods of generation and fecundation, male in some countries and female in others, who presided over love and the act of generation.

From this sprang the cult of the different deities worshipped, according to the country, under various names, which bear relation to the god *Eros* and the goddess *Venus*: deities which in their origin and for a long time after were represented only under the form of a landmark, of a crude boundary-marker. Such were the Venuses of Syria, Arabia, Paphos, etc., and the Eros of Thespia. Such still are the majority of the deities in India which preside over generation[7]. Afterwards, a revolution came about in religion, caused by the adoption of the worship of the dead, and gradually, first in part and then in totality, human forms were substituted for those crude objects of public veneration. After the *beaux-arts* had reached their perfection in Greece, Venus was everywhere represented under the figure of a young woman, resplendent with grace and beauty; everywhere, except at Paphos where her ancient form was preserved to her and she continually remained a stone boundary-marker[8].

When the need for an increase of population ceased to make itself felt, when the institution of religious prostitution had become useless, even when the progress of civilization and enlightenment made its indecency obvious, this prostitution still continued. Force of habit, the attraction of pleasure, the interest of the priests, and the superstitious ideas that attached themselves to these practices, maintained them for a long period. Venus, they said, severely punished young girls who scorned her worship; she was cruel in her vengeance. An erotic madness would lay hold of them and lead them to the greatest excess; such was the punishment reserved for these unbelievers. The priests cited terrible examples on this score. A person was able to appease this goddess, avoid her caprices, her furies, and assure the security of his or her life, only by various sacrifices worthy of her.

The cult of Venus, and of other corresponding deities, goes back to the first stages of religion. It existed well before that of the *Phallus* or Priapus, which is only one of the results of astronomic religion. Fable also indicates this priority of Venus in making her the mother of Priapus; and this last deity, who is only an extension of the cult of the *Phallus*, is not even placed in the ranks of the gods by Hesiod, so recent was his acceptance in Greece. All this evidence, therefore, demonstrates the indisputable fact that the need for an increase of population was the sole origin of these cults.

Chapter 18

TWO animals, signs in the zodiac, which marked the spring equinox and which in Egypt bore the same name, the celestial Goat and Bull, worshipped in representation and then worshipped alive n Egypt, were the origin of this cult; and their genital members, the expressive symbol of the sun fecundating nature at this bright season of the year, became the models for Phalli. These models were considered as sacred objects endowed with the generative power of the star of day, as powerful talismans whose beneficial influence brought abundance and life to plants and animals, and preserved them from harmful ills. Full of these ideas, the ancients placed the Phallus in all places where fecundity was desired, in all places where sterility was feared. The *Goat-Phalli* and *Bull-Phalli* were multiplied. They were affixed to tree trunks, to boundary-markers which bordered on cultivated lands, as a protective and beneficent talisman for harvests; they were rendered divine honors; they were placed in temples; they formed part of religious ceremonies, in the mysteries consecrated to various deities.

Up till then the Phallus was isolated, or was joined only to boundary-markers and tree trunks. But when the worship of the dead had brought in idolatry or the worship of human figures, it wrought a general change among the peoples of antiquity in all their objects of worship. These various objects gradually received the form of man. However, the metamorphosis was not so complete that they did not preserve some attributes, some characteristics that revealed their origin and primitive form. I shall not here set forth the effects of this religious revolution. I must confine myself to the objects that relate to the cult of the *Phallus*.

The two animals to which the *Phallus* owes its origin,

222

underwent the same general law and received some parts of
the human figure in their representations. The sacred Bull
was often represented, as is still to be seen in many ancient
monuments, with a man's head, surmounted with the horns
of the animal. The metamorphosis was carried even further: the whole upper portion of the figure had a human
form, whilst the rest represented the body, back, and legs
of a bull. This monstrous assemblage was named *Minotaur*,
a fictitious being, a fruit of the early progress of idolatry,
about which the Greeks spread extravagant fables and
which ancient and modern mythologists have explained in
diverse manners.

The sacred Goat underwent the same metamorphosis: it
was represented with half a human body, whilst its lower
portion retained the form of a quadruped, and the human
head preserved its ears and horns. This monstrous figure
became the deities Pan, Faunus, Silvanus, Satyr, etc. which
were frequently confused with Priapus, because often they
had his Phallus.

The boundary-markers and tree trunks felt the effects
of this change. A human head was placed at their extremity, and later half of the human body. Thus made up, these
boundary-markers and tree trunks constituted the Hermes,
Termini, Mercurys, and such idols as our artists name, very
improperly, *figures en gaines* [terminating figures]. But
as these landmarks and tree trunks for the most part already
carried Phalli, they were preserved to them in this new
make-up; and the identical deities, Hermes, Terminus, and
Mercury, were consequently often confused with Priapus,
whose characteristic feature they bore. Sometimes, however, they were distinguished from this last deity by a particular name. They were named *Hermes casmilus*, and
sometimes *Mercury of the erect member*.

After a time the origin of these various composite figures
was almost effaced from the memory of man. As they had
common figures and attributes, and similar virtues, each of

them was distinguished by a particular name determined by the place assigned to him. The idol with the Phallus and goat legs, placed in praires and cultivated lands, became the god Pan; placed in forests and on mountains, it was Faunus, Silvanus, and Satyr; in the vineyards, it was *Bacchus of the stiff sinew*; on territorial boundaries, on roads, at the entrance to houses, the idol with the Phallus received the name of *Hermes casmilus*, or *Mercury of the erect member*; and finally, the same idol set up in orchards and gardens constituted the god Hortanes or Priapus.

Thus, kept in temples, brought out in the mysteries, carried in religious ceremonies, the *Goat-Phallus* and *Bull-Phallus*, remaining isolated and preserving their primitive form, became sacred objects merely and secondary for worship. But when joined to different bodies, to landmarks and tree trunks, and annexed to various parts of the human figure, they contributed in making up true deities, whose names, as I have just explained, varied according to the places these idols occupied.

The Phalli, sacred objects of ancient worship, must not be confused with the *ex-votos* which resemble them. These latter figures were offered to Priapus by persons afflicted or enfeebled in such parts of the body over which this god presided: the offerings were images of it. The people persuaded themselves that by hanging these *ex-votos* near the divine idol, the latter would feel the effects of this proximity, or that the god having the image of the sick member before his eyes continually, would have to remedy it. Sometimes the phallic *ex-votos* were, as we have noticed, monuments of gratitude. Those men or women who had distinguished themselves in amorous combat by numerous exploits, devoutly attributed their vigor to the assistance of Priapus, and paid him homage with as many Phalli or wreaths as they had carried off sexual victories.

The phallic amulets owed their virtue to their shapes. Suspended from triumphal chariots, from the neck or shoulders of women and children, they were attributed the power of warding off the baneful effects of envious glances; but this virtue took on more strength when, as is still practiced in India, they were blessed by a priest.

Isolated at the time of its origin, isolated in the mysteries and religious ceremonies, the Phallus was a *sacred symbol*. Isolated and reduced to a small size, it was a *talisman*, an *amulet*. Hung on idols or in the chapels of Priapus or of other beneficent deities, it was an *offering*, an *ex-voto*. Having become a part of any body whatsoever, it was a god, and served to create many deities.

Such are the variations of worship and form which the Phallus underwent during the gradual development of superstition and the arts.

Chapter 19

LET us terminate this work with some observations on popular belief relative to the cult of the obscene deities and to the means of rendering them propitious, and on a peculiar attitude of faith whose origin must be imputed to the numerous errors which constituted the earliest religions of the world. It seems that the ancients held views on the means of increasing the preservative and fecundating virtues of the *Phallus* which appear so strange in our eyes. They doubtless believed that the more animated the scenes in which they represented it in sculpture or painting, the more refinements and excesses of debauchery they offered, the more the deity was flattered by them, the more his attention was caught, his benevolence brought on, and the more disposed to comply with the prayers of mortals. The most extreme indecency was proof of the most fervent devotion.

This opinion, which appears revolting to us, is nevertheless the natural consequence of the belief attributing particular tastes to each deity, and that each distributed his blessings to a greater or lesser extent according as his favorite tastes were more or less humored. The firstlings of the most beautiful flowers and the finest fruits were offered to the deities who presided over these productions of nature. The cruel gods wanted blood; animals and even men were sacrificed to them; and the more to satisfy their sanguinary tastes, the greater number of victims were offered. Thus people were persuaded that the more blood that was spilled, the more satisfied was the deity; that the crueler one was, the more religious he was.

If we apply this belief to other deities, to other religious objects, to the cult of Venus, to that of the *Phallus* or Priapus, we shall certainly obtain the same results. These deities, presiding over the propagation of mankind, over the generation of beings, over the particular act itself that procures this propagation and generation, received the most excessive evidence of devotion from their most zealous worshippers. If pictures of voluptuousness and libidinous scenes flattered these gods and were believed necessary in order to win their favor in greater abundance, one had to exceed the ordinary measure of homage paid them and offer their sensual tastes no end of pictures of the most studied voluptuousness. That is why the places consecrated by religion, the temples and tombs, in the countries in which the cult of the *Phallus* and Priapus existed or still exists, offered and offer numerous evidences of this improper display in their bas-reliefs, paintings, and other art products.

Can the most disordered imagination, one wholly given over to the extravagances of debauchery and blunted senses, conceive of scenes as lascivious, as revolting to European eyes, and especially of the Europeans of our century, as those presented by the majority of the places in India consecrated to the deity? There are few pagodas which do not offer these licentious pictures. The excesses which have procured a shameful celebrity for the inhabitants of Sodom, for the Phœnician women, the Lesbian women, etc., are retraced there without any veil beside the most holy objects of religion. Such are, for example, the bas-reliefs of the pagodas of Elephanta, *Tricoulour*, *Tréviscarré*, and others of which I have spoken[1].

The Mexicans had the same custom, and their temples often offered the most varied manners in which the union of man and woman can be achieved. The Greeks and Romans likewise carried this form of devotion to excess. The monuments of their Bacchanalia and Priapeia which remain to us are such that at first glance one is tempted to attribute these productions to the delirium of a corrupt imagination, to the intention of awakening desire, of inflaming the senses, whilst for the most part they are evidences of piety, a faithful picture of what was practiced during the religious fêtes and ceremonies of this diverse worship.

On the cover of an ancient urn, which appears to have been employed for sacred uses, an enormous Phallus can be seen with the figure of a woman entwined with her arms and legs. Sketches of the paintings on two Greek vases of the Portici museum have been published. They represent a vendor of Phalli who is offering a basket filled with them to a woman, who is going into ecstasies at the sight of their extraordinary size[2]. Another woman is enraptured in admiration of a young man, naked, who is showing himself to her in the most energetic and indecent condition. Another subject represents a vigorous man completely occupied with the action that Onan was reproached with, upon which Tissot has composed a work very useful for youth, and which, in the interest of society, should form part of the daily reading of young men[3]. Another scene, finally, offers a man and woman executing that impure and sterile coupling, that crime against the cult of Venus by which that deity received an unpardonable outrage.

Antiquity offers us a very great number of examples of similar scenes. The reader will doubtless thank me for not tainting his imagination by additional descriptions of this sort. Those I have just offered him will suffice to give him an idea of the nature of this cult, of the opinion the ancients held of it, and of the extreme license brought into the composition of objects consecrated to it.

The vases, whose lascivious paintings I have just indicated, were religious objects. They are in the Museum of the King of Naples, at Capo di Monte. They were discovered in tombs near Nola; and it is known that among the ancients, tombs were as sacred as the sanctuary.

The learned author who has described these vases, and published sketches of their paintings, comes to the support of my opinion. "A multitude of *Priapées*," he says, "are to be met with in the monuments; some are even to be found in places least susceptible of receiving them: which proves how familiar the Greeks were with these images which, according to our manners, we name *obscene*. The *Priapées*, represented as religious objects, are very great in number. Whatever system one holds to on this score, one must always come back to this principal idea, that the ancients saw in it only a symbol of fecund nature and of the reproduction of the beings that serve in the composition and maintenance of the universe. It is to this idea that we owe those Priapi of all forms that are to be encountered in cabinets, and those offerings of all sorts which recall the cult of the god of Lampsacus."

The same author speaks of ancient lamps which offer licentious images, several of which are preserved at the Bibliothèque royale. He believes that they must have been applied to religious uses. He cites engraven stones, and even some medals, called *spintrian*, which probably represent the debauches of Tiberius on the island of Capri and the bizarre couplings to which he gave the name of *Spintriæ*. This author ranks as the most celebrated ancient productions of this sort the group of the Satyr and she-goat of the Portici Museum, which can be seen only with special permission; another group, almost similar, found at Nettuno, sold by Cardinal Alexander Albani to the last King of Poland, and at present kept at Dresden; the Priapus of the museum of Cardinal Albani, with the inscription *Saviour of the World*; and the Priapus of the Museum of Florence.

He ends by saying that "the two Greek vases I describe, having been found in tombs, prove that licentious representations could themselves be applied to religion, because then there was seen in them only the symbol of the fecundating and reproductive power, represented in whatever manner they might be. In the Bacchanalia, in the initiations, many ceremonies were related to this idea. Thus it is not astonishing that *Priapées* are to be found in the tombs of the ancients, as pictures of the Bacchanalia are to be met with there[4]."

If we are less astonished that the religions of the ancients commanded human sacrifices, the greatest crime against society, than we are that they consecrated the act of reproduction, the act preserving mankind; if it appears less strange to us to see man, through piety, misuse his inclination to cruelty than to see him, through the same motive, misuse his natural propensity for the pleasures of love, we should satirize our own opinions and confess our preference for a cult which destroys and gives death to one which preserves and gives life.

TEXTUAL NOTES

TEXTUAL NOTES

NOTE ON J. A. DULAURE

1. *It is inexact to say, as is to be read in the* Catalogue des ouvrages condamnés *by Drujon, and elsewhere, that this second edition was suppressed* although the author had made some retrenchments in it. *Dulaure had retrenched nothing ; he had, on the contrary, added. What can be said is that none of those additions, simple developments of ideas or facts already exposed, was of a nature to justify a condemnation if the work, such as it had originally appeared, in no way outraged morality. In this reprint the text of 1825 has been followed, more complete, more correct, and which the author had striven to render definitive.*

AUTHOR'S PREFACE

1. *Montaigne censures, according to his custom, this unreasonable disposition of our manners; a disposition which, since the century when he lived, has but grown worse: "Each one flees seeing him born," he says in speaking of man, "each one runs to see him die. To destroy him, people seek a spacious field in full daylight; to construct him, they lurk in a gloomy pit, and the most cramped possible. It is one's duty to hide in order to make him, and it is glory, and gives birth to various virtues [honors] to know how to unmake him. The one is affront, the other is credit."* Essais de Michel de Montaigne, *bk. 3.*

2. *One will notice that I am far removed from the sentiment of a monk of the* IX *century, who wrote various theological treatises, and who, in order to free himself of the restraints of decency, pretends that there is nothing shameful in nature. "That which is useful is honest," said he, "and that which is honest is not indecent; everything that has been created has nothing of the indecent." And he adds:* "Igitur et mulieris vulva non turpis, sed honesta siquidem partes omnes creaturæ honestæ." (Ratramni monachi Corbiensis, liber de eo quod Christus ex Virgine natus est, cap. 3. Spicilegium d'Achery, *vol. 1, p. 53.*)

CHAPTER I

1. *The French here is* bouc, *which means* he-goat. *As a free translation,* buck *is too definite and* he-goat *is too awkward; be it understood that throughout* goat *signifies* he-goat. —Trans.

Textual Notes

2. *Bulls, oxen, and cows play a large rôle in mythology as emblems of the restoring and regenerating sun. Many bulls were adored in Egypt under different names. The bull* Apis, *the most celebrated of all, was at Memphis; the bull* Mnevis, *at Heliopolis; the bull* Onuphis *or* Bacis *was, according to Macrobius, at Hermuntis, a city of upper Egypt. Among the Greeks we find the* bull of Marathon, *tamed by Hercules, and of which Pasiphæ became amorous, etc. The Hebrews borrowed the* golden calf *from the Egyptians, which was destroyed by Moses, as well as the calf of Samaria, against which the prophet Hosea declaims (chap. 8 and 13.). The Romans had their expiatory, restorative bull, which they slaughtered in the sacrifices called* tauroboles, *and whose blood effaced the sins of those on whom it was spread. The symbolic monuments of the sun-god* Mithra *offer a bull whose blood is spilled for the same object. The Cimbri and the Teutoni had their sacred ox, on which they pronounced their oaths; the Scandinavians adored* Thor *or the bull, whose idol was at Upsala in the Temple of the Sun. The bull is adored in Japan, at Meaco. The rabbis speak of a gigantic ox called* Behemoth, *reserved for the feast of the Messiah, etc., etc. Cows were honored almost as much as bulls.* Io *was changed into a cow by Jupiter, who became amorous of her.* Iphianassa *was likewise metamorphosed into a cow through the effect of her sisters' jealousy. The Hebrews sacrificed and had the* red cow [vache rousse] *burned, whose ashes, mixed with water, served in expiations. Among the Indians the ashes of cow-dung are likewise employed in expiations. These people have for precept to love cows and the Brahmins.*

3. *I wonder if Dulaure thoroughly understands his zodiac? He speaks of the Goat and the Bull as if they were equally signs bordering the vernal equinox.* Taurus *indeed is, or was, for due to the precession of the equinoxes the sun now first enters it on April 20. However, the Goat,* Capricornus, *receives the sun on December 21, which plainly prohibits any connection with the spring. The sign immediately preceding* Taurus *is* Aries, *the* Ram, *into which the sun now enters on March 21. The constellation of the Charioteer, or* Auriga, *is found somewhere in the neighborhood of* Taurus, *and it contains the star* Capella, *or she-goat. There is also a constellation called the* Bull,

234

*which originally gave its name to that section of the zodiac.
So I suppose the discrepancy here is only a slight confusion
of language in that Dulaure fails properly to distinguish between stars, constellations, and signs of the zodiac.* —Trans.

4. *Herodotus*, Euterpe, *bk. 2, p. 41.*

5. *Dulaure seems to think that these are two names for
the same place, but decidedly they are not. Thmuis was a
city of Lower Egypt, on the eastern side of the Mendesian
mouth of the Nile. Chemmis was a large city of Upper
Egypt, of the Thebais, on the east bank of the Nile. Both
were famous seats of the worship of Pan or Mendes.*
—Trans.

6. *Saint Jerome tells us this of the word Thmuis.* —Trans.

7. *Plutarch*, Treatise On Isis and Osiris, toward the end.

8. *Iamblichus*, de Mysteriis, *chap. 17, sec. 1.*

9. *Lucian*, Astrology, *vol. 4, p. 65 of the last translation
[the French translation] of his works.*

10. *Dulaure is a bit confused here, I believe. Achelous
could hardly have been the son of Harpocrates; he is commonly said to have been the eldest of the three thousand
sons of Oceanus and Tethys. He was the god of the river
of the same name, the largest river in Greece. He fought
with Hercules for Deïanira, and when he lost, he took the
form of a bull, but was again conquered, Hercules depriving him of one of his horns. Achelous later recovered his
horn by trading the horn of Amalthea. According to Ovid,
the Naiads changed Achelous' lost horn into the horn of
plenty. Harpocrates, on the other hand, often identified
with Horus, was the last-born and weakly son of Osiris.*
—Trans.

11. *People commonly say the ox Apis [boeuf Apis]; but,
authorized by history, and especially by the opinion of the
savant de Caylus, I shall say the bull Apis [taureau Apis]. "I
am resolved," says that celebrated antiquary, "not to give
any false ideas, and always to say bull." (Recueil d'Antiquités, tom. 3, p. 28.)*

12. *Eusebius*, Preparat. evangel., lib. 3, cap. 13; *Amm.
Marcell.*, lib. 22, p. 245; *and Dupuis*, Origine de tous les
Cultes, *tom. 2, p. 114.*

13. *Herodotus*, Euterpe, *liv. 2, p. 42.*

14. *Herodotus, liv. 2.*

15. *Diodorus Siculus*, lib. 1, sec. 88.

16. *The Latin name for* phallus *was* fascinum, *the god it signified in the connection Dulaure here refers to was commonly called* Fascinus. *Also what he gives as* Tutunus *is usually given as* Tutinus. *—Trans.*

19. Suidas, ad verbum Priapos.

18. *See figure 26 of the* Recueil de Chifflet.

19. *The third member of the Hindu trinity is usually given as* Siva. *If this is another name for the same god, I have never heard of it. —Trans.*

20. Atlantic, *lib.* II, *part* II, *pp. 236, 251, 384.*

CHAPTER II

1. *Diodorus Siculus, liv. 1, sec. 85.*

2. *Herodotus,* Euterpe, *sec. 46.*

3. *According to the common legend, this would be impossible. Venus was in love with Bacchus and went to meet him on his return from India. She soon left him and went to Lampsacus to give birth to his child. Juno, being displeased with her conduct, caused the child to be extremely ugly. This child was Priapus. —Trans.*

4. *Lactantius,* De falsa religione, *liv. 1, chap. 21.*

5. Arrectis ita membris, ut hirci naturam imitentur. *(Diodorus Siculus, liv. 1, sec.* II.)

6. *The Satyrs, or Satyri, were a group of minor gods of the field and forest, and not a distinct god like the others, as Dulaure's phrasing might lead one to think. A group of Satyrs usually accompanied Bacchus. They were said to represent the luxuriant vital powers of nature. The older ones were usually called Sileni, although there was a particular Silenus. —Trans.*

7. Notes sur l'Histoire d'Herodote, *by Larcher, t. 2, pp. 267-268.*

8. *Strabo, liv. 17;—Clement of Alexandria,* Protrept., *p. 27.*

9. *Herodotus,* Euterpe, *liv. 2, sec. 46.*

10. *Plutarch,* Moralia, *dialogue entitled:* Beasts have the use of reason.

11. Voyage de Vivant Denon, *t. 2, p. 319.*

CHAPTER III

1. Second Mémoire sur les anciens philosophes de l'Inde,

etc., *by the Abbé Mignot. (Mém. de L'Acad. des Inscriptions, tom. 31, p. 141.)*

2. *Herodotus,* Euterpe, *liv. 2, sec. 48.*

3. Voyage à la côte occidentale d'Afrique, *by L. de Grandpré, officier de la marine Française, tom. 1, p. 118.*

4. *Among the Egyptians the epagomenal days were what, during the Revolution, the five* complémentaire *days were in France.*

5. *Plutarch,* Moralia, *Treatise on Isis and Osiris.*

6. Voyage de Vivant Denon dans la basse et haute Egypte, *tom. 3, and the* Atlas, *pl.* cxiv, *n. 47 and 54.*

7. Voyage de Vivant Denon, *tom. 3,* Atlas, *pl.* xcviii, *n. 35.*

8. *Such of note are the paintings on the two Greek vases preserved in the Portici Museum of the King of Naples and which were found in tombs near* Nola. *I shall speak of them at the end of this work.*

9. *Lib. 5, cap. 7, sec. 4, tom. 3, p. 205.*

10. *P. 431.*

11. Tom. *1, p. 499, and* tom. *2, pp. 504-505.*

12. Traduction d'Hérodote, *by Larcher, last edition, tom. 2, pp. 270 and 272.*

13. Histoire ecclésiastique, *by Fleury, liv. 19, p. 600.*

14. *Dulaure's stand on the matter of the cross is indeed hard to understand in a man otherwise so keen and open. There can be little doubt as to the phallic origin of the cross; but I shall not dispute our author here, as those interested can find ample material on the origin of the cross. The "handled cross" he refers to here is technically known as the* crux ansata *and is an out and out phallic and fertility symbol. The circle represents the female element, the cross the male element, and the two thus joined symbolize the act of generation, which is the quintessence of fertility. There are other similar symbols, as the Seal of Solomon, the two superimposed triangles. The* crux ansata *is also known as the Great Egyptian Key of Life. —Trans.*

15. An Account of the Remains of the Worship of Priapus, *etc.*

16. Voyage dans la basse et la haute Egypte, *Atlas, pl.* cxxv, *n. 15.*

17. Antiquités de Caylus, *tom. 3, p. 52, and pl.* xiii, *n. 2, 3, & 5. (Also see the plates in John Davenport's* Aphrodi-

siacs and Anti-aphrodisiacs *for examples of such figures.*
—Trans.)

18. Voyage dans la basse et la haute Egypte, *by Vivant Denon, pl. 98, n. 36 &37.*

19. Antiquités de Caylus, *tom. 3, pl.* I *&* III, *tom. 6, pl.* I *&*II.

20. Dictionnaire de la Fable, *by Millin, at the word* Osiris.

21. Voyage de Denon, *Atlas, pl.* LI, *n. 1, 2, &* 3; *pl.* CXXI, *n. 5; pl.* CXXVI, *n. 4; pl.* CXXVII, *n. 10; pl.* CXXXIII, *n. 4, & pl.* CXXXIV.

22. *Caylus,* Antiquités, *tom. 6, pl.* XV, *n. 1.*

23. Voyage dans la basse et la haute Egypte, *Atlas, pl.* XXXIII, *n. 7.*

24. Voyage de Denon, *Atlas, pl.* CXXVI, *no. 12.*

25. *The majority of the ancients who relate this tragic adventure say that Typhon cut Osiris into fourteen parts. Diodorus Siculus asserts that his body was cut into twenty-six parts, which were distributed to the Titans.*

26. *On this fable, that I have reported only in substance, one can consult the* Treatise on Isis and Osiris, *by Plutarch;* Diodorus Siculus, *liv. 1, cap. 22, or tom. 1, liv. 4, chap. 3, of the translation [French] of Terrasson; Jablonski, in his* Panthéon Egyptien; *Court de Gébelin, in his* Histoire religieuse du Calendrier, *etc.*

27. *Socrates, lib. 5, cap. 16;* Histoire ecclésiastique, *by Fleury, liv. 19, p. 595.*

CHAPTER IV

1. Baal, Beel, *is only an honorable qualification given an object of worship, which among the Chaldeans was the equivalent of the word* Lord. *The Samaritans called this deity* Baal, *and the Babylonians* Bel *or* Belus. *From this word the Greeks made* Abello, Apollo; *the Gauls,* Belenus, Belisama, Bellus-Cadrus, *etc. It seems unfailing that the adjectives* fine, beautiful [beau, belle,] *derive from the name of these sun- deities.*

2. Numbers, *ch. 25, v. 1 & 2.*

3. Idem, ibid., *v. 3 & 4.*

4. Numbers, *ch. 25, v. 5 & 9.*

5. Idem, *ch. 25, v. 17 & 18.*

6. *This frightful butchery recalls that which Moses had*

done against the worshippers of the golden image of the bull Apis, *commonly called the* Golden Calf. *Moses addressed himself to those of the tribe of Levi:* "Put every man his sword by his side, and go in and out from gate to gate throughout the camp, and slay every man his brother, and every man his companion, and every man his neighbor." *The children of Levi did what Moses had ordered them, and there were about twenty-three thousand men killed that day.* (Exodus, *ch. 32, v. 27, 28.*) (*The Bible gives the number killed as three thousand. —Trans.*)

7. *Saint Jerome in his* Commentary *on chapter 9 of the prophet Hosea; Isidorus, in his* Origines; *Rufinus, in his book 3 on Hosea. Another commentator on the Bible also says* "BEEL-PHEGOR Hebræis deus turpitudinis, ut PRIAPUS Romanis." *(Note on chap. 25 of the book of Numbers, v. 3.)*

8. *Hosea, ch. 9, v. 10.*

9. *Beyer on Selden,* cap 5, syntagm. 1, Baal-Poor.

10. *Solomon Jarchi, in his* Commentary *on the book of* Numbers, *chap. 25.* Hottinger (Hist. Orient., *p. 155) expresses the same thing. On this religious custom one can consult* Selden, de Diis Syris, Syntagm. *1, cap. 4; Beyer,* Addimenta ad Selden, *p. 244-245; Elias Schedius,* de Diis Germanis, *p. 84-85,* Antiquitates Gronovii, *tom. 7, chap. 13, etc.*

11. *Kings, bk.* III, *ch. 15, v. 12.*

12. *Idem, ibid., v. 13, and* Paralypomenon, *liv. 2, v. 16.*

13. *Rabelais makes* Mipheletzeth *the sovereign of an island peopled by the* Andouilles. *Pantagruel and his companions, after having disembarked on this island, had terrible combats to support, and put an infinitude of* Andouilles *to the sword. The carnage was so great that the* queen *of the* Andouilles *saw herself forced to ask peace of Pantagruel, who granted her it.*

14. *The* high places *were sanctuaries established on the tops of various mountains. There were altars there of rough stone, varieties of pillars or crude obelisks, the objects of worship of various peoples.*

15. Fecisti tibi imagines masculinas et fornicata es in eis. *Ezekiel, ch. 16, v. 17.*

Textual Notes

1. *This city is today named* Bambich *or* Bambouck [Mambedsck *or* Bambig]. *It was Seleucus who gave it the name of* Hierapolis. *Earlier, the Syrians called it* Magog [Bambyce *or* Mabog]. *It must not be confused with another* Hierapolis *situated in Asia Minor.*

2. *This treatise was attributed to Lucian, and is still found among his* Works; *but the extreme credulity that is noticeable in it proves that it does not belong to that incredulous author.*

3. *The* orgie *is a measure of six Greek feet. The Greek foot having 11 inches 4½ twelfths* [linges] *Parisian measure, the* orgie *ought to have 5 feet 8 inches 3 twelfths.*

4. *The towers of Notre-Dame at Paris have a height of 204 feet. They therefore surpass that of the Phalli only by about 33 feet.*

5. *Homer thought to honor Juno in giving her ox-eyes; but Bacchus, in this offering, gives us a much greater idea of this goddess. It's a case of exclaiming:* O altitudo!

6. *See the* Glossaire *of* Du Cange, *the word* Phalæ.

7. *This opinion is related to the symbolic monuments of the cult of* Mithra, *sun-god of the Persians. This god is represented holding a bull upside down under him, whose throat he is cutting, while a scorpion is biting the genital parts of the bull. This scorpion acts on the extremity of the bull's member as it acts on the extremity of those Phalli. This identity of action on two similar objects reveals the mystical connections which exist between these two objects, and concurs in establishing the affinity of the genital member of the bull with the worshipped Phalli.*

8. *Caylus,* Antiquités, *tom. 7, pl.* VII, *n. 1 & 2.*

9. *Works of Lucian.* Treatise on the Syrian Goddess.

10. *See above, chap.* III.

11. *Selden,* de Diis Syris, syntagm. *2. Ausonius, epigram 29.*

12. *Meursius,* de Festis Græcorum, *liv. 1,* Adonia. *The Hebrews rendered a cult to* Adonis *under the name of* Tammuz. *Ezekiel complains of the women who came to seat themselves at the North door of the temple, and to weep for the death of Tammuz. This god Tammuz appears to be the same as* Chamos *or* Chamosh, *whom the Canaanites*

240

(or Phœnicians), the Moabites and the Midianites wor-
shipped, and to whom Solomon built a temple that Josiah
later destroyed. As for the name Adonis, it signifies lord,
master, *as well as* Adon *and* Adonaï.

13. *Alexand. Polyhist., in* Chald., apud Syncell., *p. 29.*

14. *Ptolemæus,* Geograph. lib. 1.

15 *See* Histoire physique, civile et morale de Paris, *tome*
1, p. 160.

16. Voyage du Bengale à Scyras, *by Franklin.*

CHAPTER VI

1. *Porphyry,* de Styge, *p. 283;* Mém. de l'Acad. des In-
scrip., *tom. 31, p. 136.*

2. *Abbé Mignot, in a second* Mémoire sur les anciens
philosophes de l'Inde, *after having cited the passage from*
Porphyry on the voyage of Bardesanes, says in reference
to this figure of the two sexes: "This species of Lingam
is found even today in India, as is seen from the figures of
the idols of that country which have been sent to M. le
marquis de Marigny." (Mém. de l'Acad. des Inscript., tom.
31, p. 136.) Another writer testifies to the existence of this
figure: "It is today called," *he says,* "Ardhanary-Eswara
[Ardanari-Iswara, *or more technically*, Arddha Nari]. *This*
mixture was made, say the Brahmins, because Eswara (*or*
Chiven [Civa *or* Siva]), *lover of* Parvati, *gave her half of*
his body." (Moeurs des Bramines, *by Abraham Roger, p.*
154.)

3. *Abraham Roger, p. 157.* Chiven *or* Siven, Sib, Seib.
Schiva Esswara, Ixora, *or even* Routren, Roudar, Mayes-
souren, Mahaden, Sangara, *etc., are names of the same deity.*
Some are alike, and are pronounced differently in the var-
ious districts of India, or differently spelled by Europeans.
This god has a great deal of connection with the Priapus
of the Greeks and Romans.

4. Essais historiques sur l'Inde, *by Delaflotte, p. 206, and*
Voyage de Grandpré dans l'Inde.

5. *In the English work entitled:* An Account of the Remains of the Worship of Priapus, *etc. by R. P. Knight, pub-*
lished in 1791, there have been engraven several ancient
monuments of India which have relation to the cult of
Priapus. Two ex-votos are seen there taken from the pagoda
of Tanjore, *one of which joins the two sexes together. Es-*

241

pecially to be noticed is the engraving of a bas-relief from the pagoda of Elephanta, *which represents a group executing the infamous act which the Latins designated by the word* irrumatio. *The proper title of this very important book by Richard Payne Knight is:* A Discourse on the Worship of Priapus and Its Connection with the Mystic Theology of the Ancients. —*Trans.)*

6. Dictionnaire de la Fable, *by* Noël, *the word* Sita.

7. *These two places, this and* Tricoulour, *have me completely baffled. I cannot even find them mentioned in the big French Encyclopædias and Atlases. Consequently, I am unable to give the English equivalents of these localities, but must merely leave them in their French form. However, in order to atone a bit for my failure here, allow me to quote Edward Sellon, from his* Annotations on the Sacred Writings of the Hindus *(pp. 37-39), at some length where he gives the twelve principal places of* Lingam *worship.* —*Trans.*

"*Twelve* Lingas *are particularly mentioned in the* Kedara Kalpa *of the* Nandiupa-puran, *as being of peculiar sanctity. In this* Puran, Siva *is made to say, 'I am omnipresent, but I am especially in twelve forms and places.'*

"*These he enumerates as follows: 1.—*Somanatha, *in* Samashtra, *i.e.,* Surat. *2.—*Malikijuna, *or* Sri Sala. *3.—*Mahakala, *or* Ougein. *4.—*Om'kala. *Shrine of* Mahadeo *(or Great God, a name of* Siva*) at* Om'kala Mandatta. *5.—*Amareswarra, *in* Ujayai, *near the Hill. 6.—*Vaidyanath, *at* Deoghur, *in* Bengal. *(This temple is still in existence, and a celebrated place of pilgrimage.) 7.—*Ramása, *at* Sethubandha, *on the island of* Ramissaram, *between* Ceylon *and the Continent. (Here the* Linga *is fabled to have been set up by* Rama.*) This temple is still in tolerable repair, and one of the most magnificent in India, with a superb gateway one hundred feet in height. 8.—*Bhomasandkara, *in* Dakini, *which is in all probability the same as* Bhimeswarra, *a* Linga *worshipped at* Dracharam, *in the* Raja Mahendri *district, and there venerated as one of the chief of the twelve. 9.—*Not known. *10.—*Tryambaka, *on the banks of the* Gomati *(*Goomtee?*). 11.—*Gantamessa—*(site uncertain). 12.—*Kedarésa, *or* Kedaranath *in the* Himalaya. *The last has been frequently visited by travellers.*"

8. Voyage à Canton, *and* Observations sur le voyage de

la Chine, de lord Marcartney, *by Charpentier-Cossigny.*

9. *This, again, I leave in the French form, having been unable to find any English equivalent of it. As the big* LAROUSE *lists it, I persume that Dulaure is correct in giving it as a name of the double symbol; the symbolic sexual union has so many names in India that this quite possibly can be among them. Some of the other names for it, given by Sellon,* op. cit., *are:* Bhava, Bhavani, Mahadeva, Mahamaya, etc. —*Trans.*

10. Voyage aux Indes et à la Chine, *by Sonnerat, from 1774 to 1781, tom. 1, liv. 2.*

11. Voyage dans l'Inde et au Bengale, *in 1789 & 1790, by L. de Grandpré, naval officer, tom. 2, p. 110.*

12. Voyage aux Indes à la Chine, *by Sonnerat, tom. 2, p. 46.*

13. Idem, idem, *tom. 2, p. 50.*

14. *As the names of Indian rites, ceremonies, and sects can be rendered in so many and varied spellings, and as I am anything but an expert in Indian ritual and mythology, I have been forced to leave some of the above names in the form in which Dulaure gives them. However, wherever a reasonably thorough search was able to bear fruit, I have supplied the most approved English rendering of the name or term.* —*Trans.*

15. Voyage aux Indes et à la Chine, *by Sonnerat, tom. 2, p. 53.*

16. Essais historique sur l'Inde, *by Delaflotte, p. 206, etc.*

17. Essais historique sur l'Inde, *by Delaflotte, p. 192.*

18. Idem, idem, *p. 206.*

19. Voyage aux Indes et à la Chine, *by Sonnerat, tom. 1, p. 311.*

20. Voyage dans l'Inde, *by Duquesne.*

21. Voyage dans l'Inde *by Admiral Van Cærden.*

22. Voyage dans le Mogol et l'Indoustan, *by Bernier, and* Essais historiques sur l'Inde by Delaflotte, *p. 218.*

23. *Several examples of them will be seen in Chapter* IX.

24. *An insane Turk ran, completely naked, through the streets of Alexandria, in Egypt. He went into the shops, took what fell to his hand without paying for it, and kept it or threw it in the street. Far from displeasing the Turkish merchants, this extravagance delighted them a great deal: they saw in this waste a proof of the protection of the*

Prophet; for in the Orient the singular opinion has long been held of regarding fools as the inspired of Heaven: they are named the saints of God, whilst in Europe all the inspired of Heaven pass for fools. While this naked Turk was giving himself up to these acts of folly, an old Mussulman woman comes up. "With one hand," says the author who furnishes me this anecdote, "she draws her veil aside in order to let him see a part of her face, and with the other she takes, kneeling, that part of the fool which decency does not permit naming, although it was dirtier than mud itself, and kisses it and carries it to her forehead. The saint makes no resistance. The woman goes on her way; and the fool, with a disdainful air, continues his nonchalant walk."
(Voyage en Orient, *by M. A. D. B., chap.* II.).

At Rosette, Pokoke saw two of these fools qualified as saints: they were naked, and women were devoutly rendering them the same homage.

25. *See chap.* VI, *note* 7. *Also, for another version of Siva's adoption of the* Lingam *as his symbol, see Dubois,* Hindu Manners, Customs and Ceremonies, *3rd ed., pp. 629-631.* —Trans.

26. Voyage de l'Ambassade de la Compagnie orientale Hollandaise vers l'empereur de la Chine.

27. Voyage en Chine, *by John Barrow, t. 2, p. 321.*

CHAPTER VII

1. Histoire des Incas, *by Garcilaso de la Vega, liv. 2, chap. 6.*

2. Histoire de la Floride, *by the same.*

3. *This manuscript dissertation was communicated to me by Moreau de Saint-Méri, conseiller d'Etat.*

CHAPTER VIII

1. *Herodotus,* Euterpe, *liv. 2, sec. 49.*

2. *Plutarch,* Treatise on Isis and Osiris.

3. *Herodotus,* Euterpe, *sec. 51.*

4. *This denomination derives, they say, from* Nysa, *a city [often given as a mountain] where Jupiter had Bacchus carried by Mercury in order there to be raised by the nymphs, or from the name of* Nysa, *daughter of Aristæus, who nursed him. These are some fables: Bacchus was raised by no one, nor in any city. Bacchus was the sun; and this*

name came to him from the country of Cous, in Thebaïs. The syllable ab *or* ba *signifies* father, master, god: *thus the name* Bacchus *ought to be interpreted as* father *or* god *of* Cous. *As for the name* Dionysus, *it is the same as* Adon, Adonis, Adonaï, *or* Dionis, *which signify* master, lord: *appellations which have always been given to the sun.*

5. *Plutarch,* Moralia, Treatise on the Love of Riches, *toward the end.*

6. Aretæus, *lib. 2. Auctorum, cap. 12.*

7. *Theodoretus, cited by Castellan,* de Festis Græcorum, Dionysia, *p. 101.*

8. Arnobii adversus Gentes opera, *lib. 5, p. 177, edit. of 1651.* Clement. Alexand. Propterpt. *Arnobius and Clement of Alexandria are not the only Church Fathers who have reported this fable: it is found with these circumstances in* Julius Firmicus, de Errore profanarum Religionum; *in* Theodoretus, Sermon 8, de Martyibus; *in* Nicetas, *on* Gregory of Nazianzus, *orat. 39, p. 829, etc. See, in addition,* Observationes ad Arnobium Gebharti Elmenhorstii, *p. 171.*

9. *Juvenal, in speaking of the extreme licence of these mysteries, says (satire 2, v. 95): ....* Vitreo bibit ille Priapo.

10. *Tertullian,* Adversus Valentitianos, Tertulliani opera, *p. 250.*

11. *Castellanus,* de Festis Græcorum, Eleusinia, *pp. 143-144.*

12. *Mélanges* de critique et de philologie, *by Chardon de la Rochette, tom. 3, p. 202. Preface by Dom Lobineau, to his manuscript translation of* Aristophanes.

13. *Arnobius,* Adversus Gentes, *liv. 5, pp. 174-175.* Godescalc. Stevech., *in Arnob. Observat. Elmenthorst., Desid. Heraldi animadversiones, etc.*

14. Histoire religieuse du Calendrier, *by Court de Gébelin, p. 436.*

15. *Today named* Laspi. *(There is no town today on the site of old Lampsacus, to the best of my knowledge, but there is a little village nearby which bears the name of* Lamsaki. —Trans.)

16. *Stobæus,* Serm. 11.

17. *This should more properly be a Naiad. Naiad is not the name of an individual, but rather of one class of the* Nymphæ, *those inhabiting fresh waters: rivers, lakes, brooks, springs, etc. Since water is so essential to all vari-*

*eties of growth and fruitfulness, it is only to be expected
that the Naiads should in some way be associated with
Priapus. —Trans.*

18. *One sees that this fable has the same basis as that
reported by the scholiast of Aristophanes on the origin of
the cult of the* Phallus *in Attica.*

19. *Lactantius*, de falsa Religione, *lib. 1, cap.21. Hyginus,*
Pœticum astronomicon, cap. 33.

20. *Pausanias, liv. 9,* Beotia, *chap. 31.*

21. *Baudelot, in his work entitled:* Utilité des Voyages,
*has given engravings of these two medals, tom. 1, pp. 343
& 344.*

22. *This city, if I do not err, was named Priapus, whilst
the surrounding district bore the names Priapus and Pria-
pene. Also, the name of the small island near Ephesus is
usually given as Priapus. However, in rendering Greek
names, —us, —os, and even —is are used almost interchange-
ably, so these differences mean little after all. —Trans.*

23. *Pliny. liv. 5, chap. 31.*

24. *Idem, liv. 5.*

25. *Pausanias, Elis, liv. 6, chap. 26.*

26. *Pausanias, Beotia, liv. 9, chap. 31.*

27. *See the work of Knight, on the cult of Priapus, where
this monument is engraven.*

28. *The Orphic rites, naturally, had chiefly to do with
Orpheus, who is said to have introduced mystic worship
into Greece. However, this worship was quite complicated
and is none too well understood today, but it is known that
it become related with the worship of many gods, especially
Bacchus. Of Phanes I can tell nothing. —Trans.*

29. *Warburton attributes the cause of this degradation
of the* Phallus *which figured in the mysteries, to the indecent allegories and nocturnal assemblies; but it is indeed
rather the human passions which install themselves, so to
speak, in institutions and corrupt them after having dis-
placed the primitive spirit which dominates them.*

30. *Iamblichus,* de Mysteriis Ægyptiorum, *sec. 1, cap. 41.*

31. *Arnobius,* Adversus Gentes, *lib. 5, p. 176.*

32. *Lactantius,* de falsa Religione, *lib. 1, p. 120.*

33. *Evagrius,* Ecclesiastical History, *liv. 2, chap. 2.*

34. *Nicephorus died about 1450. His History extended
from the birth of Christ to the death of Phocas, 610. —Trans.*

Textual Notes

35. *Nicephorus Callistus*, Ecclesiastical History, *liv. 14, chap. 48.*

CHAPTER IX

1. Dictionnaire *of Pitiscus, the word* Deus.

2. *The* Corybantes *were priests consecrated to various deities, and particularly to Cybele; but, as Clement of Alexandria also names them* Cabiri, *it is probable that the priests who went into Etruria were attached to the cult of the* Cabiri *gods, established from the time of the greatest antiquity in the island of Samothrace, and where the* Phallus *formed an essential part of the mysteries, as Herodotus tells.*

3. *Clement of Alexandria,* Protrept.

4. *St. Augustine,* de Civitate Dei, *liv. 6, chap. 9.*

5. Civit. Dei, lib. 7, cap. 21.

6. Ibid., lib. 7, cap. 24.

7. Dictionnaire abrégé *of Pitiscus, at the word Senaculum.* Geniales dierum, *of* Alexander ab Alexandro, lib. 3, cap.18. Pompeius Festus, *at the word* Mutinus, *and the Commentaries on this article.*

8. *The engraving of this antique stone is to be found in the collection entitled:* Du Culte secret des Dames Romaines. *(The proper title of this work is:* Monumens du Culte secret des Dames Romaines, *and it is commonly attributed to the antiquary Pierre d'Hancarville. —Trans.)*

9. *The emperor Heliogabalus, on the report of Lampridius, had an edifice erected on the Quirinal to serve for the assemblies of the Roman ladies, who gathered first of all in this place at the time of the solemnity of the Phallus. This edifice was called* Mæsa, *from the name of his ancestor [his grandmother], who presided over these assemblies with* Sœmias, *the mother of this Prince. He made of it a place of debauchery.* Crinitus *has preserved for us the text of the ordinance which established the rights and privileges of this feminine senate.*

10. *See the details of the excesses of the Bacchanalia in the following chapter.*

11. *The names* Mutinus, Tutinus, *are found variously spelled in the manuscripts of the ancient authors. In the verses of Lucillius,* Mœtinus *is taken as a sort of talisman; there one also reads* Mutinus. *In Festus one finds* Mutinus

and Titinus; *in Arnobius and in Saint Augustine*, Mutunus, Motunus, Mutinus, Tutunus; *in Lactantius and Tertullian*, Mutunus *and* Tutunus. *But some manuscripts and one old edition of Tertullian carried* Futinus, *which has perhaps given rise to* Saint Foutin, *who will be spoken of later. Jean Guillelme thinks that one must read* Mutonus, *from which has been made, he says,* mutoniatus, *which signifies a man strongly constituted in a certain respect. Some scholars are divided on the question to know if one of these names means* muet [*dumb*], mutin [*obstinate*], *or* mouton [*sheep*]. *It may be that* Tutunus *has given birth to those caressing names of* tonton, toutou [*pet*]. *It would be more important to know if these two words express two things or only one. The ancient authors always unite them to express the figure of the* Phallus. *It is probable that two varities of* Phallus *existed, the figures of which were distinguished by differences which are unknown.*

12. *This god presided over the marital act, but he was not the only one: the Romans were accustomed in this affair, as well as in a great many others, to call many gods to their aid. Meursius presents a list of these conjugal deities* (Antiquités, *tom. 5*, de Puerperio), *which Beyer enlarges* (Addimenta ad Selden, *cap. 16.*) *Saint Augustine* (Civit. Dei, *liv. 4, chap. 11*) *has completed the catalogue of these obscene deities. Among many others, there are to be noticed the god* Jugatinus, *who brings husband and wife together; the goddess* Virginiensis, *who detaches the virginal girdle of the newly married bride;* Volupia, *who excites to voluptuousness;* Stimula, *who stimulates the desires of the husband;* Strenia, *who gives him the vigor he has need of; and this great Saint does not forget* Mutinus *and* Tutunus *in his nomenclature. He says elsewhere that the god* Liber *is thus named because, in action, he procures for the men who invoke him the advantage of a reproductive emission.* Libera, *whom he believes to be the same as Venus, grants the same favor to women: that is why the figure of the masculine sex is placed in the temple of Liber, and that of the feminine sex in the one of Libera.* (De Civitate Dei, *liv. 6, chap. 9*)

13. *Saint Augustine*, Civit. Dei, lib. 6, cap. 9.

14. Lactant., de falsa Religione, lib. 1.

15. *Arnob.*, lib. 4, p. 131.

16. Dictionnaire *of Pitiscus, the word* Mutinus.

17. *Meursius,* Græciæ Feriatæ, *tom. 5,* de Puerperio.

18. *Arnob., lib. 4, p. 133.*

19. *Festus, the words* Mutini, Titini, Sacellum.

20. *Varro,* de Lingua Latina, *lib. 6.*

21. *Pliny, lib. 29, cap. 4.*

22. *Pliny, lib. 28, cap. 4.*

23. *Much speculation has been expended on the significance of these little bells so often used in the worship of some of the ancient gods, especially Bacchus and Priapus; to say nothing of the cymbals of Cybele and the sistrum of Isis. R. P. Knight is probably crediting the ancient mind with too great metaphysical powers when he sees in these only symbols of the motion of the elements. However, he is doubtless nearer the truth when he adds that the ringing of bells and clashing of metals were generally employed in worship as a charm against the destructive and inert powers; that is, as a general stimulant. He further asserts that the name* Priapus *itself seems merely to be a corruption of the Greek word* clamorous. *See* Symbolical Language, *sec. 181. —Trans.*

24. *Baudelot,* Utilité des Voyages, *tom 1, p. 346;* Antiquités de Caylus, *tom. 4, p. 231.*

25. *See above, chap. 3.*

26. *Notes furnished by Dominique Forgès Davanzati, a prelate of Canosa.*

27. *See above p. 64.*

28. *M. de Chaduc, an Auvergnian antiquarian, had collected more than three or four hundred ithyphallic engraven stones of the most curious sort, according to Baudelot, "which, except for a few," he says, "are not found in the fine manuscript I saw: it appears evident that those into whose hands it has passed have removed them."* (Utilité des Voyages, *tom. 1, p. 343.) The collections of archeologists, and even certain printed collections, offer a very great variety of* Phalli, Fascina, *and* Priapi.

29. *See above, chapter 8, note 9. An ancient scholiast of Juvenal says that these Phalli of glass were named* Drillopotas.

30. *Pliny,* lib. 14, cap. 22, et Prooemium, lib. 33.

31. Ælii Lamprid. vet. ant. Heliogabal. Hist. Augustæ, *t. 1, p. 829.*

Textual Notes

32. Jul. Capitolini in Pertin. Hist. Augustæ, *t. 1, p. 553.*

33. *For this reason Priapus was often called* ruber *or* rubicundus. —*Trans.*

34. *Columella,* de Cultu hortorum, *lib. 10.*

35. *This is expressed by the two verses of the first piece in the collection entitled* Priapeia. *See also Horace, liv. 1, satire 8.*

36. *Horace, satire 8, liv. 1, v. 5.*

37. *This prerogative of the god Priapus over the roads is indicated by the twenty-ninth piece of the* Priapeia: *See the Commentary of Joseph Scaliger on this piece.* Priapeia, *p. 141.*

38. *If Dulaure means to say that these things made up the only differences between the representations of these gods, he may be correct; but if he means to imply, as his words seem to indicate, that these were the only differences between the gods themselves, he is so obviously in error that I feel it unnecessary to point it out in detail.* —*Trans.*

39. Petronii Satiricon.

40. *This custom is attested to by piece 37 of the* Priapeia, *entitled:* Voti solutio.

41. *Several antique monuments, and especially some engraven stones, represent similar offerings. In the collection entitled:* Du Culte secret des Dames Romaines, *a monument is to be seen which gives an idea of it. A piece of verse of the* Priapeia *(No. 40) speaks of a celebrated prostitute, called Telethusa, who, overwhelmed with the favors of love and the profits of prostitution, makes a similar offering to Priapus, qualified by* holy *in the poem. In piece 50, a young girl promises some wreaths to Priapus, if he hearkens to her prayers.*

42. *This practice is represented on an engraven stone* (Culte secret des Dames Romaines), *and is mentioned in piece 43 of the* Priapeia.

43. *Virgil,* Georg. lib. 4.

44. Priapeia, carm. 73. *Horace,* sat. 8, lib. 1.

45. *This fact is proved by several pieces in the* Priapeia. *It even seems that the* Priapeia, *and this is the opinion of savants who have annotated this work in a scholarly fashion, has been made up of different pieces gathered from the walls of the chapels of Priapus. It is probable that they are*

not the work of Virgil, as many have believed because they have been found placed at the end of his works.

(I am surprised that Dulaure entertains the thought of even the bare possibility of Virgil's being the author of the Priapeia. The authors of the majority of the pieces are un-established. Not only were little dedicatory and sportive epigrams to be found on the walls of various chapels to Priapus, but his hermæ, even when very crude, usually carried one or more of them. It was not uncommon for col-lections of these epigrams to be made by various poets, these collections being known as priapeiæ. *Only one of these col-lections has been preserved to us, and it is known as the Priapeia. The authors of the majority of the pieces are un-known. —Trans.)*

CHAPTER X

1. Genesis, *chap. 9, v. 1 & 7.*
2. Genesis, *chap. 16, v. 1 ff.*
3. Idem, *chap. 22, v. 24.*
4. Idem, *chap. 19, v. 8 ff.*
5. Idem, *chap. 19, v. 31 ff.*
6. Idem, *chap. 29, v. 28-29; chap. 30, v. 1 & 9.*
7. Idem, *chap. 35, v. 22.*
8. Idem, *chap. 38, v. 8, 13 & ff.*
9. Kings, *Bk. 3, chap. 10, v. 23.*
10. Kings, *chap. 11, v. 1, 2, 3 & ff.*
11. Jephthah *is the name of the father; the Bible does not give the daughter's name. —Trans.*
12. Judges, *chap. 11, v. 37-38.*
13. Voyage aux Indes et à la Chine, *t. 1, p. 123, 2nd edi-tion.*
14. *On the origin of this cult and of the deity Venus, see the work entitled:* Des Cultes qui ont précédé et amené l'idolâtrie, *chap 21.*
15. Temple de Gnide, *first canto.*
16. *Baruch, chap. 6, v. 42-43.*
17. *Strabo, lib. 16.*
18. *Herodotus, Clio, chap. 199.*
19. *Justinus, lib. 18.*
20. Selden de Diis Syris, Syntagm. 2, cap. 7, p. 234; Addimenta Beyeri, p. 310; *Elias, Schedius,* de Diis Ger-

manis, cap. 9, p. 123; *third* Mémoire *on the Phœnicians,* tom. 38, p. 59.

21. *Valerius Maximus,* lib. 2, cap. 6, sect. 15, p. 235.

22. Treatise on the Syrian Goddess, *in the works of Lucian.*

23. *Saint Augustine,* Civit. Dei, lib. 4, cap. 10.

24. *Eusebius,* Vita Constantini, lib. 3, cap. 53 & 56; *Theodoretus,* Ecclesiastical History, lib. 1, cap. 8. *The temple of the Aphacians was very ancient. The author of the Treatise on the Syrian Goddess speaks of it as of a venerable antiquity. Eusebius paints a frightful picture of it. It was, according to him, old ruins, surrounded by shrubbery and dense brush, to which no road or path led. The priests of the temple there held a school of debauchery. Effeminate men, shameless, in order to appease the demon which presided there, mutually gave themselves up to the excesses of the most shameful libertinage. Moreover, married men and women mingled there, confused themselves together, and assuaged the violence of their desires. . . . He relates similar things of the temple at Heliopolis, and says that the inhabitants there prostituted their daughters to the strangers who passed through their country.*

25. Deuteronomy, *chap. 23, v. 17-18.*

26. Mém. de l'Académie des Inscriptions, *tom. 38, p. 59-60.*

27. Kings, *bk. 4, chap. 23, v. 7. (Dulaure's version of this differs slightly from the King James' version, which is: "And he brake down the houses of the sodomites, that were by the house of the Lord, where the women wove hangings for the grove." These "hangings" were probably no more than the bright ribbons and garlands with which it was the custom to "hang" Priapus and other fertility gods. —Trans.)*

28. *Strabo, lib. 2.*

29. *Ælianus,* Varia Historia, *liv. 4, chap. 1.*

30. *Herodotus,* Clio, *chap. 93.*

31. *The Augilæ, if I mistake not, were not a different people from the Nasamones, as one might be led to believe from Dulaure; but rather were they a tribe of the Nasamones. This tribe got its name from the custom of going every year to the oasis of Augila, in the Great Desert of*

Africa, in order to gather the fruit from the date palms which abounded there. —Trans.

32. *Herodotus,* Melpomene, *chap. 172.*

33. *Herodotus,* Euterpe, *chap. 135. There can here be added the example offered by the Gindanes, a people of Libya, neighbors of the Macæ. Their women each wear around their ankles as many bands of leather as men they have known: the one who has most is the most esteemed as having been loved by the greatest number of men. (Herodotus,* Melpomene, *chap. 176.)*

34. *Pausanias,* Corinthia, *chap. 34.*

35. *These two names are entirely unknown to me, so I leave them in their French form. They can scarcely be daughters of Prœtus. He, in truth, had three daughters, usually called the* Prœtides, *but their names were Lysippe, Iphinoë, and Iphianassa. These girls were stricken with madness for reasons which are variously related: some say it was because they despised the worship of Dionysus; others, because they presumed to consider themselves more handsome than Hera, or had stolen some gold from her statue, etc. As these were all the daughters Prœtus had, in fact, all his children except for a son Megapenthes, I cannot imagine what Dulaure intends by the above names. —Trans.*

36. *Ælianus,* Varia Historia, *liv. 3, chap. 42. When the ancients had forgotten the motive of the primitive institutions, the cults maintained themselves only through fear of the anger of the gods. In the* Hippolytus *of Euripides, Phædra is represented as an unfortunate victim of the anger of Venus: the lawless love which torments her is the work of this persecuting deity. Racine has entered into the sense of the Greek tragedian, in having his* Phèdre *told: C'est Vénus tout entière à sa proie attachée. (It's Venus wholly intent upon her seized prey.).*

37. *The public courtesans were, at Rome as in Greece, priestesses of Venus. Ovid testifies to it in his* Fasti, *on the occasion of the vinic and floral fêtes consecrated to this goddess. "Young girls, devoted to public pleasures, celebrate the divinity of Venus, honor her with an assiduous worship; this goddess procures wealth for those who make a profession of giving themselves up to the caresses of the vulgar. Ask of her, incense in hand, beauty, the favor of the people, the art of enticing gestures, of seductive words,*

etc." (Fasti, *liv. 3.) In the same book of the* Fasti, *Ovid says of the floral fête: "But why does the troupe of courtesans celebrate these games?"*

38. *Herodotus,* Clio, *chap. 182.*

39. Voyage dans le Mogol et l'Indoustan, *by Bernier.—* Essais historiques sur l'Inde, *by Delaflotte, p. 218.*

40. *See the* Voyage en Orient *by Bernier, and especially that of Henri Grosse, as well as the note of Langlès on the* Voyage Norden, *p. 319.*

41. *Multas illa facit, quod fuit ipsa Jovi.*

42. *Aut apud Isiacæ potius sacraria lenæ. (Satire 6, v. 489.)*

43. *Satire 9, v. 22.*

44. *Herodotus,* Euterpe, *chap. 64.*

45. *Satire 9, v. 24.*

46. *Livy, fourth decade, liv. 9, or the edition of* Drakenborchius, *liv. 39, chap. 8, 9, 10, & 11.*

47. *Doubtless Juvenal, using his privilege as a poet, has overdrawn the picture; but, suppressing the exaggerations I suppose in him, enough facts will remain to us, especially if there is added to them what Livy has preserved for us of the ancient Bacchanalia, to decide that the Romans had abused this cult as indecently as had the Greeks and Orientals.*

48. *Vita Sancti Romani. Thesaur. anecdot., tom. 3, p. 1656.*

49. *After so much unimpeachable testimony, so many combined proofs of the existence of religious prostitution, one will doubtless be astonished to learn that a man, justly famous for his philosophy, for his genius, for the brilliance and universality of his talents, that Voltaire, in his* Dictionnaire philosophique, *at the word* Babel, *has treated what Herodotus and his translator Larcher report on this subject, as fables, as tales from the* Thousand and One Nights. *"These tales of Herodotus" he says, "are today so decried by all honest people, reason has made such great progress, that even old women and children no longer believe such foolishness." It would be easy to be right against Voltaire here: to his opinion, devoid of proofs, could be opposed the testimony of the whole of antiquity. But a refutation in due form is not necessary: the numerous authorities I have just cited are a sufficient answer; I hold myself to that. I merely*

*wish to place here, for the instruction of the reader, some reflections made by a man who has more fully observed the manners of the different oriental nations and who has travelled more than Voltaire: "One judges ancient peoples badly when he takes as a basis of comparison our opinions and our customs. . . . he gratuitously gives himself hindrances of contradiction in supposing in them a wisdom in conformance with our principles: we reason too much according to our ideas, and not enough according to theirs." (*Voyage en Syrie et en Egypte, *by Volney, tom. 1.)*

50. *Herodotus,* Euterpe, *chap. 102; Diodorus Siculus, liv. 1, sect. 65.*

51. *Diodorus Siculus, liv. 1. This act recalls that of Catherine Sforza. Her subjects, in rebellion, having seized her children and threatening to kill them, this woman, more courageous than modest, uncovered herself before the eyes of the rebels and said to them: "There is the wherewithal for having other children."*

52. Kings, *bk. 2, chap. 6, v. 14 ff., 20, 21, & 22. This reference should be to Samuel. —Trans.*

53. *On this matter, I scarcely need call the readers attention, I imagine, to the similarity between the words* testimony *and* testicles, *or to the fact that in Latin the word* testis *is used to express both* witness *and* testicles. *—Trans.*

54. *Mémoires sur l'Egypte, published during the campaigns of Bonaparte, second part, p. 195.—Extract from a letter of Adjutant-general Julien to Citizen Geoffroy, a member of the* Institut d'Egypte, *of Rosette, 20th of Vendémiaire, year 7.*

55. Voyage dans le département du Finistère, *tom. 3, p. 233.*

56. Leviticus, *chap. 18, v. 3, 6, etc.*

57. Leviticus, *chap. 18, v. 24-25.*

58. *Herodotus,* Euterpe, *chap. 60. What is remarkable is that, almost to the last detail, this custom was also practiced in France; and the banks of the Seine, like those of the Nile, offered similar assaults, similar responses.*

59. *Justinus,* Hist., lib. 1. cap. 7.

60. *Plutarch,* Moralia, Treatise on Courageous Actions of Women, *chap. 6.*

61. *Tacitus,* Annales.

62. *Tacitus,* Hist., lib. 2, cap. 3.

63. *Frenchmen who have travelled recently in Egypt have experienced this complete difference between the various objects which affect the modesty among the Egyptian women and the European: they have noticed Egyptian women, occupied with work in the fields or on the banks of a river, who, at the approach of a man, and especially a foreigner, hasten to raise their clothing and uncover their backsides in order to hide their faces.*

64. *Plutarch, Life of Lycurgus, chap. 21 & 22. There has been much argument about the institutions of Lycurgus, and especially about those of which I have just spoken. There has been a great cry against the indecency of those girls offered naked to public view, and even on the still more provoking indecency of their ordinary costume, which left a part of their thighs uncovered. In order sanely to judge of such institutions, one ought to begin by stripping himself of his prejudices, then to become acquainted with the situation, the character of the people among whom they have been established, their relation with neighboring peoples, and the various characteristics of these latter; by carrying oneself back, if possible, to the time in which the legislator lived; to learn his data and means. . . . Lycurgus felt the necessity of forming for his republic men of an extraordinary stamp, of a strength of body and soul capable of making his work prosper. He knew that the women contributed a great deal in a nation to form the character of the men; he extended his institution to the sources of existence. He needed neither delicate, prudish, nor timid women, but* viragoes *whose greatest virtue was love of the fatherland. This republic of Sparta, which has received the admiration of the ancients and moderns, lasted more than five hundred years.*

65. *Plato, Laws, tom. 1, liv. 6; and tom. 2, liv. 8.*

66. *Christian writers in their declamations have made us acquainted, better than the pagan writers, with the details of this cult.*

CHAPTER XI

1. *Manuscript* Mémoires *on the antiquities of Alsace and Mount Donon, accompanied by drawings. This singularity recalls another of the same sort to my mind. The bas-reliefs*

Textual Notes

on the tomb of King Dagobert, formerly to be seen at Saint-Denis and since in the gardens of the Museum of National Antiquities, represent the soul of this King at grips with devils. On one of these latter there is to be seen in place of the sex a human face.

2. No Celtic monument proves that this cult was established there before that period; for the supposed Phalli that Borel says he discovered near Castres must not be considered as productions of art, as objects of worship. Here is how this author expresses himself: "The second wonder of the country is the mountain called Puytalos, *which we can name mountain of the* Priapolithes, *because it is full of long round stones in the form of virile members.* ... *Besides conforming to the virile member, if they are cut a conduit is found in the center of crystal, which seems to be congealed sperm. To some testicles are found attached; others are covered with veins; and others show the balanus, and are eaten away as if having escaped from some venereal disease; and there are even stones found among them having the figures of the shameful parts of women, and sometimes they are found joined together; and some are found with a straight shape, others which are bent, etc.*" (Les Antiquités de la ville de Castre, *by Borel, bk. 2, p. 69.*)

It is probable that these are products of nature; varities of stalactites whose forms, extremely varied, often approach works of art.

3. Odin, or Woden or Godan, is evidently an Oriental deity, whose very name has scarcely been altered by the Germans. They have made the word Gott *of it, the generic name for deity, the adjective* gut, *good, fine, and* gotz, *idol. The signification of* joy *is given to this word, which is an emanation of deity; and the Latins take it in this sense, making their word* gaudium *from it. It is the same deity as the* Gotsuten-oo *of the Japanese, the* Godan *or* Wodan *of Hindustan, and the* Pout, Boutan, Bœda, Boudham, *and* Gadma *or* Godam *of the Singhalese and Siamese.*

4. Thor was a sun-deity. Here, as in the Orient, the cult of the Phallus was united with that of this star.

5. Atlantic., *tom. 2, pp. 293-294.*

6. De Bello punico. *lib. 3, v. 395.*

7. Antiquités de Nîmes, *by Gautier, p. 60, and* Descriptions des principaux lieux de France, *tom. 2, p. 162.*

Textual Notes

8. Nouveaux Mélanges de l'Histoire de France, *tom. 2, p. 28.*

9. *Details furnished by M. le baron Caila, the author of the discovery of this amulet.*

10. *Bulletin of the excavations made, by order of the King, of a Roman city on the little mountain of the Châtelet, p. 18.*

11. *Ibid., p. 51.*

12. *Archeology of* Mons Seleucus, *a Roman city in the country of the* Vocontii, *today Labatie-Mont-Saléon, prefecture of the Hautes-Alpes, at Gap, 1806, p. 35.*

13. *Vialart de Saint-Morys has had the kindness to send me a copy of this in wax. Grivaud has had it engraved in his* Recueil d'antiquités.

14. Monuments antiques, *unpublished, by A. L. Millin, tom. 1, p. 262.*

15. *See the letter which Aldegore, Archbishop of Magdeburg, and the prelates or secular princes wrote to the bishops of Saxony, Lorraine, and France, in vol. 1, p. 625-626 of the* Amplissima Collectio veterum scriptorum.

CHAPTER XII

1. Judicia sacerdotalia de criminibus. (Veterum scriptorum amplissima collectio, *vol. 7, p. 35.*)

2. *Burchard, lib.* 10, cap. 49.

3. Statuta Synodalia Ecclesiæ Cenoman. (Amplissima collectio veterum scriptorum, *vol. 7, p. 1377.*)

4. Supplément au Glossaire de Du Cange, *by Carpentier, the word* Fascinare.

5. *The drawings of this artist, intended for the* Académie des Belles-Lettres, *have passed, no one knows how, into the hands of an individual who is depriving the public of them.*

6. Voyage aux Indes et à la Chine, *tom. 1, p. 322.*

7. Genesis, *chap 30, v. 14 ff.*

8. *See in the depository of the manuscripts of the* Bibliothèque royale, *section of Baluze, roll n. 5.*

9. Journal de Paris, sous les regnes de Charles VI et Charles VII, *p. 121.*

10. *Here is what Jacques Grevin, a doctor, relates on the preparations to which this* little man, *formed from the root of the mandragora, is subjected: "The imposters carve out of the said (plants), whilst they are still green, the*

form of a man or woman, and six grains of millet or barley at the places where they want hair to be. Then, having made a hole in the ground, they bury it and cover it over with fine sand, until the little grains have thrown out their roots, which they say to be perfect in the space of twenty days at most. Then they take it up again, and with a very sharp knife they trim the little filaments of the grains and adapt them so well that they resemble the beard, head hair, and other hairs of the body. They make the simple people, stupid and foolish, believe that these roots representing the figure of a man can be taken from the earth only with great peril and danger to life, and that in order to extract them they attach a dog to them, and that they stop up their ears with wax for fear of hearing the cries of the root; which heard would make them all die, without a single one of them being able to escape. The virtues which are related as being in this little man, thus made and forged, are strange: they say that it is engendered beneath a gibbet, from the urine of a hanged thief, and that it has great power against storms and I know not what other calamities. All these are but follies." (De l'imposture des Diables *by Jacques Grevin, liv. 4, pl. 339.*)

(This is a bit vague and incomplete. After the root is partially exposed and a dog tied to it with a cord, the men were supposed to retire to a safe distance, stop up their ears, and call the dog. The dog, evidently immune to those horrible shrieks the root would give out, would come running, trailing the root after him. As for the root's being the product of a hanged thief's urine, this is a bit inexact. As is known, a man when hanged dies with his penis in erection, and frequently ejaculates his sperm before dying. As thieves in the old day were hanged out in the open, this sperm was said to penetrate the earth and there to give birth to a mandragora. —Trans.)

The author of the Maison rustique, *at the word* Mandragore, *says that there were males and females of them; that the forms of the two sexes, masculine and feminine, were easily given them. "One of these roots,"* he adds, *"is named* hand of glory. *Shut up preciously in a box, everyday it doubles what money one has. These roots pass as an assured remedy against sterility." It is here to be seen that they have the property of* Phalli; *and* main de gloire [*hand of*

Textual Notes

glory], *from which perhaps is derived the word* mandragoire *or* mandragore [*mandragora*], *recalls the* main ithyphallique [*ithyphallic hand*] *of the antiquarians.*

"I have seen," says Abbé Rosier (Cours complet d'Agriculture, tom. 6, p. 401), "mandragoras which represented the parts of men and women well enough; and this resemblance is readily achieved. To this end a mandragora is chosen with a sturdy root which, after a distance of several inches, splits into two branches. As this root is soft, it easily takes any iimpression that is desired to give it, and preserves it on drying." The same author then speaks of the proper procedure for bringing about hairs: it is the same as that of which Jacques Grevin speaks, and which I have just cited.

11. *The Syracusans, says Athenæus, at the time of the Thermophoria, sent through all Sicily, to their friends, cakes made of honey and sesame. These cakes had the form of the feminine sex. The Romans made breads with wheaten flour which presented the figure of one or the other sex. Martial speaks of one in this verse of bk. 9, epig. 3:* Illa siligineis pinguescit adultera cunnis. *He makes mention of the others in his epigram 69 of book 4, which has for a title:* Priapus siligineis.

12. Tractatus de superstitionibus, D. Martini de Arles.

13. Malleus Maleficorum, fratris Jacobi Sprenger, *part 2, quest. 1, chap. 7, entitled:* Quomodo membra virilia auferentur. *Brother Jacques Sprenger adds, as is his custom, a little tale. Here it is: "It is reported that an individual, having lost his virile member through diabolical art, went to a sorceress in order to recover it. She showed him a nest at the foot of a tree which contained many members, and told him that he could take the one which pleased him. He wanted to take a very large one. 'Do not take that one,' says the sorceress, 'it is not for you. It belongs to a common workman.' " Master Inquisitor of the Faith was facetious.*

14. Essais *of Montaigne, liv. 3, chap. 5.*

15. Idem, ibid.

16. *I am going to cite only one of these magical operations. Our chaste language would not be able to support the translation of the others which Burchard, Bishop of Worms, has transmitted to us in the Latin of the Church: "Have you not done what certain women are accustomed*

*to do? They strip themselves of their clothing, anoint their
naked bodies with honey, spread a sheet on the ground
on which they scatter some wheat, and roll on this over and
over again. Then they carefully collect all the grains which
have fastened on their body and place them on a mill-stone,
which they turn in the reverse direction. When these are
reduced to flour, they make a bread of it which they give
their husbands to eat, in order that they may weaken and
die. If you have done this, you shall do penance for forty
days on bread and water." (Burchard,* de Pœnitentia, Decretorum lib. 19.)

17. *(Burchard,* de Pœnitentia, Decretorum lib. 19.*)*

18. Collectio antiqua Canonum pœnitentialium. Thesaurus Anecdotorum, *tom. 4, p. 52.*

19. Glossary of Du Cange, *the word* Machinamentum.

20. *Burchard,* lib. 19, *8 vol. ed., p. 277.*

CHAPTER XIII

1. *In several pieces of the* Priapeia *this god is qualified
as* saint [holy]. *Ancient inscriptions are to be found in
which Bacchus and his companion Eleutherus bear the
same title.
(I know of no companion of Bacchus by the name of
Eleutherus. One of Jupiter's surnames is* Eleutherius, *but
he could hardly be termed a companion of Bacchus. I
wonder if Dulaure could have become confused on Saint
Eleutherus, who was a Pope of the second century.
—Trans.)*

2. Journal d'Henri III, *by L'Etoile, tom. 5;* Confession de
Sancy, *liv. 2, chap. 2; and the notes of Le Duchat on this
chapter.*

3. Idem.

4. Confession de Sancy, *liv. 2, chap. 2, and the notes of
Le Duchat.*

5. Histoire religieuse du Calendrier, *p. 420.*

6. *Extract from a* Mémoire addressé à l'Académie Celtique, *by M. L. R. . . .*

7. Thæses inaugurales de Vinginibus; Facetiæ facetiarum,
p. 277.

8. St. Guerlichon *or* St. Grelichon, *as Pierre Viret names
him in his* Traité de la vraie ou fausse Religion *(liv. 7, chap.
35.) Le Duchat believes that this name has come to him*

261

from gracilis (grelot) [*a small bell*]. *For the rest, this name is yet today a trivial injury, applied ordinarily to a base man, or attached shamefully to a prostitute.*

9. Apologie pour Hérodote, *chap. 38.*—Traité de la vraie et fausse Religion, *by Pierre Viret, liv. 7, chap. 35.*

10. *Extract from a letter of Pastureaud de Vaux.*

11. *Le Duchat, in his notes on the* Apologie pour Hérodote, *thinks that the fecundating power is attributed to* St. Gilles *because his name bears a relation with* eschilles, *which signifies little bells.*

12. *St. René was set up as Priapus because of the relation of his name with the word* reins [*loins*]. *For the same reason, similar honor was paid* St. Regnaud.

13. *Some persons will be thankful to me for not reporting the verses cited by Le Duchat on the powers of Saint Regnaud.*

14. Tableau des differentes Religions, *by Sainte-Aldegonde, tom. 1, part. 5, chap. 10.*

15. *This Saint, called* Guinolé, Guignolé, Guignolet, Gunolo, Vennolé, Guingalais, Winwalœus, *was the first Abbot of Landevenec, in Basse-Bretagne, in the year 480. His various legends offer ridiculous fables. It is doubtless the relation which is to be found between his name and the word* gignere, *to engender, that has won the attributes and powers of Priapus for this Saint.*

16. Anecdotes relative à quelques personnes et à plusiers événements remarquables de la Révolution, *by M. J.—B. Harmand (de la Meuse), former deputy and ex-prefect of the department of the Bas-Rhin, 1814, pp. 90-91.*

17. Voyage dans le Finistère, *fait en 1794 et 1795, tom. 2, p. 150.*

18. *Cambry, author of the interesting* Voyage dans le Finistère, *has furnished me this last circumstance and has assured me of having himself seen the Saint and his peg. He has authorized me to publish his testimony.*

19. *Extract from a letter addressed to the author by Barailon, Doctor of Medicine, corresponding member of the* Institut, *and member of the* Corps Législatif.

20. Johannis Goropii Becani, Origines Antwerpianæ, *1569, lib. 1, pp. 26 & 101.*

21. Johannis Goropii Becani, Origines Antwerpianæ, *lib. 1, p. 101.*

Textual Notes

22. Itinerarium Belgico-Gallicum, *p. 52*.

23. Itinerarium Galliæ, Jodoci Sinceri, *p. 234*.

24. *See above, chap. 8, p. 96*.

25. *These breads were named* p. . . .; *the solemnity was known by the name of the* fête des pin. . . . *(The word intended here is* pinne; *a popular and vulgar term for* penis. —Trans.)

26. *"Where is the pillar that makes women fertile?" asked a simple village woman of a bulky canon of this church. "It is I," he answered, striking himself on the chest, "it is I who am the pillar."*

27. *In the middle of this chapel is a tomb in the form of a camp bed on which the figure of Saint-Antoine-de-Paule is to be seen, lying in a coffin in the habit of the Order. Sterile ladies are introduced, one after the other, into this place. They kneel down, say some prayers, make the circuit of the tomb three times, lie down upon it, and then retire. A writer, an enemy to the monks of this monastery, who has employed three volumes in revealing their pious frauds, says that they also introduced, for money, into this secret place the lovers of the ladies who came to invoke Saint Antoine, and that the miracle took place without the Saint's meddling in it; but this is perhaps a calumny.*

28. *This expression, of course, comes from the old days of doublet and hose; and the* point *was the string used to tie them together. Consequently, knotting this string would leave a man handicapped in various ways. The expression was applied figuratively to men who found themselves suffering from certain inabilities; to imply that to all intents and purposes they might just as well have their point tied up. A modern equivalent might be,* button up the flap; *or more emphatically,* sew up the flap. *For an excellent account of this matter, see John Davenport's* Aphrodisiacs and Anti-aphrodisiacs. —Trans.

29. *There still existed in this country some years ago a famous* fascinier, *named Gabriel Roux, alais Damiens. He was a petty farmer at the place of Petit-Cros, in the canton of Chambon, commune of Châtelet. He was killed on the 11th of Fructidor of the year 10, by a miller who had been married for three years without being able to have any children, and who accused the* fascinier *Roux of his impotence. A curé of this country has assured the one who*

has communicated this fact to me that several fasciniers whom he converted pronounced, in order to work their charms, some Latin words, and were careful to slip into the food of the husbands a powder coming from the dried sexual parts of a wolf. . . . As for the saint vinage, it was and still is in great use in many villages of France. I have discovered in an old ritual manuscript the orison that the priest recited to bless it. It is entitled: Benediction of the love of Saint John the Evangelist.

CHAPTER XIV

1. *This, alas, is now sadly changed. I was amazed, and a bit stunned, at Rome a few years ago, to see that the present Pope was having plaster of Paris fig-leaves carefully cemented over the genitals of the ancient Greek and Roman statues of the Olympian gods reposing in the Vatican; as well as over those of all other ancient art works which to his fine, clean mind required expurgation. But most of my sympathy went to the old gods. What an ignoble present for beings with such a glorious, robust past! In short, their conversion to Christianity has become complete. I expect on my next trip there to find that he is having the Sleeping Ariadne supplied with a brassière. Honi soit. . . etc. —Trans.*

2. *Note furnished by Dominique Forgès Davanzati, prelate of Canossa. (This ithyphallic or phallic hand when made with one's own hand—either by inserting the thumb between the middle and index fingers, or by extending the middle finger and clenching the rest of the hand—was a gesture of contempt when made toward some person. As Dulaure tells, the Italians call this* fica *or* fig; *and the reader will doubtless be surprised to learn that the apparently harmless expression, "I don't give a fig for you," is really a verbal manner of making this gesture and, properly understood, fighting words. —Trans.)*

3. *Suidas, at the word* Priapus.

4. *It is to a Neapolitan, Dominique Forgès Davanzati, nephew of the archbishop Davanzati and prelate of Canossa, that I owe this anecdote.*

5. *In the text of R. P. Knight the date is given as September 27. —Trans.*

6. *It is not I, but the Italian author who comments thus.*

7. *This Italian account is to be found inserted in an English*

work entitled: An account of the remains of the Worship of Priapus lately existing at Isernia in the Kingdom of Naples, *etc., by* R. P. Knight. *A terrible occurrence has just nearly annihilated the city of Isernia, and with it perhaps the last remains of the ancient cult of the* Phallus *in* Europe. *An earthquake which caused frightful ravages in a great part of the Kingdom of Naples, on the 7th of Thermidor, year 13 (or July 26, 1805), has reduced this city to a heap of ruins. More than fifteen hundred persons, they say, lost their lives there.*

CHAPTER XV

1. "Laudator temporis acti." Art of Poetry, *v. 173.*

2. *According to the author of a little volume called* Padlocks and Girdles of Chastity, *these facts relating to the end of da Carrara are "embellishments" added by Dulaure, and he advances reasonable evidence to support his contention. This small work referred to above is very interesting and informative on this subject, but can, I think, in no sense be said to be a profound or even serious study of the matter. The American edition, which came out a few years ago, is a translation of the French original published by Liseux back in, I think, the 90's but for some unknown reason the fact of its translation is not acknowledged. More detailed information on this can be found on p. 48 of Esar Levine's* Chastity Belts, Panurge Press, *1931. I cannot recommend this volume too highly as being the only really serious attempt ever made to gather together all the significant material on chastity girdles, and I refer the reader to it for all matters relating to them. —Trans.*

3. *Misson,* Voyage d'Italie, *tom. 1, p. 217.*

4. *Brantôme,* Dames galantes, *tom. 2, pp. 112-113. Rabelais speaks of these girdles, which he names* à la Bergamasque: *"The deuce . . . take me . . . if I do not buckle my wife in the Bergamask fashion when I go out from my seraglio." (*Pantagruel, *bk. 3, chap. 35.)*

5. Tableau de l'Amour considéré dans l'état du mariage, *part 2, chap. 2, art. 3.*

6. *Frequently called, especially by English writers, the* Judicial Congress. —Trans.

7. Discours sur l'impuissance de l'homme ou de la femme, *by Vincent Tagereau, Angevin, chap. 6.*

8. Traité premier de la Dissolution du Mariage pour l'impuissance et froideur de l'homme ou de la femme, *by Antoine Hotman, p. 63. One may consult on the same subject the* Traité de la dissolution du mariage pour cause d'impuissance, avec quelques pièces curieuses; *the* Dictionnaire *of Bayle, article* Quellenec; *the* Congrès de Cythère, *by the Marquis de Maffei, etc., etc.*

9. *I report a single example of this variety of penalty, taken from a cartulary of Champagne: "The woman who shall speak villainy of another, as with putage, shall pay five sols, or she shall carry the stone in procession quite naked in her chemise, and the other shall prick her in the buttocks with a needle." (Glossary of Carpentier, at the word* Naticæ.)

10. *For these different customs, see the Glossary of Du Cange, at the words* Processiones publicæ, Vilania, Lapides catenatos ferre, Putagium; *the Supplement to the said Glossary, by Carpentier, at the words* Approbatus, Forus, Naticæ; Les Coutumes et établissements du château Clermont-Soubiran, *printed at Agen in 1596. There is also to be seen there a wood-cut which represents this chastisement. See also Olaus Magnus,* De ritu gentium septent., *lib. 4, cap. 6.*

11. Fureteriana, *p. 224.*

12. *See the Glossary of Du Cange, at the word* Marcheta.

13. Histoire du Quercy, *by de Cathala-Coture, t. 1, chap. 10, p. 134 ff. I cannot share the opinion of the historian of Quercy. The dishonor is for him alone who orders and believes himself right in committing violence. The one who endures them in spite of himself is dishonored only in the mind of the common fool. The assassin and not the victim is criminal, and incurs public infamy. It is necessary to repeat this principle which, though very evident, has not yet entered into all heads, as is here instanced.*

14. Description historique, etc., des Etats de Parme, *by Moreau-Saint-Merry. (A manuscript.)*

15. Camillus Borellus, Bibliotheca Germ., *tom. 1;* Essais sur Paris, *by Saint-Foy, tom. 2, p. 172.*

16. Bœrius, Decis, *297, n. 17; Du Cange,* Glossaire, *at the word* Marcheta.

17. Essais historiques, *by Saint-Foy, tom. 5, pp. 157-158. The absurd, ridiculous, and indecent privileges to which*

the lords of the good old days *subjected their serfs or vassals, would offer a curious enough picture. I shall here report a single example of them, which is to be found recorded in the registers of the Chambre des Comptes (file 21
of the* Aveux du Bourbonnais, aveu de la terre de Breuil,
*given by Marguerite of Montluçon, September 27, 1398.)
After having established the privilege that these lords had
over women who beat their husbands, the act states: "Each
public woman who gives herself to any man, when, she enters the city of Montluçon for the first time must pay four
deniers on the bridge of that city, or there give* un pet
[*break wind*]," (Traité de la police, *by Delamare, tom. 1,
p. 493;* Glossaire of Du Cange, *at the word* Bombum, *etc.)*

There is to be found in this Glossary another example of
such a vulgar fine. He who, in England, held in fief lands
of sergeantship, in the territory of Hemingston, county of
Suffolk, was obliged to come to the court each year on
Christmas day and do a jump, whistle, and break wind before the King.

18. Glossaire *of Du Cange, at the word* Abatissæ, *and its*
Supplément, *by Carpentier, at the same word.*

19. De Gestis rerum Anglorum, Willelmi Malmerburien-
sis, *lib. 5, p. 170.*

20. Histoire générale du Languedoc, *tom. 4, Preuves, p.
370.* Ordonnances des Rois de France, *tom. 7, p. 327.*

21. Histoire générale du, Languedoc, *tom. 4, p. 465.*

22. Essais historiques sur Paris, *tom. 1, pp. 97-98.*

23. Histoire générale de Provence, *by Abbé Papon, tom.
3, pp. 180-181;* Description des principaux lieux de France,
tom. 1, p. 187; the Pornographe, *p. 350.*

24. Libertas et Franchesia Villæfranchæ, Description des
principaux lieux de France, *tom. 6, p. 170.*

25. *The above to be more nearly correct should read,
"places of prostitution of both sexes" rather than "for
both sexes." While houses of male prostitution catering to
the female trade are by no means unknown, still the very
great majority of them are for men. This is just as true today
as it was in the time when Rome was in its glory, although,
I confess, perhaps to a somewhat lesser degree. However,
let no one imagine that male prostitution is today dead, or
even of negligible proportions. Space prohibits my going in-*

to details on this, but they are plentiful and not hard to find. Dulaure's assumption that his time can offer no such "examples" is rather naïve. Paris, today as formerly, has always been the Mecca for perverts of all kinds. Shortly after Dulaure wrote this, from 1820 to 1826 to be exact, the famous male establishment of the Rue du Doyenné, near the Louvre was in full flower. This place solicited both the male and female trade. (See Untrodden Fields of Anthropology.) *Naturally, no big city is exempt from this sort of thing, but Berlin, I suppose, deserves honorable mention. —Trans.*

26. Pornographe, *p. 354;—Machiavelli*, Life of Castruccio Castracani.

27. Journal de L'Etoile, *tom. 1, p. 205.*

28. Chronique de Louis xi, *in the year 1461. The same writer says that after this indecent scene a man was seen, a bit below the Ponceau Fountain, on a cross, representing Jesus crucified between two thieves. It is presumable that the toilette of those who played the rôles of Jesus on the cross and the two thieves was the same as that of the Sirens.*

29. Récréations historiques, *by Dreux du Radier, tom. 1, pp. 270-271. Monstrelet, in describing a fête which the Duc de Bourgogne gave in 1453, says that there was to be seen "a virgin who poured forth hippocras in great bounty from her breast; and beside the virgin was a young child who gave out rose water from his little spike." (Chroniq. vol. 3, fol. 55, v.)*

30. Pontus Heuterus, in car. Pugnace, *lib. 5, p. 386;* —Récréations historiques, *by Dreux du Radier, tom. 1, p. 272.*

31. *See* Recueil de plusiers farces tant anciennes que modernes, *Paris, 1612.*

32. Pugatory, *canto 23.*

33. *Philelphus, ninth decade, satire 10.*

34. Sermo communis de tempore prædicabilis; sermo 3, de pœnitentia, sine paginatione.

35. Sermon 4, Tuesday before Advent, *fol. 13.*

36. Sermo 29, third Sunday of Advent, *fol. 79, verso. See also the same reproaches in sermon 38, fol. 98, sermon 41, fol. 106, verso. Also Sermon of the first Sunday of Lent, part 2, fol. 41.*

Textual Notes

37. *Menot, sermon for the second week-day after the second Sunday of Lent, fol. 25.*

38. Idem, *third week-day after the first Sunday of Lent, fol. 94, verso.*

39. Sermones discipuli de tempore et sanctis, sermo 84, ad finem.

40. Essais de Montaigne, *tom. 2, liv. 2, chap. 12, p. 220.*

41. Essais de Montaigne, *liv. 3, chap. 5. I have seen in Switzerland, in the church of the abbey of Muri, a pen sketch which represented a large procession. The men wore their braguettes quite apparent. A recent hand has sought to do away with this incongruity of costume which the progress of decency rendered too daring.*

42. *Maillard, tom. 1, sermon 6 of the first Sunday of Adfol. 48, verso.*

43. *Maillard, sixth sermon of the first Sunday of Advent, fol. 48, verso.*

44. *Lent-sermons preached at Saint-Jean-en-Grève, by Olivier Maillard, 1498, sermon 26 of the second Sunday of Lent, fol. 60.*

45. Idem, ibid, *fol. 74.*

46. *Sermon 38 of the fourth Sunday of Advent, fol. 98. (The French word so coyly abbreviated above is* maquereau, *literally* mackerel, *which is a common term for pimp or panderer. —Trans.)*

47. *Sermon 23 of the Saturday of the second Sunday of Advent, fol. 73, verso. In sermon 36 of the third Sunday of Lent, fol. 88, he says that Suzanne did not dare even to show her legs. "And you," he adds, "you are not ashamed to appear stark naked before others; and to give yourself over to your dissoluteness."*

48. *Sermon 17, the sixth week-day of the first Sunday of Advent, fol. 51.*

49. *Sermon 3 of the third Sunday after Penetecost, fol. 14.*

50. *One cannot, without breaking all the rules of decency, give otherwise what the bold monk dares express, unnecessarily, in a sermon. See* Fructuosissimi atque amœnissimi sermones fratris *Gabrielis Barlette,* dominica prima Adventus Domini, *fol. 266, verso.*

51. Chroniques *by Froissart, vol. 1, chap. 14, p. 11.*

52. Histoire de Louis XII, *by Jean d'Auton, chap. 59, p. 221.*

53. *See* Recreations historiques, *tom. 2, pp. 185-186.*

54. Tractatus 3 de credulitate dæmonibus adhibenda, doctoris felicis Hemmerlein, Malleus maleficorum, *tom. 2, p. 311.*

55. *Let one read, if he can without indignation, the voluminous* Commentaires de Blaise de Montluc, *and he will see aspects of his cruelty on almost every page. It is not an enemy who accuses Montluc of them; he himself boasts of them. Here are some of his titles to glory: In spite of the treaties which permitted the Protestants of Cahors to assemble for preaching, the clergy and Catholics of this city set fire to the building in which members of that religion were together, and as these unfortunate people escaped from the flames they were massacred. The Court, upon news of a similar crime, named a commission to try the guilty. Many canons, and even the Bishop of Cahors, were convicted of being the authors of this fire and the murders. Montluc, Lieutenant of the King in Guienne, arrived when a canon named Viole, whom, in his Gascon idiom, he calls Bieule, was about to be condemned to death. He addresses himself to the president and tells him that if he pronounces the sentence he will kill him. "At the first word," he says, "he utters, I shall kill him." Then he says to him: "You will declare here before me what I demand of you, or I myself shall take you in hand; for I have hanged a score of more worthy people than you, or than those who have attended the sitting." After this discourse, worthy of an angry executioner, Montluc put the tribunal to flight and saved the criminals. He was always accompanied by two executioners who were called his* valets-de-chambre. *He took credit to himself for this. "I secretly obtained," he says, "two executioners, who were called my lackeys, because they often followed me about." Having seized a Protestant named Verdier, he informs us that he had two well-equipped executioners with him, and that he himself aided in the execution of this unfortunate. A Protestant minister one day hazarded coming to implore his protection. "I began to swear," says Montluc, "and grasped him by the collar, telling him: 'I do not know what keeps me from hanging you myself from this window, lewd fel-*

low; for with my own hands I have strangled a score of more worthy people than you....' I can say with truth that there is no Lieutenant of the King in France who has had more Huguenots put to the knife and rope than I; and if I have not done enough of it or as much as I wished, it is not my fault." It would take a volume to report all the acts of injustice, perfidy, and inhumanity with which this old soldier honors himself in the long Memoirs that he wrote during his old age. I have never done more painful reading.

The betrayals, perfidies, and cruelties of Simon de Montfort perhaps surpass those of Blaise de Montluc. I shall cite only one example of them. Simon de Montfort, by order of the Pope, made war on Raymond vi, Comte de Toulouse. In order to seize some lands of this Count and despoil him of his property, Simon de Montfort found need to have some troops pass through Quercy. This was not easy by force: he had recourse to perfidy, and the legate of the Pope took betrayal upon himself. He made propositions of peace to the Comte de Toulouse and invited him to come to the church of Narbonne, in order there to cement the peace at the foot of the altar. The Count believed in the sincerity of this prelate, suspended hostilities, and came, along with his principal officers, to the church of Narbonne. The ceremony took place with the usual solemnities; religion seemed to stand security for the sincerity of their mutual oaths. These oaths, and the religious display which ought to have rendered them more sacred, were only a sacrilegious comedy that the legate had played in order to facilitate the passage of Simon de Montfort's troops through Quercy. This act of villany on the part of this warrior, who performed many another, is less astonishing than the immorality and effrontery of the contemporary writer who relates it. "Whilst the legate," he says, "amused and inveigled, by a pious fraud, the enemies of the faith assembled at Narbonne, the Comte de Montfort was able to advance into Quercy and Agénois, and there to receive reënforcement which came from France, and with advantage to combat the enemies of Christ. O pious fraud! O fraudulent piety of the legate!" Petrus Val., cap. 78.

I shall not make any particular observation here; the text suggests enough. But I shall remark that in general our old nobles, after having committed all sorts of violences during the course of their lives and seeing themselves approaching the end, began to have fear of Hell, and believed to escape its torments and absolve themselves of their numerous crimes by giving property to the monasteries. It is thus that Punch of the marionette players strikes or kills without reason all who come before him, and ends by trembling before the Devil when he appears. Simon de Montfort and Blaise de Montluc, as well as Catherine de Médicis and Cardinal Richelieu, were placed in the old gallery of the Palais-Royal, in the ranks of the illustrious men of France.

56. Sermonum dominicalium totius anni fratris GUILLELMI PEPIN; sermo 2, Dominica 23, post Trinitat. fol. 251.

57. Amours des Rois de France, *by Sauval.*

58. *I have seen at the* Bibliothèque royal, *in the depository of the Manuscripts, some* Hours *written in the sixteenth century, ornamented with beautiful miniatures some of which, located at the beginning of the volume, represented the four seasons. Winter was figured by a room in which were seen seated, on both sides of a fireplace, a man and woman in the costume of the time. The lady was represented raising her dress as much as it was possible to do while seated. The miniatures of the books and manuscripts of the church often offer still more revolting indecencies.*

59. Concilium Parisiense, art. ix. Amplissima collectio, *tom. 8, col. 1021.*

60. *The group of the Three Graces, by Germain Pilon, was placed in a chapel of the former church of the Celestines, at Paris.*

61. Voyage dans la ci-devant haute et basse Auvergne, *tom. 1, p. 246.*

62. Essais historique sur Paris, *by Saint-Foix, tom. 1, p. 218.*

63. *An inquiry manuscript, composed by more than eighty witnesses, and of which I have a copy, contains the strangest and most scandalous facts. The abbot was Charles de Saint-Nectaire; he died in 1560. The cabinet in which these nudities were painted bore the name of foir de monsieur. The genealogists and the authors of Gallia Christiana tell us that this abbot, who authorized all sorts of crimes and debauches in his monastery, was as illustrious for his*

nobility as for his piety. *Seek truth in certain histories; it is as if one sought it in the exaggerated compliments, among men of slight acquaintance, which is the common custom of civilized society.*

CHAPTER XVI

1. Boudin *also means sausage, but usually a special, dark, blood sausage or pudding. Captain Bourke, in his remarkable book* Scatalogic Rites of All Nations, *points out that this word, though it commonly meant blood-pudding, also had the vulgar meaning of* excrement. *He futher maintains that the eating of boudins at this feast was a symbolical eating of excrement, which ceremony had doubtless in bygone days been carried out to the letter. —Trans.*

2. *See* Mémoires pour servir à la fête des Fous, *by Dutilliot.*

3. De sacra episcoporum autoritate, *J. Filesac, p. 365;* —Glossaire *of Du Cange, at the word* Palmata; —Glossaire *of Carpentier, at the word* Disciplina.

4. *The priests sold the confession. It happened that young girls who wished to earn their Easter sacrament and who did not have money to pay the confessor, prostituted themselves in order to get it. Here is what Dom Carpentier reports in his Supplement to the* Glossaire *of Du Cange, at the word* Confessio: *"The suppliant, having encountered a young girl of fifteen or sixteen years, required of her what she wished that he might have her carnal company, which was granted him by her; for which he promised her a robe and hood, and to supply her with money so as to go to confession on Easter Day."*

5. Histoire des Flagellants, *by Abbé Boileau.*

6. *France, it is true, may have been somewhat less affected by this wave of flagellation than other countries, but to say that it was "untouched" is, I think, stretching the facts a bit. Reference to almost any of the fairly numerous works on flagellation will convince the doubtful on this point. —Trans.*

7. *On these various uprisings of floggers, see the* Glossaire *of Du Cange, at the words* verberatio, pœnitentiarum redemptiones, gesta Trevirorum, archiepiscoporum, sub anno 1296; —Amplissima collectio, *tom. 4, p. 362, 419;*

—Chronic Alberti continuatio; —Altera Chronici Guillelmi de Nangis; —Spicileg. d'Achery, *tom. 3, p. 111;* —Anonymi Carthusiensis, de religionum origine; amplissima collectio, *tom. 4, p. 81;* —Thesaurus anecdotorum, *tom. 2, p. 906, etc.*

8. *It is Tertullian especially who makes game of the* nudipedalia, *and of many other pagan practices and that the Christians have since imitated.* See Tertulliani Apologeticus, cap. 40 ad finem.

9. *Guillaume Guyart, in his book entitled* La Branche aux royaux lignages, *says on this subject: People, private and from foreign lands, through Paris, bare-foot and in swaddling-bands, went, and of them only three were shirted.*

10. Amplissima Collectio, *tom. 4, p. 1101.*

11. Histoire de Saint Louis, *by Joinville, edition of 1761, p. 27.*

12. Vie de Saint Louis, *by the confessor of Queen Marguerite, p. 326.*

13. *See the* Glossary *which follows the* Vies, Annales, Histoires et Miracles de Saint Louis, *at the word* langes. *See also the* Supplément au Glossaire de Du Cange, *by Carpentier, at the words* linguis *and* roba lingia.

14. Supplément au Glossaire de Du Cange, *by Carpentier, at the word* camisia.

15. *Supplement to the* Glossaire *of Du Cange, at the word* linguis.

16. Continuatio Chronic. de Nangis, *year 1315;* Spicilegium d'Achery, *tom. 3, p. 70.*

17. Guilbe *is certainly the same as* guimple, *of which we have made* guimpe [*wimple*]. *A* guimple *was a band of linen with which women covered their throats, and which knights placed over their casques.* (See Du Cange, *at the word* Guimpla.) *Thus the curé Pigenat, one of the most famous fire-brands of the League, must have been but very scantily covered by this slender drapery.*

18. Journal des choses advenues à Paris, *from December 23, 1588 to the last day of April 1589; printed among the* Preuves du Journal d'Henri III, *t. 2, p. 459.*

19. Journal d'Henri III, *by l'Estoile, for the year 1589.*

20. Mercure de France, *May 1735, p. 898.*

21. Fragmentum statutorum ecclesiæ Nivernenis; Thesaur. anecd., *tom. 4, p. 1070.*

Textual Notes

22. Supplément du Glossaire de Du Cange, *at the word* Pentecoste.

23. Concilium Nanetense, anno 1491, *Supplement to the* Glossaire *of Du Cange, by Carpentier, at the word* Prisio.

24. Pantagruel, *liv. 5, chap. 12.*

25. *Alphabet of the French author following the* Pantagruel *of Rabelais, at the words* fouetteurs du Rivau.

26. Les Escraignes Dijonnoises, *liv. 1, sect. 18.*

27. Mémoires de la Societé royale des Antiquaires de France, *tom. 4, p. 156.*

28. Epistolæ Pontificiæ selectæ ex registro antiquo Urbani Papæ IV. Veterum scriptorum amplissima collectio, *tom. 2, col. 1260.*

29. Jo. Sleidani, de Statu religionis et reipublicæ, lib. 4, anno 1524, p. 62, verso. *This custom adopted by bishops of selling inferior priests permission to have concubines finds further verification by a piece composed in 1522 by the Diet of Nuremberg, printed in the* Catalogus testium veritatis, *and entitled* Centum gravamina. *Here is what is to be read there, in Article 75:* "The officials, in drawing annual tribute from monks and secular priests, permit them publicly to keep concubines and femmes-de-joie, by whom they have children." *In Article 91, one also reads:* "The majority of the bishops and their officials not only permit priests to have concubines, on paying a tribute, but even if there are some wise priests who wish to live in continence, they must equally pay the tribute of concubinage, under the pretext that Monsieur the Bishop needs the money."

30. Rerum Leodiensium, *etc.,* amplissima Collect., *tom. 4, p. 1225 and the note.*

31. *On these two facts,* see Silvæ nuptialis Joannis de Nevizanis, *bk. 1, p. 70-72; and* Nicolas de Clémangis, de Præsilibus Simomiacis, *p. 165, col. 1.*

32. Chronic. Guillelm. de Podio Laurent., *chap. 6; and* Histoire générale du Languedoc, *by Dom Vaissette, tom. 3, liv. 21, p. 121.*

33. Francisci Joannis Nider, ordinis prædicatorum, de Maleficiis, cap 9, ad finem.

34. Speculum humanæ vitæ, lib. 2, cap. 19.

35. Nemoris unionis tractatus, cap. 35, p. 377.

36. Nemoris unionis tractatus 6, cap. 34, p. 374. *The*

preachers Barlette and Maillard also speak of these murders committed by nuns.

37. De reformatione Ecclesiæ; sect. de reformatione cæterorum ecclesiasticorum.

38. Petri de Aliaco, cap. de reformatione religionum et religiosorum; Johannis Gersonis, in declaratione defectuum virorum ecclesiasticorum, *p. 65.*

39. Hist. Anglic. Henri III, *p. 105.*

40. *I dare not go into details about the shameful tastes and infamous habits to which many members of the clergy were given over. However, my moderate assertion is, so to speak, cuirassed with proofs. Besides the works already cited on this matter, general and particular proofs of the corruption of the clergy will be found in almost all histories of the thirteenth, fourteenth, fifteenth, and seventeenth centuries. One can consult Bermond Chauveron, canon of the cathedral of Viviers, who composed a large book entitled:* De publicis concubinariis, *which treats only of the concubinage of the priests; and Paul Olearius of Heidelberg, the author of a little treatise entitled:* De fide concubinarum in sacerdotes, *in which he speaks of the arrogance and dominating spirit of the priests' concubines. He says that they were absolute mistresses in their houses, and that they wanted to have the most distinguished places in church.*

41. *Platin.,* de vitis Pontificum.

42. *The manners of which I have just given a scanty sketch relate very nearly to only the fourteenth, fifteenth, and sixteenth centuries. The eulogists of bygone times, scarcely knowing where to place the happy period in which innocence and virtue reigned, will perhaps say that it existed in the preceding centuries. If my subject had allowed me to speak of the manners of the tenth, eleventh, and twelfth centuries, what frightful pictures of crimes, absurd errors, and misfortunes I should have had to offer! Contagious diseases, famines, and wars desolated France almost continually during those three centuries; no law, no public administration. The strongest ruled; crimes remained unpunished or sometimes honored; religion was magic; a great portion of the States remained uncultured; human flesh was sold publicly in the markets; the stupidity and ferocity of the people equalled the public misery.*

Textual Notes

43. *A dozen fore-skins of Jesus Christ have been counted. One of them is with the monks of Coulombs, another at the abbey of Charroux, a third at Hildesheim in Germany, a fourth at Rome, in Saint John Lateran, a fifth at Antwerp, of which I have spoken in this work, a sixth at Puy-en-Velay, in the church of Notre-Dame, etc.*

The navels of God were quite as manifold. I cannot refrain from citing on this head a little known anecdote. At Châlons, in the collegial church of Notre-Dame-de-Vaux, there was a holy navel of God *which performed a great many miracles. The Bishop of the diocese, J.-B. de Noailles, took it into his head in 1707 to have the reliquary containing it opened in the presence of various experts. In place of the holy navel, three grains of sand were found in it. The surgeons and other professional people drew up their report on it. The canons, furious at this discovery, which was injurious to popular devotion, appealed against the indiscreet Bishop, and maintained with some heat that those three grains of sand were the holy navel. There were many proceedings on this matter, which can be read in a printed document entitled:* Lettre d'un Ecclesiastique de Châlons aux Docteurs de Paris.

As for the ass's tail, *preciously preserved at Genoa, in the church of the Dominicans, it is mentioned in a church book containing the service for Holy Week. Here are the expressions:* "Degno è ancora di sapere come la coda d'uno di quei duo animali, in questo atto adoperati dal Signore, senza arte humana incorreptibile si conserva hoggidi in Genoa presso dei padri di San Dominico, facendo pia remembrenza dell' humilità c'hebbe il figliolo di Dio per noi in questa intrata." (Jeaninus e Capugnano ord. Prædicatorum, in declarationibus super officium hebdomadæ sanctæ. Venetiis, *1736, p. 12.*)

CHAPTER XVII

1. *See above, chap. 12, p. 129.*
2. *The love of crude and savage peoples does not resemble that of civilized peoples, or, to explain myself more exactly, love among robust individuals whose muscular system predominates over their nervous system, is different from love among weaker persons in whom the nervous system is superior. With the former it is an imperious need,*

a purely brutal passion; with the latter it does not limit itself to a single point: it occupies, so to speak, the entire capacity of an individual, all his sensitive system. It is indeed the need to enjoy; but this need is preceded, is disguised by that of being loved. That delicate sentiment, those innocent and enchanting preludes, which make up the charm and vexations of youth, belong to a peaceable condition, to an advanced civilization, to gentle manners, but are not the share of savage man.

3. *See above, chap. 10, p. 139.*

4. *A fact of modern history comes to the support of my conjectures. In 1707, an epidemic carried off a great portion of the inhabitants of Iceland. In order to repeople it, the King of Denmark permitted each girl to have as many as six bastards without her honor suffering from it. The women made extremely good use of the permission. The island was soon repeopled. The evil was repaired; but the women still continued the remedy. It required another law to abolish the first.* (Esprit des Usages et des Coutumes, *tom. 2, pp. 291-292.*)

5. *It is known that among the Mussulmans, husband and wife are notified from the top of the minarets at a certain hour of the morning to be about their conjugal duties. The Jesuits, for the same reason, had the same custom established among the tribes of the Guaranis: "They had," says Fèlix de Azara, "a large bell rung at midnight in order to awaken the Indians and stimulate them to propagation."* (Voyage dans l'Amérique méridonale, *tom. 2, chap. II, p. 175.*)

6. *Kamul is a district of the province of Tanguth, formerly under the dominion of the Grand Khan of Tartary. The inhabitants have a particular language, and worship idols. When a traveler arrives in this country, the master of the house where he has chosen his domicile enjoins his wife, his daughters, and his relatives to satisfy all the stranger's desires. He then leaves his house, doubtless in order not to be a troublesome witness, and does not reënter his home until the stranger has gone away. This method of exercising hospitality is regarded as an act of religion by this people. The beauty of the women of this country ought to increase the devotion of the travelers.*

When Mongu Khan ascended the throne in 1251, he

ordered the abolition of this custom. For three years it was not observed; but in this interval, the crops having failed and various other misfortunes having fallen on the inhabitants, they sent ambassadors to Mongu Khan charged with soliciting the reëstablishment of this custom. The Khan granted it, making this answer: "I know that it is my duty to place limits to this scandalous custom; but since you take glory in your shame, you can cover yourselves with it, and your wives continue henceforth to render their charitable services to strangers." Marco Polo, who reports this anecdote, and who travelled in that country about the end of the thirteenth century, says that this custom still existed in his time. (Histoires des Voyages et Découvertes dans le Nord, *by Forster, tom. 1, pp. 117-118.*)

The town of Martaouan, situated ten leagues from Aleppo, is famous among European travelers because of the same custom which even today is in vogue there. The chief of the country, as well as every father, every husband, and even every lover, comes to offer strangers his daughter, wife, or sweetheart. The travelers are embarrassed only as to choice, and are held to mark their gratitude only by a few pieces of money. A Frenchman who passed through this place reports the following anecdote of it: "The inhabitants do not forget," he says, "to cite to strangers the story of a good old missionary who, going into India, passed through Martaouan. This pious sexagenarian, preserved by his age from the temptations of all these sirens, believed the next day that his young colleagues had been wiser than the companions of Ulysses; but he had the pain of seeing himself forced, as treasurer of the company, to pay these hosts the price of their complaisance." (Mémoires historiques du Voyage de Ferrières-Sauvebeuf.)

There is the same custom at Chichiri, in Arabia Felix; and a slight recompense suffices the young girls who honor themselves by giving their favors to strangers. The Tschuktschs likewise offer their wives to travelers; but these latter, in order to render themselves worthy of it, must submit to a disgusting test. The daughter or wife who must pass the night with her new guest, presents him with a cup full of her urine: he must rinse his mouth with it. If he has this courage, he is regarded as a sincere friend; if not, he is treated as an enemy of the family. In Africa there is the same practice on the Riogabou Coast [?]. In the kingdom of Juida it is an act of religion to establish places of prostitution for strangers. During Cook's visit to Otahiti, the islanders offered the English of his expedition the spectacle of a religious sacrifice made to Love by a young boy and girl of eleven or twelve years of age,

I could compose a volume of similar customs, but here I must not go beyond the limits of a note.

7. On the origin of these gods of generation represented by boundary-markers, see the work entitled: Des cultes qui ont précédé l'idolâtrie, *chap. 21, p. 415 ff.*

8. Corn. Taciti Historia, lib. ii, cap. 3.

CHAPTER XIX

1. *See above, chap. 6, pp. 83-86.*

2. *It is very likely that this painting furnished the idea for an ingenious allegorical composition, and much more decent, found in the ruins of Herculaneum, which has been engraved under the title of* The Vendor of Cupids.

3. *The terrible sin hinted at here in so circumlocutory a manner, is simply masturbation. The "sin of Onan," so often used, even by professional men who should know better, as a synonym for masturbation, is quite another thing. It is known technically as "withdrawal" or* coitus interruptus, *and consists simply of the withdrawal of the virile member immediately before orgasm with the consequent ejaculation of the sperm outside the vagina. Of the two, doctors agree that onanism is by far the more deleterious to health.* —Trans.

4. *Description of three unpublished paintings of Greek vases of the Portici Museum.*

INDEX TO NOTES

PUBLISHERS' NOTE

The original French edition of this work was published in Paris in 1805 and printed in the classic type of that period. This limited American edition is the first translation ever done into English. Since this volume is certain to be commented upon widely, the publishers have chosen S.A.Jacobs to arrange its format, to prepare its composition, to see it through the press and plan its binding. The resultant beauty is as simple and chaste as it is effective. The interested reader will note herein a number of unusual departures from contemporary book-design and particularly the unobtrusive illusion of type-size variety although the entire work has been printed from 10 point Linotype Janson face

*